INTERNATIONAL INSTITUTIONS and POWER POLITICS

INTERNATIONAL INSTITUTIONS
and POWER POLITICS
POLITICS

BRIDGING THE DIVIDE

ANDERS WIVEL and T.V. PAUL, Editors

Georgetown University Press / Washington, DC

The publisher is not responsible for third-party websites or their content. URL links were active at time of publication.

Library of Congress Cataloging-in-Publication Data

Names: Wivel, Anders, editor. | Paul, T.V., editor.
Title: International Institutions and Power Politics : Bridging the Divide
   / Anders Wivel and T.V. Paul, editors.
Description: Washington, DC : Georgetown University Press, 2019.
Identifiers: LCCN 2018058553 (print) | LCCN 2019980424 (ebook) | ISBN
   9781626167001 (hardcover : alk. paper) | ISBN 9781626167018 (pbk. : alk.
   paper) | ISBN 9781626167025 (ebook : alk. paper)
Subjects: LCSH: International agencies—Congresses. | International
   relations—Congresses.
Classification: LCC JZ4850 .I5837 2019 (print) | LCC JZ4850 (ebook) | DDC
   341.2—dc23
LC record available at https://lccn.loc.gov/2018058553
LC ebook record available at https://lccn.loc.gov/2019980424

♾ This book is printed on acid-free paper meeting the requirements of the American National Standard for Permanence in Paper for Printed Library Materials.

20 19   9 8 7 6 5 4 3 2   First printing

Printed in the United States of America.

Cover design by Jeremy John Parker.

Contents

Illustrations

Acknowledgments

This book is the product of a joint realization that the intimate relationship between power politics and international institutions has not been properly studied in international relations. While many realists ignore institutions as epiphenomena of power politics that thus do not play a significant independent causal role in world politics, institutionalist scholars on the other side of the spectrum focus on showing how institutions operate independently of power politics or how the latter has limited impact, especially after the creation of institutions. Linking these two crucial elements in international politics requires an eclectic approach that we have adopted in this project. The volume is the product of a series of conferences and workshops, in particular in Copenhagen in November 2015 and in Montreal in December 2017. We also held panels at the International Studies Association (ISA) conferences in New Orleans and Baltimore in 2015 and 2017. During these meetings several discussants commented on the papers, making the end product better. The valuable comments by the two external reviewers helped us much in revising the papers. The discussants included Mark Brawley, Krzysztof Pelc, Fernando Nunez-Mietz, Hamish Van der Ven, and Erik Kuhonta. We thank Donald Jacobs, senior acquisitions editor at Georgetown University Press, for his strong interest in the volume. We also appreciate the financial support from the Fonds de recherche du Québec–Société et culture (FRQSC), the James McGill Chair at McGill University, and the Department of Political Science, University of Copenhagen. The following research assistants helped us at various stages, and we thank them all: Alexander Funch Adamsen, Jean-Francois Belanger, Alice Chessé, Jakob Dreyer, Jai Jaeyoung Kim, Philip Larsen, Apoorva Malepati, Erik Underwood, and Line Jæger Winther. Finally, we thank our respective families for their unwavering support throughout the work of this project.

Anders Wivel, Copenhagen
T.V. Paul, Montreal
October 2018

Part I

Introduction

CHAPTER 1

Exploring International Institutions and Power Politics

Anders Wivel and T.V. Paul

The study of international institutions has waxed and waned along with major changes in the international order over the past century. The interest in institutions was prominent in the immediate post–Cold War era, as the scholarly attention on great power rivalry and nuclear deterrence became less salient. This is aptly captured by Michael Barnett and Martha Finnemore when they wrote: "International organizations have never been more central to world politics than they are today" (2004, 1). Today, we may echo their assessment with the confidence that the institutional order they recognized seems even more comprehensive, more complex, and more robust than it did back then. The complexity and detail of institutional arrangements have deepened at the same time as the issues covered by institutions have continued to widen to the extent that most policy issues are now encapsulated by transborder agreements. Institutional complexity, it seems, leads to even more complexity as "the proliferation of international agreements multiplies the number of actors and rules relevant for any given decision of international cooperation" (Alter and Meunier 2009, 13). Even so, institutions can decline or can lose their strength, in particular when major powers violate the norms, principles, and rules inherent in them or engage in self-seeking policies that ignore them. The reluctance of powerful states to commit to international institutions is a recurrent phenomenon in international relations. It has recently been highlighted by the choices of the Trump presidency and their repercussions for the global and North American institutional orders (Ikenberry 2017; Stokes 2018) and by the British decision to leave the European Union with potentially important consequences for Europe's institutional order (Diamond,

Nedergaard, and Rosamond 2018). Institutions can still linger on as new ones are created, while old ones survive or perish through efforts at reforms or negligence.

This introductory chapter proceeds in five steps. First, we provide a brief over-view of the institutionalization of world politics, demonstrating the continuing close relationship between international institutions and power politics. Second, we define what we mean by international institutions and power politics and unpack how our definitions relate to these concepts as usually understood in the study of international relations. This book focuses on formal institutions. Third, we situate this volume's attempts to understand the relationship between inter-national institutions and power politics in the study of international relations and specify how we add to the current research agenda. Fourth, we identify the major research questions of the volume and briefly introduce the chapters to follow. Finally, we address the significance of this volume and set out a future research agenda.

The Growth and Resilience of International Institutions in a World of Power Politics

The idea of "international organization," a term sometimes used interchangeably with "international institutions," is as old as organized politics: The Greek city-states Athens, Sparta, and Macedonia used a common currency, reflecting a high degree of international cooperation and coordination, and military alliances and trading agreements were common, as was war and military conflict (Pease 2003, 19). However, it was not until the nineteenth century that international organi-zations (IOs) began to play a major role in international relations, reflecting the consolidation of the state system and increased interdependence creating demand for higher levels of cooperation and coordination. The Rhine River Commission, set up in 1804 between France and the German confederation to govern the increasing traffic on the river Rhine, is often referred to as the first modern international organization with the power to establish international rules and the competency and staff to secure their implementation (Archer 2015, 11). While the Rhine River Commission may be seen as a functional response to technical problems generated by increased cross-border communication (How do we ensure that ships do not collide as traffic on the river increases?), other inter-national institutions were more directly linked to war and power politics. The Congress of Vienna (1815–22) initiated the Concert of Europe, which is "gener-ally seen as an important forerunner of today's international organizations" (Rittberger, Zangl, and Kruck 2012, 36), especially the UN Security Council. The Concert of Europe successfully organized cooperation and secured peaceful relations among the European great powers until 1853 but existed in a weaker format beyond that period. Mirroring the balance of power, Great Britain, Prus-sia, Russia, Austria, and France "decided on meeting as it were in concert on a regular basis, in order to discuss questions of concern and to draw up agreements and treaties. From this activity, documents with legal force evolved" (Neumann and Gstöhl 2004, 3). The aim of the concert was to restrain through institutional norms the power political ambitions and warlike dispositions of the great powers of the day and to restrain revolutionary movements with the great powers system. Smaller states had no say in the concert or its institutional decisions.

As illustrated by Rittberger, Zangl, and Kruck (2012, 37), war and power politics have often stimulated the establishment or development of IOs from the European Concert and onward.[1] The Napoleonic Wars were an important stimulus for the establishment of the European Concert, the first Geneva Convention, and the Hague Convention. World War I inspired the League of Nations and the Kellogg-Briand Pact, and the end of World War II was the starting point for the United Nations, the Arab League, and the Organization of the American States. The Cold War stimulated the creation of several security institutions, such as the North Atlantic Treaty Organization (NATO), the Warsaw Pact Organization, the ANZUS Security Treaty between Australia, New Zealand, and the US, as well as the Southeast Asia Treaty Organization (SEATO), the Central Treaty Organization (CENTO), and the Conference on Security and Cooperation in Europe (CSCE). It was also a main driver behind the establishment of organizations for economic cooperation and trade, such as the Council for Mutual Economic Assistance, the European Economic Community (EEC), and the General Agreement on Trade and Tariffs (GATT). Groupings such as SEATO and CENTO did not survive beyond a few years. The end of the Cold War was an important stimulus for reforming and transforming the institutions of the Cold War: the EEC into the EU, GATT into the World Trade Organization (WTO), and CSCE into the Organization for Security and Cooperation in Europe (OSCE). The closure of the Warsaw Pact resulted from the collapse of the Soviet Union and the end of Cold War systemic rivalry, even though NATO survived by adapting its institutions and strategic objectives to the new strategic environment (Rynning 2005; Wallander 2000). The end of the Cold War was also the impetus for reforming NATO and stimulated the creation of institutions such as the African Union and the Association of Southeast Asian Nations (ASEAN) Regional Forum.[2]

Recently, observers have argued that the long-term trend toward increased institutionalization of world politics is giving way to a return of the transactional self-help politics of the past (Patrick 2017). Provoked by the Trump administration's questioning of institutional commitments in NATO as well as the faltering nuclear agreement with Iran and the US withdrawal from the Trans-Pacific Partnership (and US intention to withdraw from the Paris climate agreement), this "back to the future" scenario has gained a significant following in American foreign policy circles (Kristensen 2017). We take issue with this reading of the current institutional order. First, it tends to juxtapose self-help and power with institutionalization and cooperation. However, institutionalized cooperation is often the result of the "power politics of peace," for example, balancing threat or power or exercising hegemony (Wivel 2004). In the history of international relations, there are numerous examples of the coexistence of power politics and international institutions and the use of institutions by stronger or weaker actors to maximize their interests and power (Paul 2018; A. Watson 1992). In the highly legalized settings of the current international order, power is often exercised in nuanced ways by setting agendas, influencing informal facts, and bargaining in the shadow of the law. In this way, the US and the EU do not win more WTO disputes, but they do appear to exert far more influence than other members over the WTO jurisprudence that results from these disputes (Daku and Pelc 2017).

Finally, the institutional order established by the end of the Second World War has proved to be extraordinarily resilient. A low point of the international trade regime in the 1970s and 1980s was subsequently counteracted by the Uruguay Round and subsequently the creation of the WTO. Since 2018 the United States and China have been engaged in a trade war, imposing tariffs worth hundreds of billions of US dollars. The long-term effects of this dispute on the institutional landscape of international trade are yet to be seen. The trade war may damage parts of the current economic order but, at the same time, strengthen other parts, for example, by creating an incentive for the EU and China to work closer together. The deep transatlantic divide over Iraq in 2003 gave way to cooperation over security and trade, for example, the attempt to create the Transatlantic Trade and Investment Partnership (TTIP). It seems that once institutional norms set in, it becomes difficult to shift back to unilateralism, even for the hegemon.[3] Thus, the current institutional order has so far proved to be robust in the face of potentially lethal challenges that sprung up during the past decades. For instance, NATO survived the deep disagreement between the United Kingdom and the United States on the one side and France and Germany on the other in the run-up to the Iraq War in 2003. Although leading security experts saw this as evidence of "soft balancing" (e.g., Pape 2005; Paul 2005; 2018, chap. 5),[4] NATO continues as a defensive alliance, as a forum for debates over Euro-Atlantic and global security between the US and its allies, and as an instrument for out-of-area missions, such as the 2011 military intervention in Libya. In 2017, during the first months of his presidency, US president Donald Trump failed to affirm his commitment to Article 5 of the North Atlantic Treaty and questioned the commitment of the US to come to the rescue of allies under attack. He scorned European members of the alliance for assigning less than 2 percent of their gross domestic products (GDPs) to defense budgets. However, even though European alliance members responded with anger and disbelief, they also responded with a strong reaffirmation of alliance commitments, which was within a few months echoed by the US administration.

From 2008, the EU, viewed by its proponents as an important cause of peaceful change and prosperity in Europe and as a model for institution building in other regions (Murray 2010), suffered a longtime and multidimensional crisis.[5] President of the European Commission Jean-Claude Juncker (2016) described the crisis as "at least in part . . . existential." It was characterized by leading analysts as "wicked crises" in which attempts to fix one type of crisis would intensify other types of crises (Dinan, Nugent, and Paterson 2017, 361). Yet despite predictions of the union's likely demise (Mearsheimer 2010; Rosato 2011), the EU emerged robust and, in some policy areas, strengthened by the crisis—even after the decision of the United Kingdom to leave the EU (Wivel and Wæver 2018). To be sure, a more robust EU may also be necessary in the future as Europe's political leaders attempt to tackle challenges, such as the ongoing fiscal problems of Italy, the long-term consequences of the 2015–16 migration crisis, and the rise of illiberal populism in several member states.

Outside the Euro-Atlantic area, the activities of organizations such as the Shanghai Cooperation Organization (SCO), the Collective Security Treaty Organization (CSTO), and Brazil, Russia, India, China, and South Africa (BRICS) exemplify the importance of organizations to those states seeking to maintain the status quo and those seeking to challenge or even revise regional and global orders. The SCO survived deep disagreements over Russia's war with Georgia in 2008, which China and the Central Asian member states feared could create a precedent, and in 2017 the organization expanded its membership to include Pakistan and India in addition to founding members China, Kazakhstan, Kyrgyzstan, Russia, Tajikistan, and Uzbekistan. In the Pacific, the Trans-Pacific Partnership (TPP) survived the withdrawal of the United States when remaining member states Australia, Brunei, Canada, Chile, Japan, Malaysia, Mexico, New Zealand, Peru, Singapore, and Vietnam successfully renegotiated the agreement and reached a partial deal in 2017.

The rising powers have been creating new institutions, especially in the economic arena. The prominent institutions have a Chinese mark to them, although other states, such as India, have been active in these groups as well. G20 and BRICS were institutional frameworks that came about in the post-2008 financial crisis. BRICS has since then created two financial institutions—New Development Bank and Asian Infrastructure Investment Bank—with members' contributions to support developmental and infrastructure needs of all member states. In fact, the rising powers have been supporters of many existing international institutions, including the UN, although they clamor for reforms, especially in financial institutions, such as the International Monetary Fund and the World Bank, and their governing structures. The rising powers have focused on institutions—existing and new—as a way to manage relations among themselves and with the established powers. In many respects, this shows institutions' value as tools for power transitions and peaceful accommodation, an aspect of institutions often neglected in realist and other systemic theories on power transition conflicts.

In sum, "cooperation under anarchy" (cf. Oye 1986) seems to be the rule rather than the exception in world politics today, and cooperation is often institutionalized in IOs—"created by the commitments made by sovereign states"—at the same time as "their purpose is to bind those states to their commitments" (Hurd 2018, 1). While the "back to the future" argument is misguided in its prediction of an imminent demise of the current institutional order and its jux-taposition of power politics and international institutions, it rightly points to the continued importance of power politics for the form and content of this order (e.g., Colgan and Keohane 2017; Ikenberry 2017; Patrick 2017). This volume attempts to examine the multifaceted relationships between power politics and international institutions in both theoretical and policy dimensions. In the next section, we define what we mean by "international institutions" and "power politics."

Defining International Institutions and Power Politics

The aim of this volume is to explore how the logic(s) of power politics are at the same time influencing and being influenced by the institutionalization of world politics. All contributions to the volume start from the assumption that power politics remains an important, even defining, characteristic in international relations and the empirical observation that international institutions are now more numerous and comprehensive than in the past. This does not mean that variations do not exist in terms of their importance or value for the conduct of international relations. But how should we understand "international institu-tions" and "power politics"?

The examples in the previous section illustrate the close relationship between power politics and international institutions as well as the diversity of interna-tional institutions. Some are military, others are economic, and yet others deal with issue areas, including security cooperation, climate change, and human rights. The examples also illustrate the need for defining what we mean by inter-national institutions in a way that is sufficiently inclusive to capture the diversity yet specifies what institutions we do not include in our use of this term.

We define international institutions as *associational clusters among states with some bureaucratic structures that create and manage self-imposed and other-imposed constraints on state policies and behaviors.* While we find previous definitions, such as that of Koremenos, Lipson, and Snidal—"explicit arrangements, negoti-ated among international actors, that prescribe, proscribe, and/or authorize behav-ior" (2001, 762)—or that of Robert Keohane—"particular human constructed arrangements, formally or informally organized" (1988, 383)—appealing, they seem incomplete. Our definition focuses on formal IOs with bureaucracies, bud-gets, and elaborate rules for decision making and membership (Archer 2015, 1–3). We focus mainly on international governmental organizations (IGOs), which "are founded either through an intergovernmental agreement or a deci-sion of an existing IGO [and] have a membership mainly composed of or domi-nated by states, usually represented by governmental agents" (Rittberger, Zangl, and Kruck 2012, 7). Our definition also includes international regimes understood as "implicit or explicit principles, norms and rules, and decision-making procedures around which actors' expectations converge in a given area of international relations" (Krasner 1982, 186). Our definition of international institutions does not include historically evolved fundamental and durable practices such as sovereignty, war, diplomacy, and the balance of power or what the English school terms primary institutions (see Buzan 2004, 167–76). These primary institutions and other social institutions (e.g., public opinion, which was discussed by classical realists in the 1950s) may affect the creation and life of international institutions as defined here, but they are not themselves part of our definition or the focus of attention in this volume. This is not because we regard primary institutions as unimportant but because the focus of the volume and of individual chapters is primarily on the simultaneous robustness and crisis of the current order of formally institutionalized international relations.

From this starting point, we seek to unpack the complex relationship between power politics and institutionalization and to explore the meaning of concepts such as power, interests, and balancing in an institutionalized setting. The volume aims to be a pluralistic endeavor, exploring how the logics of expected consequences and the logics of appropriate action interact in the institutionalization of world politics (cf. March and Olsen 1998). Likewise, we understand power politics in a way that allows for exploring both logics when analyzing the relationship between international institutions and power politics.

"Power politics," writes Martin Wight, "is a colloquial phrase for international politics" based on the assumption that we are dealing with independent political units with "continuous and organized relations between them" (1995, 23). As argued earlier, today these "continuous and organized relations" are often taking place within international institutions. IR scholars typically define power as "power over resources" (Waltz 1979) or "power over outcomes" (Hart 1976). If power is understood as "power over resources," it is measured by material resources, such as military power, population, or size of territory. Some scholars, most notably structural realists, argue that power is fungible and that power in one realm translates into power in another; it is therefore meaningful to speak of aggregate power (Waltz 1986). This view is challenged by scholars arguing that material power is always filtered through the perceptions, misperceptions, and imperfect knowledge of others (Jervis 1976; Wohlforth 1993) or that it makes little sense to decouple materialist measures of power from the way policymakers understand power and the legitimate use of it to further state goals (Guzzini 1993; Thorhallsson 2006). If power is understood as "power over outcomes," it runs the risk of becoming tautological by deducing power from outcomes: winning a conflict is seen as proof of power (Hill 2014). The "power over resources" and "power over outcomes" understandings of power are both compatible with Robert Dahl's (1961) classical definition of power as A getting B to do something B would not otherwise have done. They are occasionally supplemented, or contrasted, with the observation that actors may exercise "agenda-setting power" based on their position within an organization (Allison 1969). This agenda-setting understanding of power may lead to analyses of how A gets B to do what B would not otherwise have done based on A's position within the organization. However, it can also go beyond an intentional goal-oriented understanding of power by pointing out how A is embedded in organizational practices such as standard operating procedures leading to a particular way of understanding and exercising power. IOs may therefore produce effects unintended by both their creators and the decision makers working within them (Barnett and Finnemore 1999). Thus, power may be nonintentional, reflecting structural or institutional characteristics (Strange 1988b), and institutional practices may therefore play an independent role in shaping, opening, and limiting the exercise of power (Manners 2002).

We define power politics as *the contestation among individual states using their particular resources and bargaining strengths to influence the structure of relations and the conduct of other actors.* In the context of institutions, power politics involves *the efforts by states to influence the formulation, application, and enforcement of the rules and regulations of a given institution as well as the control of bureaucratic positions and allocation of resources within it.* Materially powerful actors could attempt to drive the agenda of the institution, but they need not always succeed. Weaker actors could form coalitions, come up with strong diplomatic arguments, take advantage of institutional measures, and convince others on the viability of their position. Thus, the mistake of the typical realist position—materially stronger actors often get their way—needs to be rectified if we want to understand the power politics of international institutions in a more holistic way.

The choice between the different concepts of power is more often than not posed as an either-or decision in favor of one or the other and is typically coupled with a discussion of whether to accept, reject, or supplement the (structural) realist baseline understanding of power as possession of material resources (Barnett and Duvall 2005, 40–41). As argued by Krasner, this is unhelpful if we are to understand and explain international relations. A "power over resources" understanding is neither fully adequate nor completely useless, and conventional approaches to power are sometimes useful but also incomplete as a point of departure for understanding international relations (cf. Krasner 2013, 340–41). Consequently, our understanding of power politics in international institutions comprises "power over resources," "power over outcomes," and "agenda-setting power." Following Barnett and Duvall (2005), we view these different understandings of power as placed along two dimensions of power rather than in terms of dichotomous choices. The first dimension concerns whether power is "an attribute of particular actors and their interactions or a social process of constituting what actors are as social beings, that is, their social identities and capacities," whereas the second dimension "concerns the degree to which the social relations through which power works are direct and socially specific or indirect and socially diffuse" (Barnett and Duvall 2005, 42–43). In sum, we subscribe to a broad understanding of power politics "as involving politics based on the use of power to influence the actions and decisions of actors that claim, or exercise, authority over a political community" (Goddard and Nexon 2016, 3). We proceed from the assumption that military and nonmilitary instruments are important for the conduct of power politics.

Power, International Institutions, and the Study of International Relations

Developments in international relations theory, and in particular theories that tend to dominate theoretical discourse at a given time, are far from a perfect reflection of the developments and transformations in real-world international relations. Rather, a general pattern seems to be "that each major rupture in the international system triggers a swing away from whatever theory dominates" (Wæver 1998, 51). Theory building need not follow the Kuhnian idea of one paradigm replacing another based on new empirical discoveries but may simply reflect the prevailing interests among scholars to address issues that come to the forefront as a result of changes to the international order of the day. Fortunately, theoretical developments are not completely detached from changes in the fabric of international relations. As the number of international institutions has risen, international relations scholars have increasingly engaged in understanding the institutionalization of world politics. Today, all major theoretical perspectives on international relations claim to be able to explain the causes, effects, and design of international institutions (Rittberger, Zangl, and Kruck 2012, 32), and in addition, a number of empirical studies of IOs seems to combine these perspectives or draw on theoretical strands outside the conventional IR toolbox.

The role and prominence of power politics and international institutions have traditionally varied among different strands of IR theory.[6] In particular, the division of labor between realist students of power and liberal students of international institutions has skewed the study of power and international institutions and has blinded each perspective from using the insights of the other. Power is at the core of the study of international relations, and the study of the use or abuse of state power in international politics has traditionally been associated with realism and equaled power politics with a realist understanding of realpolitik (Finnemore and Goldstein 2013, 5). In the words of Barnett and Duvall, "the discipline of international relations has tended to treat power as the exclusive province of realism" (2005, 40). In contrast, liberal theory has traditionally been associated with the development of international institutions. International institutions constituted the third leg of Immanuel Kant's liberal vision of perpetual peace, the two others being democracy and economic interdependence (Russett, Oneal, and Davis 1998). Twentieth-century IR liberalism can be read as a continuous engagement with international institutions. Beginning in the early twentieth century with the writings and political engagement of Norman

Angell to the functionalist and neo-functionalist integration theories of David Mitrany and Ernst B. Haas in the 1940s, 1950s, and 1960s, to 1970s interdependence theory and the neoliberal institutionalism of the 1980s and 1990s, liberals have grappled with the institutionalization of world politics (Grieco 1990, 4; see also Georg Sørensen's contribution to this volume). Likewise, constructivists, some of them inspired by the early work of Ernst B. Haas (1958), have a strong engagement with understanding international institutions and their effect (e.g., Adler and Barnett 1998; Barnett and Finnemore 2004; Bjola and Kornprobst 2011), while poststructuralists have been less concerned with international institutions (as defined previously) and more focused on power.[7]

The relationship between power and institutions played an important role in the "so-called debates of the '-isms'" (Adler 2013, 112), which played a constitutive role in developing what we understand as IR today. The first debate in the interwar years between realists and idealists took place in the context of the hopes that liberals had for and the ultimate failure of the League of Nations, with realists warning of utopian ideas for a transformation of the international realm. The relationship between power and institutions played a more marginal role in the second debate between traditionalists and behavioralists but an important role in the so-called interparadigm debate of the 1970s. Pluralists (focused on the consequences of interdependence), Marxists (focused on structural inequality), and realists (focused on the power politics of the great powers) assigned very different roles and importance to international institutions. However, they all tended to subscribe to an instrumental view of the institutions, whether they were seen as tools for managing interdependence (pluralists), tools for disciplining the weak (Marxists), or tools for maximizing the power and security of the great powers (realists).

The neorealism versus neoliberal institutionalism debate over the origin, role, and importance of international institutions served as a focal point for defining and shaping theoretical divisions in the 1980s and 1990s (e.g., see Baldwin 1993). This debate contributed to a hitherto unknown theorization of international institutions (Martin and Simmons 1998), which was inspired by the robustness of international institutions during the global power shifts and international crisis in the global political economy in the 1970s (Martin 2017, 3). The (in time partly overlapping) debate between rationalists and reflectivists also kept institutions firmly on the agenda as a focal point for theoretical disagreement (Adler 1997; Keohane 1988; Koremenos, Lipson, and Snidal 2001; Mearsheimer 1994, 1995; Wæver 1995). However, in this debate realists sticking to a view of international institutions as epiphenomenal and merely mirroring the interests of the great powers (most forcefully Mearsheimer 1994) were increasingly cornered and marginalized, while constructivists and liberals were busy discussing when, how, and why institutions mattered.[8]

Today, international institutions have largely disappeared as a focal point for debates between realists and their critics.[9] Realists do not deny the existence of international institutions, but most realists are skeptical about their effect on state behavior, and the two most prominent strands of realist theory today—structural realism (including the offensive realist variant) and neoclassical realism—tend to ignore the issue of international institutions altogether. Structural realists begin from the assumption that the structure of the international system is anarchic and therefore power politics tend to dominate relations between states. In a world where power and interests are "the predominant forces driving world politics," international institutions are—in the structural realist view—understood as "mere facilitators, translating the interests of powerful states directly and unproblematically into international outcomes" (Gruber 2000, 15). As summed up by John Mearsheimer, "Institutions have minimal influence on state behaviour" because they "are based on the self-interested calculations of the great powers" (1994, 7), and for this reason they are usually ignored in structural realist theory (Waltz 1979; Mearsheimer 2001).[10] Neoclassical realists accept the structural realist starting point in international anarchy but argue that there is rarely a perfect fit between structural incentives and foreign policy (Rathbun 2008; Ripsman, Taliaferro, and Lobell 2016). Thus, if we are to shift our analytical focus from international outcomes—for example, the occurrence of war (Waltz 1988), to foreign policy—we need to focus on the "transmission belt" between anarchy and policy (Rose 1998). This move allows neoclassical realists to explain deviations from neorealist expectations (Schweller 2003) and to fill in the blanks left by structural realism by pointing to domestic political variables and individual-level ideational variables, which allows them to explain why one policy option was chosen over others even when the international incentives were indeterminate (Ripsman 2009). By doing this, neoclassical realism significantly expands the role for domestic institutions in realist analysis (e.g., Zakaria 1998) but tells us little about the potential role of international institutions (Wivel 2017).[11]

This volume does not seek to update or replay the debate between realists and institutionalists (cf. Wæver 1996), nor to go another round in the eternal boxing match between realists and their critics on how, why, and to what extent institutions matter. Rather, the contributions to this book seek to move beyond paradigmatic debates and answer recent calls to address specific and important real-world problems of international relations by midlevel theorizing, accepting that this may lead to a more eclectic, but also more open, understanding of international relations (Lake 2013; Sil and Katzenstein 2011). Thus, we discuss how power travels with unequal effects through institutional landscapes and how these landscapes condition the use of power.

By doing this we add to a growing literature that has moved significantly beyond the simple question of whether institutions matter in order to explore how institutions limit or enable the pursuit of power and influence of states in the international system and which institutional strategies states use in pursuit of the national interests. This literature has mainly taken three forms.

First, several studies seek to explore how a particular international institution shapes power processes in international relations and how power politics shapes institutional change and innovation. These studies focus on, for example, the International Criminal Court (Bosco 2014), G20 (Cooper 2010), ASEAN (Eaton and Stubbs 2006), and the US-India Nuclear Pact (Pant 2011). A second branch of recent institutional literature looks at the interaction between power politics and particular phenomena related to international institutionalization, such as networks (Avant and Westerwinter 2016), regime complexity (Drezner 2009; Hafner-Burton 2009), commercial flows (Costalli 2011), legitimization (Finnemore 2009; Hurd 2008; Oates 2017; Pelc 2010; Zürn and Stephen 2010), and norm diffusion (Katsumata 2011). A third branch focuses on the role of particular intra-institutional mechanisms and the way they shape power politics at the same time as they are shaped by the power and interests of member states. These mechanisms include, for example, categorization (Ella 2016), membership (Hwang, Sanford, and Lee 2015), coalition building (Monteleone 2015), sanctions (Urpelainen 2013), representation (Cogan 2009), and delegation (Haftel and Hofmann 2017).

While this literature adds significantly to our understanding of international institutions, it also tends to lose sight of some of the fundamental debates over the nature of international relations, which were the focus of the previous debates over international institutions. Therefore, the ambition of this volume is to build on our present knowledge of international institutions and reconnect it to more general discussions and concerns on the nature of international relations and state behavior. This is reflected in the research questions to which we now turn.

Research Questions and the Contents of This Book

The research questions of this volume are organized into two clusters. The first cluster of questions considers the instrumental use of power and international institutions: How do states use international institutions to maximize influence? Which institutional strategies do great powers and other states use in pursuit of the national interest? What determines the choice of institutional strategies? How do institutions limit the pursuit of power and influence of states in the international system?

The second cluster of research questions considers the contexts of power politics and international institutions: How do global and regional orders affect institutionalization, and how does institutionalization affect global and regional orders? How does the institutional setting affect how power is understood and how power is exercised? What is the effect of lessons of the past and institutional memory on the exercise of power and the likelihood of institutionalization? How does the relationship between power politics and institutionalization vary across different policy areas?

Exploring these research questions, the following three sections of the volume are organized in accordance with Barnett and Duvall's (2005, 42–43) two dimensions introduced earlier. In each part we begin with analyses viewing power as an attribute of particular actors and their interactions and understanding social relations through which power works as direct and socially specific. We then move toward analyses at the other end of the two dimensions, viewing power as a social and constitutive process and understanding social relations through which power works as indirect and socially diffuse. Consequentially, the first cluster of research questions will play a larger role in the first chapters of each section, whereas the second cluster of research questions will play a larger role toward the latter part of each section.

Part 2, "Theorizing Power Politics and International Institutions," unpacks the relationship between international institutions and power politics in major theoretical approaches to international relations. In their discussion of classical realism and the design of international institutions, Samuel Barkin and Patricia Weitsman argue that classical realists—critical of the ambition to fix or repair international relations by rational human design—warned that formal institutionalization would not end or even mitigate the importance of power politics for interstate relations. They acknowledged the importance of the state as a social institution depending on its ability to create a loyalty of its citizens going far beyond rational individual interest maximization and material means of coercion. In the following chapter, Norrin Ripsman gives an empirically informed neoclassical realist answer to the question: Why do states spend so much time and so many resources on international institutions? Responding to the critique that neoclassical realists have so far said little about the role of international institutions, Ripsman argues that political decision makers located at the nexus between international and domestic politics engage in an ongoing negotiation over legitimacy and resources. In this context international institutions are useful tools for legitimizing foreign policy decisions, overcoming domestic opposition, easing the demands on domestic resource mobilization through burden sharing, and generating domestic pressure on other states. Thus, even though a "realist" starting point has typically led to a focus on the state as a unitary actor (Martin and Simmons 1998, 742–43), this does not necessarily follow from a focus on power politics and may even limit our understanding of how states use power in pursuit of the national interest.

In the following chapter, Georg Sørensen discusses how liberals understand international institutions and power politics and the relationship between the two. Liberalism offers a fundamentally optimistic perspective on the perennial challenges of taming power in international relations through institutionalization, but there is considerable variation in how much taming is possible and which means are the most effective. Using the contemporary challenges of international society as a prism, Sørensen discusses the tension between "good enough governance" or "gridlock" in financial crises, climate change, and security from a liberal perspective. This is followed by Ben Rosamond's constructivist reading of the political economy of international institutions. Rosamond shows how international political economy (IPE) scholarship seeks to question and go beyond conventional understandings of international institutions and power politics. He argues that it is useful to think about structures and structural power in terms of collective understandings and intersubjectivities and that intersubjective structures can be made "real" through the design and maintenance of institutions that internalize their logic. From this point of departure, Rosamond explores the discursive relationship between globalization and anarchy and what this means for our understanding of power politics and international institutions.

Chapters in part 3, "The Processes of Power Politics and International Institutions," focus on soft balancing, information, and networks in order to explore how these processes affect the relationship between international institutions and power politics. Anders Wivel and T.V. Paul discuss how institutions enable states to pursue power more effectively and restrain states' threatening behavior but at the same time how this pursuit is transformed by processes associated with developments of social institutions and the increased importance of structural modifiers favoring nonmilitary means to maximize power and interests. Institutional soft balancing provides a platform for states to incur costs from other states by speaking on behalf of a collective (preferably the international society) and at the same time provides a shield against retaliation. In comparison with other soft-balancing strategies, institutional soft balancing is typically more cost-effective and legitimate while allowing for a flexible response to aggression. Austin Carson and Alexander Thompson look within formal IOs to show how information accessibility and information-processing capacity affect how institutions limit and enable the pursuit of power. Within these institutions, as noted by Carson and Thompson, even formal organizations that appear to be inclusive on paper may in practice have informal practices that are exclusionary. They argue that information is an important source of power and that the design and practices of institutions have important consequences for how material power disparities are translated into policy. In her chapter, Stacie Goddard applies a network approach, arguing that it is useful in analyzing institutional orders and revisionist politics. From this point of departure, she conceptualizes under what conditions revisionism is likely to occur, which states are likely to engage in revisionist behavior, and what instruments states are likely to deploy in pursuing revisionist policies. Discussing how revisionist politics play out in different institutional orders, she argues that revisionism is not limited to aggressive attacks on the institutional order and that we can nuance our understanding of the relationship between revisionist policies and institutional change by conceiving of institutions as networks.

Part 4, "The Power Politics of Global and Regional Institutions," presents three empirically grounded studies of international institutions and power politics. Using the nuclear Non-Proliferation Treaty (NPT) and the International Atomic Energy Agency (IAEA) as examples, Steven Lobell and Brad Nicholson point out how norms and institutions affect the process and pace of socialization and competition in international anarchy. Like technology and geography, social institutions can be understood as structural modifiers, but unlike technology and geography, norms and organizations are nonmaterial. From this starting point, Lobell and Nicholson explore the effect of shared norms and organizations on making the security environment less competitive and thereby limiting the pursuit of power. In the following chapter, Sarah-Myriam Martin-Brûlé, Lou Pingeot, and Vincent Pouliot analyze the power politics of United Nations peace operations. They demonstrate how informal practices within and around the Security Council lend structure to UN power politics in the realm of peace operations and show how the power politics of peacekeeping permeate decision making and the implementation of peace operations on the ground. Finally, John Hall and Frédéric Mérand analyze the interaction of power and institutions in the world's most comprehensive regional institution, the European Union. Identifying five crises—Brexit, the Eurozone, migration, internal protectionism, and Russia—Hall and Mérand explore how the parallel growing authority of European institutions and member states has affected the relationship between power politics and institutionalization and what this will mean for European policymaking in the future.

Part 5, "Conclusions," sums up and critically discusses the contributions to the volume. Annette Freyberg-Inan, using the preceding contributions to the volume as a platform, discusses how we might at the same time continue to view power politics as a fundamental characteristic of international relations—even if it is characterized by increasingly institutional complexity—and allow for political transformation. Taking a neo-Gramscian approach, she argues we need to theorize material and ideational power together rather than keeping them as two separate dynamics with independent effects. Accordingly, we can use the concept of hegemony to comprehend the mixture of force and consent central to understanding not only international institutions but also international relations and politics in general. Finally, in the last chapter of the book, Daniel Nexon uses the contributions to the volume as a point of departure for reflecting on the nature of international institutions and power politics.

Significance and Future Research Trajectories

This volume seeks to make a major contribution to the advancement of the study of both international institutions and power politics. Both these strands of literature have evolved in somewhat independent tracks, and as a result they have paid insufficient attention to the value of each other. Our effort in this volume is to bridge the long-neglected links that exist between these two crucial dimensions of world politics. IR theory, in particular, realism and liberalism, have made major advances in analyzing the importance of power politics and institutions respectively, yet we still lack an adequate appreciation of the mutual influences of the two. In that way, we are also advancing eclectic approaches to analyzing world politics (Sil and Katzenstein 2011).

Future research trajectories in this area could be developed on both theoretical and empirical linkages more specifically. For example, we still do not know adequately how rising powers use institutions for power transition purposes, especially of a peaceful nature. Knowing how rising powers shape or reshape existing institutions and how new institutions are created to include norms and practices rising powers want will be significant additions to peaceful transitions literature. Institutional decay due to power politics among major power actors is another issue area that demands our attention. Similarly, institutional regeneration due to the efforts of both major powers and nonmajor powers should be a vital area of research. Further empirical studies are required on almost all issue areas of the institutions literature in order to see how power politics is related to the creation, functioning, and evolution of international institutions.

Notes

A previous draft of this chapter was presented at a workshop at McGill University, December 1, 2017. We thank the workshop participants, and Krzysztof Pelc, in particular, for useful comments.

1. The following examples are mainly drawn from Rittberger, Zangl, and Kruck (2012, table 3.1), although they focus exclusively on security institutions when discussing the relationship between power politics and international institutions.

2. The end of the Cold War was not only the catalyst behind institutional reform and the construction of new institutions. Eastern bloc organizations such as the Treaty of Friendship, Cooperation, and Mutual Assistance, informally known as the Warsaw Pact, collapsed with the Soviet Union's Cold War empire and ceased to exist in 1990, and the Council for Mutual Economic Assistance was disbanded in 1991. Thus, the number of intergovernmental organizations peaked in the last years of the Cold War with 378 IGOs in 1985, up from 37 in 1909 and 123 in 1951. Union of International Associations, "Figure 2.1: Number of International Organizations by Type," 2015, https://uia.org/sites/uia.org/files/misc_pdfs/stats/Number_of_international_organizations_by_type_2014.pdf. Assessments of the current number of IGOs vary with classification criteria, but assessments by the *Yearbook of International Organizations* and *Encyclopaedia Britannica* place the number close to 250. See the discussion in Richard Woodward and Michael Davies, "How Many International Organizations Are There? The Yearbook of International Organizations and Its Shortcomings." *Political Insight* (blog), October 11, 2015, https://www.psa.ac.uk/insight-plus/blog/how-many-international-organisations-are-there-yearbook-international.

3. The US learned this at its own cost when it tried to coerce Japan to change its trade policies through unilateral means in the 1980s in ways that ran counter to the trade regime's

norms. Its threats faced widespread normative condemnation and disproportional resistance and proved less effective than working through formally authorized channels (Pelc 2010).

4. See Paul (2018) for the theory and history of soft balancing and Wivel and Paul's contribution to this volume for a discussion of the causes, characteristics, and effects of institutional soft balancing.

5. See Hall and Mérand's contribution to this volume for an analysis of power politics and the institutionalization of Europe.

6. For the unusual argument that international institutions are generative of power politics, see Pouliot (2016).

7. For a discussion of how the poststructuralist conception of power compares with a realist understanding of power, see Sterling-Folker and Shinko (2005). For a collection of essays analyzing the institutionalization of Europe from constructivist and poststructuralist points of departure, see Kelstrup and Williams (2000).

8. For realist discussions of how and why institutions have played and continue to play an important role in realism, see Schweller and Priess (1997) and Samuel Barkin's contribution to this volume.

9. See, e.g., the overview of critique raised against neoclassical realism and the neoclassical realist response in Ripsman, Taliaferro, and Lobell (2016, 175–83) on the issue of international institutions.

10. Some structural realists allow for systemic factors modifying the effects of international structure, thereby, in principle, creating room for international institutions, but the specific implications for state action are rarely spelled out (Buzan, Jones, and Little 1993; Snyder 1996).

11. However, as argued by Ripsman, Taliaferro, and Lobell (2016), neoclassical realism has a potential for explaining IGOs as a result of international power relations by analyzing how systemic pressures on national policy choices are conditioned by domestic-level intervening variables affecting how decision makers perceive external challenges and formulate and implement their responses. See also Norrin Ripsman's contribution to this volume.

Part II

Theorizing Power Politics and International Institutions

CHAPTER 2

Realist Institutionalism and the Institutional Mechanisms of Power Politics

J. Samuel Barkin and Patricia A. Weitsman

The George W. Bush administration's security policy choices were often understood through a discourse that revolved around the dichotomy of unilateralism versus multilateralism. Bush was seen as a unilateralist who eschewed global opinion almost universally. Yet what became clear during this period of US foreign policy is that states use institutions to advance their strategic goals. This is the heart of what, following Ronald Krebs (1999), we call realist institutionalism: the use of multilateral apparatuses by states for strategic or power gain. Realist institutionalism argues that states use institutions as vehicles to achieve their aims as much as, or even rather than, to create harmony or cooperation for its own sake. The approach builds on the conceptual space that many classical realists left open for international institutions. It brings to that space both an acknowledgment that the world is a more multilateral and globalized place than it was in the mid-twentieth century and a recognition that the tools available for the study of institutions in international relations (IR) have improved significantly since then.

Realist institutionalism argues that institutions are essential conduits for states to realize or actualize power or force in their security interests. Institutions do this in various ways. Global organizations such as the United Nations (UN) may serve as vehicles for transmitting information regarding the intentions of the policy purveyor, determining the level of international support, and seeking endorsements (Thompson 2010). Institutions may serve to achieve strategic ends more explicitly too. Military alliances and coalitions, for example, are institutions that facilitate the actualization of power capabilities. It is not enough to possess a sophisticated military arsenal; one must have the wherewithal to effectively bring those capabilities to fruition. Institutions promote that capacity through command structures, assets, established working relationships, joint training, forward basing, and so forth. That the United States has command structures that span the globe is a critical component of its hegemony: it is not only its power capabilities or gross domestic product (GDP) that matter; it is the capacity to bring those resources to bear in the event of crisis, the actualization of power, that is essential. This perspective underscores the insight that Robert Dahl (e.g., 1957), David Baldwin (e.g., 1979), and others have emphasized, which is that power is a relationship, the capacity to get others to do one's bidding, not simply a static indicator of what one possesses.

Realist institutionalism posits that institutions are not simply separate bodies with independent influence; nor are they mere reflections of power. Instead, as states seek to exercise power and to influence the decisions and choices of others, institutions are one vehicle for them to do so. Institutions augment power and security not simply by assisting in straightforward capability aggregation but also by helping states achieve foreign policy goals in other ways. This perspective stands in contrast to that of realists such as John Mearsheimer who argue that institutions are hollow and ineffective for states' pursuits of security (Mearsheimer 1994). The approach of realist institutionalism suggests instead that institutions, as conduits of capability—akin to what Thompson (2010) calls "channels of power"—foster the realization of state capacity. In our view realism needs to recognize the important element of power actualization that takes place through institutions and to see institutions as vehicles of capability rather than as empty shells that are nothing more than reflections of the distribution of capabilities in the system.

This chapter proceeds in three sections. The first offers a disciplinary history of realist institutionalism that shows how contemporary neorealism came to see international institutions as irrelevant to security studies despite a recognition of the centrality of institutions in both classical realism and some early neorealisms (classical realism is understood here as what Kenneth Waltz [1979] calls first-image, while neorealism is a shorthand for third-image realism). The second discusses the relationship among realist theory, national power, and international institutions. The final section highlights three different mechanisms through which institutions affect state power and security: institutional design, the effects of international institutions on the material bases of state power, and the effects of those institutions on the legitimacy, both domestic and international, of state security policy.

A Disciplinary History of Realist Institutionalism

A dichotomy has developed over the past several decades in the field of international relations in regard to the utility of institutions. Keohane and Martin (1995), for example, speak of a divide between realist and institutionalist theory.

Nonetheless, we are surely not the first to see institutions as strategic spheres for states. While many contemporary realists and neorealists are dismissive of international and intergovernmental institutions, classical realists were much less so. This observation is not a novel one—Schweller and Priess (1997) argued two decades ago that John Mearsheimer's rejection of the utility of international institutions is a departure from realist tradition, and Ronald Krebs (1999) argued, with reference to military alliances, that institutions can be a tool of power. The relationship between realism and institutionalism is more complex than simple acceptance or rejection. A brief discussion of the role of institutions in classical realist thinking, and its development in neorealist thought, can help to illuminate this complexity.

Social institutions, broadly defined, are central to realist theory. The state, after all, is a social institution, and realism is premised on the state's ability to draw on the loyalty of its citizens to a far greater degree than those citizens' rational utility calculations would allow for. But this still leaves open the question of the relevance of international institutions to outcomes in international relations. The early classical realists of the mid-twentieth century certainly saw a role for social institutions loosely defined, such as international public opinion (e.g., Carr 1946, 132–45). They also saw a clear role for alliances in the making of effective foreign policy (e.g., Morgenthau 1985, 201–12). Alliances vary broadly in their level of organizational institutionalization (Weitsman 2014). But all alliances are formal institutions—if not, if they were merely reflections of what states would do in their national interest anyway and would not be worth negotiating in the first place (see, e.g., Grieco 1990).

These early realists had less to say about formal intergovernmental organizations other than military alliances. The network of institutions for international cooperation that we take largely for granted now did not yet exist at the time. The most visible such institution of the interwar period, the League of Nations, failed at its core task, and there were few countervailing organizations to point to. Thus, these scholars focused little attention on formal intergovernmental institutions because they were neither common in nor particularly important to international politics before midcentury. Some classical realists of the following generation, writing when formal intergovernmental institutions were better established, did see them as playing a potentially central role in international relations (e.g., Claude 1962).

Realism is, nonetheless, often seen as being anti-institutionalist. How did this view develop, given the key role of some kinds of institutions in classical realist theory? Classical realists argued that all the institutions they saw as important, such as states, alliances, and informal institutions like public opinion, were mechanisms of power. These institutions allow states to aggregate and deploy power more effectively by acting as foci for political identity, as mechanisms to cumulate power across states, and as ways for states to make power politics more palatable abroad. These scholars at the same time argued against what E. H. Carr

(1946) called utopianism and what Hans Morgenthau (1946) associated with "scientific man," the idea that political institutions could replace power politics.

This idea points to the difference between the tension between realism and some kinds of liberal institutionalism on the one hand and the recognition by classical realists of the importance of some kinds of institutions on the other. The institutionalism that the classical realists were arguing against was the belief that we could design international institutions well enough to remove the role of power politics from the international system. The "scientific man" against whom Morgenthau argued is one who believes that he can design perfect institutions of governance, ones that can replace or prevent a need for power politics. Domestic institutions in liberal democracies are designed in this way, to obviate power politics as much as possible.

Whether or not we see these institutions working at the domestic level, the classical realists argued that the conditions did not then exist for such institutions to work at the international level. States were the social institutions that effectively dominated power in international politics, and until this basic fact of the international system changed, power would continue to be the ultimate arbiter of relations among those states (Carr 1946). To the extent that this is still true, the logic of classical realism still holds—international institutions will ultimately be unable to constrain powerful states in the absence of countervailing power.

This classical realist argument is not ultimately about the relative importance of power and of institutions in international relations, but rather about the relationship between the two. The institutionalism that Keohane and Martin talk about, and that Mearsheimer rejects, is a belief in the ability of institutionalism to replace power (Mearsheimer 1994). But to argue that international institutions cannot replace power as the ultimate arbiter of outcomes in international politics is not the same as arguing that these institutions do not affect power (e.g., Barnett and Duvall 2005). The classical realist argument is that institutions provide the mechanisms for power. In other words, the argument is not about whether we should be thinking about institutions but about how we should be thinking about institutions.

The concern for institutions, both domestic and international, in realist thinking was for the most part displaced in the transition from classical to neorealism in the 1970s and 1980s (Barkin 2010). Neorealism, in its focus on the effects of system structure, pays little attention to the actual mechanisms of power as put to use in the conduct of foreign policy. Whereas classical realism took states to be the central actors in international relations as an empirical observation and focused on how those actors generate and use power, neorealism assumes that states are the central actors and that they will learn to maximize security, either through conscious emulation or evolution (Waltz 1979). But when one begins by assuming that states will in the end maximize power, one does not need to focus in any real detail on the mechanisms for doing so. The mechanisms are, in Waltz's terminology, reductionist and, in Mearsheimer's, epiphenomenal.

The question of the particular role that international institutions play as mechanisms of power therefore becomes largely irrelevant in neorealist thinking. Alliances can be assumed to be important as aggregators of power in a multipolar world because the assumed job of alliances is to aggregate power. Collective security organizations, similarly, can be assumed to not matter because the assumed job of these organizations is to replace power as the core mechanism for settling disputes among states. And institutions that do not focus on major international security issues can be ignored because neorealism focuses only on issues that affect or are affected by the structure of the international system.

Not all neorealists ignore the role of institutions as both sources and targets of state power. Robert Gilpin's version, for example, looks to institutions, broadly defined to include sets of explicit and implicit rules of international exchange as well as formal international organizations, as the motivating element in hegemonic wars (Gilpin 1981; see also Wivel 2004). A state, in this argument, can use a hegemonic position in international politics to create rules and institutions that give it a structural advantage (either political or economic) over other states. This advantage reinforces its hegemonic position. Over time, however, the costs of maintaining the system, as well as the vagaries of differential growth rates, mean that other states will eventually come to rival existing hegemons in power. Because hegemony brings with it control over institutions, and institutions in turn are a source of hegemonic power, control over international institutions is worth fighting over. This explains great power wars in a way that balance-of-power neorealist theories, like those of Waltz and Mearsheimer, cannot.

The literature that focuses on an opposition between realism and institutionalism builds directly on the Waltzian tradition of neorealism, however, rather than on either the Gilpinian tradition or earlier classical realism. Not only Mearsheimer's offensive realism but also Keohane's neoliberal institutionalism draw directly on, and are to a large degree self-described variants of, Waltzian theory. The study of international institutions within realism, as seen from both within and without the realist scholarly community (e.g., Legro and Moravcsik 1999), has thus to a large degree become a victim of the Waltzian focus on systemic constraints at the expense of the classical realist, and Gilpinian, concern for policy mechanisms and institutional effects.

Institutions and Power

The discussion to this point has made the case that the debate between realists and institutionalists about whether international institutions can be seen as replacing power as the central determining factor of outcomes in international relations misses the possibility that institutions can be seen as mechanisms of state power. The three sections after this one will discuss more specifically the role of institutions in politics among states and the mechanisms through which institutions affect state power. This section looks more broadly at the concepts of power and institutions. Given the centrality of the concepts of power and institutions to this argument, a reasonable question to ask at this point is, Why speak of realist institutionalism rather than power and institutions more broadly? To answer this question, we must begin by looking at the concept of power in international relations.

As discussed in the introduction to this volume, there is an extensive literature in international relations about what power is. Much of the literature on the question in American political science looks at power as a relational attribute, as the ability of an actor either to get other actors to do things that they would not otherwise do or to achieve goals against opposition by others (e.g., Baldwin 2002). Defined as such, power can be identified only in hindsight, limiting its conceptual utility as an analytical and policy prescription tool. Realist theory has generally adopted this relational understanding of power. However, it has tended to focus on the resources and attributes that are understood to generate power capabilities in the first place rather than on power outcomes, in order to overcome the limitations of post hoc analysis.

Various realist scholars have associated different sets of attributes with power capabilities. The most common attribute is military resources, ranging from simple counts of personnel and equipment to more nuanced and subjective analyses of training, quality, morale, and so forth (e.g., Mearsheimer 2001). Some scholars have simply spoken of capabilities and assumed that it would be obvious which states have them and which do not (e.g., Waltz 1979). Others have included a much broader range of capabilities, ranging from economic output and resource base to attributes such as national morale, political will, and ability to sway public opinion (e.g., Morgenthau 1985). Counting capabilities in this way allows for comparison and prediction that operationalizing power as outcomes does not. But it creates its own questions. What is the relationship between capabilities and outcomes? What resources are effective in which circumstances or with reference to which goals? To what extent are the less tangible power resources depleted or reinforced by use?

To complicate these questions, many other types of power have been suggested in the political science literature. The power to set agendas and, more broadly, the terms of discourse are difficult to quantify but point to a role for international institutions much more clearly than do, for example, military capabilities (on the power to set agendas, see Bachrach and Baratz [1970]). And critical theorists speak of structural power, which is the constraint that social structures put on the ability of individuals to act (Barnett and Duvall 2005). Power, in other words, can mean a variety of different things, and these things relate to each other in potentially enormously complex ways. A project addressing the general question of the relationship between power and institutions in international relations would therefore lack focus. To be tractable, it would have to begin by specifying the type of power being discussed and the context of that power.

In this context, a discussion of realism helps to specify the scope of the argument. We focus here on the use of international institutions by states as mechanisms for aggregating or projecting power and more broadly the effects of those institutions on that power. Power here is understood, therefore, as relational. The concerns with states as central actors and with relational power match those of realist theory, as does the focus on foreign policy, on the intentional use of power by states. Realism serves as a useful shorthand for these specifications and focuses on an understanding of power that is somewhat narrower than that provided in the introductory chapter.

Furthermore, a focus on international institutions is a necessary corrective for realism. There is already an extensive literature on the relationship between power and institutions—discussions of structural power, for example, assume ex ante that social institutions are mechanisms of power. But realists as a research community have for the most part eschewed discussion of international institutions as mechanisms of power since the transition from classical to structural realism in the 1970s and 1980s. To the extent that this research community occupies an important position in the international relations literature and that international institutions play an important role in international politics, encouraging the realist research community to come to terms with these institutions is a worthwhile undertaking.

The second concept that needs specification at this point is that of institutions. That social institutions can matter in realist theory is axiomatic—the state, the central unit of analysis in realism, is an institution. The focus of this project is more specifically on international institutions. But even then, "international institutions" can refer to a broad variety of different things. The definition proposed in the introduction to this volume—*associational clusters among states with some bureaucratic structures that create and manage self-imposed and other-imposed constraints on state policies and behaviors*—is a narrow one, focusing on formal multilateral institutions. This definition excludes not only many informal international regimes but also most military alliances, which, even if they have formal organizations, are not multilateral.

Somewhat more broadly, "international institutions" can be construed to include any formal institution that has states as members (it could also be construed to include international nongovernmental organizations [NGOs], but we do not look at NGOs here). Even more broadly it can also be construed to include social institutions that are not anchored in formal organizations. In this way, the concept overlaps with that of international regimes, "implicit or explicit principles, norms, rules and decision-making procedures around which actors' expectations converge in a given area of international relations" (Krasner 1982, 185). Institutions, in this sense, are sets of behaviors that are recognized and expected by the relevant actors.

An example from the field of security studies is proportionality. The idea of proportionality appears in international jurisprudence, but it is not formally institutionalized, and there are no international organizations formally charged with overseeing the implementation of proportionality. Furthermore, proportionality is difficult to specify in practice, for a variety of reasons. States often respond to provocations in a disproportionate way, and more or less get away with it. Yet, the idea of proportionality of military response has a constraining effect on state behavior because ignoring it has diplomatic and reputational repercussions. States engaging in military responses that are clearly disproportionate have been known to try to justify their actions in the language of proportionality. The effect of proportionality as a social expectation in international politics is certainly not determinative—states can ignore it when they choose. But nor is it irrelevant (Gardam 2004).

These sorts of social institutions, broadly defined, can have a constraining effect on foreign and security policy, but they can also have a differentially empowering effect. An example can be found in international norms against intentionally targeting civilians in war. The norm limits targets of force but not the effects of force. An attack that is targeted at a military installation, but that incidentally kills dozens of civilians, falls within this norm, but an attack aimed at a soft target by people who do not have the ability to penetrate hard targets, and that kills fewer civilians, falls outside it. This difference empowers capital- and technology-intensive militaries at the expense of poorer armies and of non-state users of force. It is by this logic that some armies can kill thousands of civilians legitimately but other uses of force are considered illegitimate despite generating far smaller headcounts (T. Smith 2002).

Social institutions understood in this broader sense provide a useful link between a realist institutionalism and constructivist methods. These methods are designed specifically to address the relationship between agency and social institutions. This relationship encompasses both the constraining and enabling effects of institutions on the behavior of actors (whether individuals or corporate actors such as states) and the ways in which actors can in turn shape the institutions (Barkin 2010). The constructivist literature has dealt with issues of power for decades, and the literature that focuses specifically on constructivist analyses of relational power continues to grow. The institutions included in this literature range from formal organizations and international law, to norms, to discursive institutions, accepted patterns of discourse that empower some actors at the expense of others and enable sets of policies while constraining others (e.g., Mattern 2005; Krebs and Jackson 2007; Goddard 2009b).

While at the level of theory the arguments underlying the realist institutionalism presented here are compatible across the range of definitions of international institutions, in practice most of the discussion that follows, in keeping with the rest of this volume, focuses on formal institutions that have states as members. The focus encompasses both those institutions that realists are most likely to embrace—alliances—and those they are least likely to embrace—formal institutions for the collective management of multilateral disputes and for collective decisions about the allocation of relative gains. Alliances, as it turns out, are about the collective management of internal disputes as much as aggregation of power against states outside the group (Weitsman 2004). And the ways in which formal institutions manage disputes, the rules and procedures through which they operate, are themselves mechanisms of power.

The Mechanisms of Institutional Power

There are several specific mechanisms through which institutions affect state power and through which state power affects institutions. The first set of mechanisms, relevant particularly to formal international organizations, involves institutional design, encompassing both the ways in which institutional design can empower some states at the expense of others and the ways that states can design institutions that give them a power advantage and maintain this advantage over time. The second set involves the effects of institutions on material resources. And the third involves the legitimacy and knowledge effects of international institutions and is relevant for both formal and informal institutions.

Institutional Design

Institutional design affects state power, and state power can affect the design of international institutions, in a variety of ways. By institutional design we mean primarily the constitutional or treaty elements that provide the legal basis and dictate the administrative structure of formal international institutions. These include rules about the powers and remit of the organization, its membership, its voting and administrative structure, and financing. Rules and patterns of behavior within an organization that do not come from a constitutional document or treaty but that are consistently practiced and entrenched within the organization can also be considered elements of institutional design.

There is an extensive literature on the design of international institutions, most notably within the neoliberal institutionalist tradition of IR scholarship (Koremenos, Lipson, and Snidal 2001). This literature focuses on ways in which institutional design can minimize the market failures of international cooperation and thereby improve the ability of states to cooperate effectively on issues of mutual concern and to maximize the absolute gains from cooperation (e.g., Keohane 1982). But the design of international institutions can also generate relative gains for some states at the expense of others, and this relative effect is less well studied in the IR literature.

Whether one is concerned with absolute or relative gains, institutional design matters because organizational structures are resistant to change and organizational histories are path dependent (Pierson 2000). Institutional structures, particularly those anchored in the constitutional documents of the organization, are difficult to change because of the nature of international law. Unless there is a mechanism for change identified in its foundational treaty, changing the basic design of international organizations requires the assent of all member states. This gives states empowered by a given set of institutional rules effective veto power over change.

In the World Trade Organization (WTO), for example, new trade rules require the assent of all members. This means that unless there is universal agreement among members, states continue to be bound by the existing rules that came into force in 1995. Any state that prefers the old rules to proposed new ones can undermine change, meaning that new rules need to be utility improving for over 150 countries at the same time. This builds a bias against change into the system. In practice, many of the smaller members could not effectively block change by themselves, although they can do so in negotiating blocks. But any state with a large economy can, meaning that there is a much lower bar for the power to block changes in the organization than for the power to create change (Gruber 2000).

This resistance to change means that institutional histories are path dependent—long-term outcomes are dependent on the initial rules of the organization (Bennett and Elman 2006). Since national power can be used to affect the structure of international organizations, and that structure is resistant to change and can affect relative state power, the organizations can become mechanisms for maintaining the status quo and slowing change in the international distribution of power. In other words, international organizations give status quo powers additional leverage, beyond what would traditionally be considered power resources, with respect to revisionist powers (on status quo and revisionist powers, see Schweller 1994).

This discussion assumes that states that are not empowered by institutions will continue to use them. Why would they not, however, simply stop participating and engage in politics in other venues or through other means? In some cases, they do indeed do so. States engage in forum shopping, looking for the international institution that will maximize their interest with respect to a particular issue (e.g., Jupille, Mattli, and Snidal 2013). Examples can be found in the United States' working through the North Atlantic Treaty Organization (NATO) when the UN Security Council failed to legitimate a particular action, as was the case in Kosovo. Sometimes states create new institutions while continuing to participate in the old ones, as China is now doing with the Asian Infrastructure Investment Bank and the World Bank. And occasionally, but surprisingly rarely, states withdraw from institutions altogether. Rarely, because nonparticipation has costs. States that withdraw from an institution forgo any benefit that might have been gained from it and lose the ability to influence change that can be made to happen in the institution (Hirschman 1970).

Furthermore, nonparticipation in existing institutions can leave states worse off than if the institution did not exist in the first place.

A more common situation is one in which a state that withdraws from an established institution ends up not only losing the benefits of that institution but finding itself in a worse situation than if the institution had not been created in the first place. Lloyd Gruber makes this point in the context of the WTO (Gruber 2000). Countries that withdraw or choose not (or are unable) to join find themselves in a world in which all of the major global economic players are in a club, and they are excluded. The rules of the WTO dictate that any concessions by a member to a nonmember must also be extended to all members. This makes bilateral trade agreements harder for the nonmember to negotiate than would be the case if there were no WTO.

States that withdraw from institutions will not always find themselves worse off than if the institution did not exist. For example, France still benefited from the public good of NATO collective defense even after it withdrew from active participation in the organization. It did, however, lose the ability to influence NATO decisions and operations, without any concomitant gain (beyond the opportunity to express some pique). When the end of the Cold War made both the organization's public goods externalities and its policy decision making more complicated, it became more clearly in France's national interest to rejoin NATO.

This set of examples suggests that there is a range of possible effects of leaving well-established international institutions. But because institutions help to define the status quo of contemporary international politics, leaving them is rarely costless. Exit usually does not eliminate the institution but leaves the exiting state without a voice in the organization and without the benefit of its rules and resources. Exit is also likely to be a more powerful tool for hegemonic powers, or states that are in some way crucial to the institution, than for other states. But this also makes institutions particularly useful to hegemons because they bind other states to the hegemon's rules. Having rules that are in a state's interest, therefore, is a source of power for that state (Gilpin 1981).

Institutions and Material Power

The discussion to this point still leaves the question of the mechanisms through which state power can affect institutional design and through which that design in turn empowers or disempowers states. The former relationship, the effects of national power on the design of institutions, is the more straightforward of the two. States can coerce or bribe other states to join institutions or provide side payments for concessions on questions of institutional design. The power resource most closely related to the issue area of a given negotiation is most likely to be effective in generating an institutional design that maximizes a state's interests. This is perhaps clearest in the structure of the UN Security Council, in which permanent membership reflected military potential at the end of World War II. With respect to issues of environmental security, China is the world's largest emitter of greenhouse gasses, giving it de facto veto power over any effective international agreement on climate change.

Institutional design can in turn empower states in a variety of ways. A straightforward example is through voting rules. Most international organizations work on a one-country, one-vote basis. This has the effect of empowering smaller countries (whether in terms of population, economy, or military resources) at the expense of larger ones. Vanuatu, for example, has the same vote in the UN General Assembly as the US or China. At the same time, there are different vote thresholds in different institutions and often for different kinds of votes within institutions. A majority-vote system empowers the median country, whereas a unanimity rule empowers the country with the most extreme views on an issue. This pattern of relative empowerment helps to explain why powerful states are more willing to allow simple majority voting in organizations (or for votes) that do not generate legally binding rules and are more likely to prefer unanimity for votes that do generate binding rules. For example, the General Assembly has simple majority voting for most resolutions, but two-thirds majorities are required for budget votes, the admission of new members, or major rule changes.

Relatively few international organizations work on a principle other than one country, one vote, but some key institutions work this way. The voting rules of the Security Council, with its five veto powers, have institutionalized the roles of those five powers as the core voices on matters of international security. Granted, they continue to be (arguably) the key military players globally. However, their role in global decision-making processes about responses to threats to international security is nonetheless more formal and central than would likely otherwise be the case (e.g., Cronin and Hurd 2008). This is probably least true of the US, which would be the central player anyway because of its unique military capabilities. But the veto is still useful to the US, particularly in situations that are predominantly political rather than military. An example is the ability of the US to veto Security Council resolutions on Israel that would otherwise pass and become international law.

Membership rules also have empowering and disempowering effects. Military alliances are by nature exclusive, empowering those within and disempowering those without. Organizations such as the Organization for Economic Cooperation and Development (OECD) set some international standards and admit members by invitation only. Countries that are not invited to join have no voice in the setting of those standards but are affected by them nonetheless. And organizations like the WTO and the European Union, for which new members need to adopt rules and standards that require approval by existing members, empower those existing members, but only until the country in question has actually joined the organization.

Other aspects of organizational structure can generate power for particular countries in ways that are less clear-cut but potentially important nonetheless. These include rules about personnel, whether formal or informal; location; and financing rules and patterns. An example of personnel rules is the historical understanding that the head of the International Monetary Fund will always be a European and the head of the World Bank an American; this convention empowers the traditional financial powers of the global north in international monetary and development issues to a greater extent than their current financial resources might warrant. Both of these organizations are located in Washington, DC, within walking distance of the White House. Whether the US is meaningfully empowered by this is unclear, but US negotiators thought it would be when they insisted the institutions be headquartered there. Similarly, the location of the United Nations Environmental Programme secretariat in Nairobi has little practical impact on Kenya's material power resources, but the Kenyan government acts as if the prestige effects are important (e.g., Ivanova 2012).

There is also the broader set of rules and issue remits of international organizations. These do not empower states in the same sort of specific way as the other aspects of institutional structure discussed previously. But they do support and reinforce particular worldviews, thereby supporting those countries that share those worldviews. For example, the UN Office on Drugs and Crime (UNODC) operates under the assumption, drawn from international law, that the international trade in narcotics is illegal. This assumption frames the UNODC's activities—its remit does not include questioning the assumption that any trade in narcotics should be criminalized. This framing of the issue reinforces the political position both of countries that favor strict enforcement over those that favor legalization and of importing countries over exporting countries. This issue framing helps to reinforce the position of US narcotics policy preferences in the international politics of narcotics control over those of many Western European countries (which often prefer a softer approach) and many Latin American countries (which would prefer that the US take more responsibility for its internal consumption problem rather than focusing on controlling production abroad).

Finally, there are the direct effects of international institutions on the material resources of states. In the traditional realm of realist politics—military power—institutions can be an effective way of magnifying the effectiveness of a given set of military tools. They can, in other words, intervene between resources and capabilities. For example, they may guide choices about weapons procurement and collaboration that enable military options to be employed. On the one hand, participation in alliances such as NATO is well-known for raising free-riding challenges. On the other hand, the NATO alliance provides an institutional framework that can prosecute wars on behalf of its member states with a collaborative decision-making framework and ready resources. Institutions enable material resources in less straightforward ways as well. One of the most important institutional resources for the US in war-fighting capacity is its command structures that span the globe. In other words: real estate. It is useful to employ unilateral drone warfare when it reduces risk and is likely to yield an effective outcome, but drones are based all over the world. The network of agreements and relationships that make this possible are key institutional effects.

Institutions can also have effects on states' economic and financial power. Trade agreements, for example, inevitably favor the trade patterns of some countries over those of others and thereby have differentially empowering effects on those countries. Large economically developed states use international organizations such as the Financial Action Task Force to better leverage financial power to win policy concessions from other states over issues ranging from terrorist financing to tax sheltering (Drezner 2008). And some multilateral environmental agreements contain mechanisms for developing states to leverage environmental power to gain financial resources—for example, the Multilateral Fund, created as part of the agreement to reduce ozone-depleting substances (DeSombre and Kauffman 1996).

Legitimation and Power

The third set of mechanisms through which international institutions can empower states is legitimation and knowledge effects. Getting others to do what one wants through the simple application of material resources is often impossible. For example, removing a government from power can be accomplished with brute force. But putting in place the sort of government one wants to replace it cannot (as the US discovered in both Iraq and Afghanistan). It is generally the case that the most efficient way to get others to do what one wants them to do is to convince them that it is what they want to do, or that it is the right thing to do. And institutions can be an effective way of creating the legitimacy and knowledge that can do this convincingly.

There is a large literature in IR on legitimation and knowledge, particularly in the context of constructivist approaches (beginning with Kratochwil and Ruggie [1986]). And constructivism was introduced into the IR literature in part as a critique of neorealism (e.g., Wendt 1987). This might seem to suggest that constructivist arguments do not fit well with realism and that therefore a realist institutionalism that draws on constructivist arguments will not work. But a realist worldview is not in fact incompatible with constructivist methodology. Classical realists wrote extensively about normative and intersubjective questions, including morale, beliefs, and legitimacy. Constructivist theory can provide useful methodologies for studying these questions in the context of a realist worldview (Barkin 2010). There is an extensive literature within constructivism on power, particularly on nonmaterial power (e.g., Barnett and Duvall 2005;

Mattern 2001; Krebs and Jackson 2007). These provide a direct link with realist theory.

Institutions help to define expectations of what will, and should, happen. They can affect actors' definitions of their own interests. And they help to legitimate some actors, ideas, and behaviors and to delegitimate others. The international regimes literature, and in particular its neoliberal institutionalist variant, focuses on actor expectations as a key to understanding the cooperative effects of international institutions (Krasner 1982). According to this argument, actors cooperate in part because institutions create conditions in which they expect others to reciprocate and in part because they know what is expected of them (Keohane 1986). What the regimes literature generally fails to discuss is that these expectations often serve some interests better than others.

For example, an expectation that international security crises will, first and foremost, be discussed at the Security Council empowers those states that have a seat there, and even more so those that have a veto. An expectation that developing states will have "differentiated responsibilities" in multilateral environmental agreements empowers developing countries, particularly larger and richer ones, at the expense of those countries categorized as developed. And an expectation that primary resources are not covered by international trade rules allows exporters of these resources to form cartels that would be deemed unacceptable in manufactured exports. Institutions also help to define actor interests in ways that affect state power. This can happen at the scale of general interests—the institutionalization of democracy and human rights as norms in the UN system probably encourages the development of these norms in populations (or at least parts of populations) globally, which not only empowers countries that can claim to respect these norms but more specifically threatens the power of governments that do not.

Institutions can also affect more specific interests through more specific mechanisms. An example can be seen in the phenomenon of election monitoring. It is increasingly becoming the case that governments in countries with limited democratic credentials allow election monitors, even when they would much prefer to have free rein to cheat, and sometimes even when they plan to cheat. Before election monitoring was an established practice, there was no opprobrium attached to not using the practice. But now that it is, there is a general assumption that governments that do not allow election monitors are planning to cheat, so governments that plan to cheat are not any worse off for allowing monitors. Expectations create an interest in monitoring, but the whole system has the effect of delegitimizing governments that cheat in elections (Kelley 2008).

Finally, institutions are often viewed as guarantors of legitimacy. States working through multilateral frameworks, especially global neutral ones such as the UN, will secure a legitimacy dividend they would not yield if undertaking a mission or operation alone. The relationship between institutions and legitimacy is not that straightforward, however; legitimacy generally inheres to the mission rather than the institutional framework that births the policy.

That which constitutes legitimate action, in terms of both behavior and ideas, is historically variable—the content of legitimacy is specific to time and place (Bukovansky 2002). Ultimately, action or ideas that are accepted as legitimate entail an element of "moral appropriateness" and are consistent with intersubjective understandings of just or correct principles—those principles, institutions, norms, or rules deemed worthy in themselves of pursuing or obeying (Clark 2005; S. Mulligan 2006; Shinoda 2000; Hurd 1999, 2008). Determining what is or is not legitimate is complex. However, to the extent that one can take world opinion as an indicator of legitimacy, one can see that the use of international institutions did not automatically lend the legitimacy participant states frequently sought to the operations undertaken by the United States and its allies in the post–Cold War world (Weitsman 2014). The conditions under which institutions provide a legitimacy dividend require further examination.

One approach to addressing the legitimating effects of international institutions is provided by Alexander Thompson, who argues that institutions have varying degrees of "neutrality" and therefore vary in the degree to which they convey legitimation and political benefit to states that work through them to advance their own goals. The more global the institution, other things being equal, the more political benefit it yields; regional organizations with less diverse memberships have less neutrality and thus fewer political advantages (Thompson 2006a, 9). Institutions serve as vehicles to transmit information regarding the intentions of the policy purveyor, help to determine levels of international support, and aid states in seeking endorsements that make the achievement of desired outcomes more likely.

More specifically, Thompson argues that international organizations can provide political advantages in many ways to states seeking to legitimize interventions. First, states can use them to signal limited intentions more credibly than they could do unilaterally. They also generate more transparency for any operation subject to the sanction of the international community via the institution. Working through an international organization can also signal to domestic audiences that there are valid reasons for intervention, which heightens support for the mission. In other words, international organizations can serve simultaneously both to legitimate action internationally and to increase its domestic legitimacy.

Conclusion

There is an enormous literature in IR on international institutions, on what they do, how they do it, how effective they are, how they interact with states, and so forth. But because the study of institutions other than the state does not fit within the most parsimonious and streamlined neorealisms, realists in general have for the most part ignored this literature for decades. As a result, international institutions are often understudied in security studies. At the same time, states, even militarily powerful states, clearly care about international institutions. They put considerable effort into creating and maintaining them and put political capital into designing and changing them. They recognize the effects of institutions on the translation of material capabilities into power and work through them even when material considerations do not warrant their involvement. If states are the central actors in realist analysis, and states act in a way that clearly signals the centrality of institutions to international relations, then realists need to address the role of international institutions more directly. Realists may well be correct in arguing that international institutions do not make states secure, but states nonetheless use institutions to make themselves more secure.

A realist institutionalism would fill this lacuna in the IR literature generally, and the realist and security literatures specifically. It would draw on the existing institutionalist literatures in IR, be they neoliberal, historical, constructivist, or new institutionalist, to better understand the role of institutions in international politics in general, and security studies in particular, and better understand how states and international institutions interact. But it would do so from a specifically realist perspective, focusing on how international institutions empower states and how states in turn empower international institutions. This would help both to bring realist theory into a twenty-first century in which institutions clearly matter in international politics and to anchor institutionalist theory in a Westphalian system in which states are still the key actors in international relations, they still prioritize security issues, and power is still the ultimate guarantor of their interests.

CHAPTER 3

A Neoclassical Realist Explanation of International Institutions

Norrin M. Ripsman

Structural realists maintain that international institutions have no independent effect on state behavior or international outcomes. To the extent that international institutions condition state behavior, realists argue, they do so merely as a reflection of existing power relations. In general, the strong will shape these institutions according to their power and interests; the weak will be more likely to obey them because they do not have the power to resist the great powers who drive the institutional bus. Consequently, structural realists dismiss institutions as epiphenomenal of great power politics. In this regard, institutions are largely irrelevant, as states will break with them if their interests so dictate (Mearsheimer 1994).[1]

This structural realist claim, while plausible, cannot explain one persistent puzzle. Over two decades ago, Robert O. Keohane and Lisa Martin (1995, 40) posed a question that has not been adequately addressed by realists, despite its importance for explaining world politics and the explanatory power of realism: If international institutions are irrelevant, why do states (including great powers) spend so much time, resources, and influence on them? How do we explain, for example, the British and French desire to create the North Atlantic Treaty Organization (NATO) in 1949 if institutions do not change the underlying dynamics of world politics? NATO Secretary General Lord Hastings Ismay's oft-quoted rationale for NATO was "to keep the Russians out, the Americans in, and the Germans down" (see Nye 2000, 53). Yet if structural realists are correct, the alliance should have been either unable or unnecessary to accomplish these goals. American power alone should have been sufficient to keep the Russians out and the Germans down, if the United States wanted. No alliance or any other institutions should have been capable of keeping the Americans committed to Europe if their interests required them to exit. So why was NATO so important? Moreover, even the US, the all-powerful unipole, was eager in 1990, 1999, 2001, and 2002–3 to get the United Nations or NATO to endorse its military operations in Iraq, Serbia, and Afghanistan. Why would it matter if these institutions have no significant effect on international politics?[2]

Neoclassical realism can offer some insights into this question that structural realism cannot. Focusing on security institutions (of the military and diplomatic variety), this chapter will explore how neoclassical realism—which argues that states construct foreign policy to respond to international imperatives but that domestic political arrangements also have an intervening influence between systemic pressures and national foreign policy responses—can clarify why even realists should acknowledge that states, even great powers, should and do care about international institutions. I focus exclusively on security institutions, such as alliances, collective security organizations, and regional security institutions, because institutional cooperation in the security area should paradoxically be the most difficult to explain from a power political perspective (e.g., Lipson 1984). After all, in an anarchic environment, where security and survival matter most, states should be reluctant to restrict their autonomy in the security area as well as to trust their security to transnational institutions. Therefore, if I can explain why, from a realist perspective, states would want to delegate authority to an international institution in the realm of high politics, it would carry more weight than explaining cooperation in an area that realists would consider peripheral and of little consequence. I focus on more formal institutions, which fits within Wivel and Paul's definition of *associational clusters among states with some bureaucratic structures that create and manage self-imposed and other-imposed constraints on state policies and behaviors.*

In general, neoclassical realists would agree with structural realists that great powers will ignore institutional demands or, in extreme circumstances, terminate their membership when national interests diverge sharply from the requirements of international institutions. These types of clashes, however, are relatively rare. Most of the time, security institutions and alliances offer states certain advantages that enable state leaders to overcome domestic resource mobilization problems, maintain their power positions, and balance their short-term power-projection needs with their need to avoid squandering long-term power resources. Consequently, it is rational for state leaders to join these institutions in order to provide maximum security at a manageable cost, thereby maximizing both their international and domestic priorities.

The chapter addresses two primary audiences. First, it addresses realists, who have been conditioned to dismiss international institutions as of little importance to international politics. Second, it addresses those who would dismiss realism because of its inability to account for consequential effects of international institutions. By conflating realism with a rather narrow version of structural realism, both groups misunderstand the degree to which international institutions can help states to achieve distinctly realist national interests, thus earning them a place—albeit a limited one—in the realist toolbox of statecraft.[3]

I begin with a brief summary of the structural realist position on international institutions. I then overview the neoclassical realist challenge to structural realism and explore how neoclassical realist insights can help explain the utility of international institutions in a manner that is consistent with realpolitik and power politics. Before concluding, I distinguish the realist logic developed in this chapter from liberal institutionalist explanations of international institutions.

The Structural Realist Logic

Structural realists claim that international institutions are of little relevance to international politics (Wivel and Paul's introduction to this volume; Stein 2008, 206). They assume that in an anarchical international system, where security is scarce, states must rely on themselves to ensure their survival. Consequently, they prefer to balance internally rather than externally, if at all possible, as they cannot trust their alliance partners to come to their assistance (Waltz 1979). Under these circumstances, states cannot afford to bind themselves to international institutions, which are also unreliable, since there is no way to compel other states—especially great powers—to honor their commitments under anarchy (Snyder 1984; Downs, Rocke, and Barsoom 1996). Therefore, while great powers may participate in international institutions, they prefer not to put too much faith in them and they are unlikely to be constrained by them. When their interests diverge from institutional demands, they will simply withdraw from the institutions, as Germany and Japan did from the League of Nations in the interwar years (see Pedersen 2015), or they will violate commitments made to them, as French president Charles de Gaulle did repeatedly until he ultimately withdrew from NATO in 1966 (see Spirtas 1999). John Mearsheimer (2001, 364) thus argues, "The rhetoric about the growing strength of international institutions notwithstanding, there is little evidence that they can get great powers to act contrary to the dictates of realism."

To the extent that institutions matter in international politics, however, structural realists follow E. H. Carr's lead (1946, 86) in assuming that they are merely a tool of great powers to exercise their dominance. As Stanley Hoffmann (1973, 49) argued, "International institutions, in their political processes and in their functions, reflect, and to a large extent magnify or modify the dominant features of the international system. Therefore, institutions are merely epiphenomenal of power relations and have no independent effect on world politics" (cf. Mearsheimer 1994, 7). Indeed, Mearsheimer (1994, 47) comments, "What is most impressive about institutions, in fact, is how little independent effect they seem to have had on state behavior." Kenneth Waltz (2000, 20) thus observes of NATO expansion, rather than its retrenchment or dissolution, after the Cold

War: "The survival and expansion of NATO tell us much about American power and influence and little about institutions as multilateral entities." Consequently, realists judge that the expectations of liberals and constructivists that institutions can restrain competition and foster cooperation in interstate politics is misplaced.

A Neoclassical Realist Explanation of International Institutions

While structural realism has dominated the realist discourse in recent decades, it represents only one branch of realism (see Walt 2002; Brooks 1997). As Randall Schweller and David Priess (1997) observe, earlier classical realists treated international institutions with considerably more respect than structural realists do, viewing them as mechanisms to exclude other states and bind their rivals (see also Samuel Barkin's contribution to this volume). While Schweller and Priess build on what was an emerging trend in the mid-1990s of "modified structural realism" to construct a theory of international institutions focusing on the motivations of states (i.e., whether they are status quo or revisionist powers) and the differing effects of polarity, I ground my approach in the culmination of that trend: neoclassical realism.

Neoclassical realists agree with structural realists that states conduct national security policy primarily in response to international constraints and opportunities. Nonetheless, they argue that structural realism presents an oversimplified view of both the international system and the states that navigate it. In particular, they charge that structural realists overestimate the clarity of the international system, the degree to which decision makers perceive systemic stimuli correctly, the rationality of decision making, and the ease with which states can mobilize societal resources to implement policy. To remedy these shortcomings, they contend that national responses to systemic pressures are conditioned by domestic-level intervening variables that affect national perception of systemic stimuli, the formation of policy responses, and the mobilization of societal resources to implement those policies (Ripsman, Taliaferro, and Lobell 2016; Rose 1998; Schweller 2003; Rathbun 2008). Neoclassical realists are not, therefore, subject to the critique often leveled against structural realists that they treat all states as identical, failing to differentiate between them (e.g., Wivel 2017, 15). Instead, neoclassical realists consider how the unique domestic political and institutional contexts of states can influence even their security behavior, at least to some degree.

An implication is that governments may select policy responses to international pressures that are more likely to overcome domestic opposition that could interfere with policymaking and to ease resource mobilization dilemmas they may face so that they are able to respond to external threats and opportunities more effectively. The motivation in this case is not domestic political, but international strategic. Furthermore, states must balance between their immediate power mobilization needs and their ability to extract resources in the future. They will consequently be sensitive to policy choices that either squander their resources or create domestic constraints that will hamper their ability to mobilize resources in the future.

Neoclassical realism fits within the realist approach to international politics because it shares the core assumptions that unite disparate realist works. Notably, it assumes that the international system is anarchical, that states are the primary international actors, that states prize security over all other goals—although security is not their only goal—that cooperation is difficult under anarchy, and that material capabilities and relative power have a predominant influence on international outcomes (Frankel 1996; P. James 2002). In addition, it assumes that states privilege the external environment when making foreign security policy. Therefore, a neoclassical realist explanation of the utility of international institutions would constitute the only realist effort to take institutions seriously, rather than dismiss them summarily.

The neoclassical realist critique of structural realism suggests several possible uses for multilateral security institutions from a realist perspective. States should be interested in institutions for several reasons: (1) to share the burden of defense with other states in order to alleviate domestic political pressures on the national leadership and preserve national power over the long term, (2) to ease resource mobilization in support of policy, (3) to help leverage the legitimacy of these institutions to generate domestic pressure on other states, and (4) to assist the state in signaling its intent, which may prevent unnecessary and wasteful conflicts. I address each of these motives in the following sections, noting that states should be eager to achieve these goods from international security institutions, provided that they do not constrain national security behavior to an unacceptable degree.

1. Maintaining Power over the Short and Long Terms

While great powers might have the power to act unilaterally and might prefer to do so, there are both short- and long-term costs to doing so. In the short run, great powers must face the domestic political costs of mobilizing resources in support of policy, especially in the event of war. As neoclassical realists point out, states do not have automatic access to the money, materiel, and manpower required to implement policy and prosecute a war; they must extract them from their population and key economic actors (Ripsman, Taliaferro, and Lobell 2016; Lobell, Ripsman, and Taliaferro 2009). Resource mobilization can, therefore, entail domestic political costs if the burden of taxation is too onerous for the population or if key economic interests are unhappy bearing the costs of the war (Barnett 1992; Cappella Zielinski 2016). In extreme cases the economic deprivation that can result from war can compel a population to overthrow its leaders, which not only is detrimental to the leadership but can also undermine the national war effort (Bueno de Mesquita and Siverson 1995; Bueno de Mesquita et al. 2003; Chiozza and Goemans 2003). Indeed, the high cost of war was a significant factor in the 1917 Bolshevik Revolution—which led to the collapse of the Russian front, dramatic Central Power advances into Russian core territory, and the disastrous peace of Brest-Litovsk (see W. Mulligan 2014)—as well as the overthrow of Kaiser Wilhelm in Germany at the end of World War I (see Wheeler-Bennett 1971; Wargelin 1997). In democratic states the costs of war mobilization can hurt a leader's reelection prospects and impose limitations on the leadership's ability to wage war. For example, growing public dissatisfaction with the Vietnam War and the mobilization of troops through the draft led US president Lyndon Johnson not to seek reelection in 1968 and to scale back the US military campaign in Vietnam (Dallek 2005; Mack 1975).

Since leaders wish not only to maximize national interests but also to stay in power and achieve their other idiosyncratic goals for which staying in power is a necessary condition, it makes sense for them to seek a means to reduce the costs of war and power projection to avoid fates similar to those of Czar Nicholas, Kaiser Wilhelm, and Johnson, as long as doing so would not jeopardize national security. International security institutions offer them the prospect of burden sharing or splitting the costs of force or power projection with other institutional members (see, e.g., Sandler and Forbes 1980), also known as "pooling" (Abbott and Snidal 1998). While institutional procedures might slow down the mobilization process and devolve some control to outside actors, it may be rational to accept these trade-offs if state leaders fear that they could lose power in an election, revolution, or coup, especially if they believe that the institution is capable of meeting the security challenge the state faces. Thus, as Gi-Heon Kwon (1995) observes, patterns of international burden sharing are often influenced by domestic political considerations.

Aside from considerations of leadership survival, which realists view as of secondary importance to national security, burden sharing can offer a state the ability to conserve its resources so that it can secure itself both now and later. Over the long run, great powers that squander their resources needlessly can hasten what Kennedy (1994, 374) calls imperial or strategic "overstretch," which he defines as "a mismatch between a Great Power's obligations and its capabilities, between its desired policies and its actual resources." In Kennedy's view overstretch is the principal force that undermines great power status (see Kennedy 1989). Therefore, since statecraft involves intertemporal trade-offs to provide security in both the short and long term, participating in multilateral security frameworks can, under certain circumstances, help great powers navigate this dilemma (see Edelstein 2002; Streich and Levy 2007; for a skeptical view, see Krebs and Rapport 2012). While they may face short-term advantages if they conduct power politics and use force unilaterally on their own terms, these advantages may be counterbalanced by incentives to utilize multilateralism and international institutions in order to conserve power resources for the long haul. In this regard, in the midst of a severe economic crisis, the Obama administration's decision to "lead from behind" and rely heavily on NATO allies to spearhead the 2011 Libya intervention reflected a desire to conserve US power resources for the longer term (K. Marsh 2014). The decision to go it alone or pursue a collaborative security policy may consequently not be as stark and simple as structural realists portray it.

An additional long-term incentive relates to the domestic mobilization of resources discussed previously. If, as Michael Barnett (1992) observes, states must frequently bargain with societal actors to secure resources to implement security policy, that too can affect long-term state power. If leaders strike short-term bargains to secure policy support and needed resources in return for devolution of state power in the future, that may constrain the state excessively and, consequently, undermine its ability both to mobilize resources and project power effectively in the future. In this manner, for example, Barnett (1992, 217–25) argues that the Egyptian war mobilization strategy in the late 1960s and early 1970s, while effective at rebuilding the Egyptian military after its devastating 1967 defeat, led to an overall decline in the power of the Egyptian state, making it far more dependent on external support for its security goals. Relying on international institutions to defray the costs of security now can help forestall political compromises that might undermine long-term state power later.

The need to preserve national power for the future can also inspire participation in institutions that can reduce the number and magnitude of challenges that the great power will face. For example, the nuclear Non-Proliferation Treaty (NPT) and the non-proliferation regime more broadly serve to discourage would-be proliferants from developing nuclear weapons.[4] This assists nuclear great powers in two important ways, both of which preserve their long-term power and influence. First, to the extent that it does prevent some states from developing nuclear weapons, it preserves the great powers' dominance vis-à-vis these weaker states at relatively low cost, without the need for costly military counter-proliferation efforts. Second, it reduces the number of targets on which nuclear powers need to squander harder power, such as economic sanctions or military coercion, to prevent them from proliferating (see Simpson 1985). Thus, while the US has had to employ sanctions and other coercive instruments against Iran and North Korea in recent years to prevent nuclear proliferation, it has not had to do this with the vast majority of countries around the world thanks in large part to the NPT. In these ways, institutional membership can help great powers manage their interests while husbanding their power resources for the long haul.

Thus, if great powers can reduce the short- and long-term costs of power projection and war through burden sharing within international institutions, that would be a rational course of action and consistent with a power-based, realist understanding of international politics.

2. Easing Policy Mobilization and Resource Extraction from Domestic Population

As mentioned, neoclassical realists maintain that leaders cannot always balance automatically—as structural realists assume—because they do not have full control over the policy process and do not have automatic access to national resources for foreign policy purposes. Consequently, they must often bargain with societal actors for these resources (Taliaferro, Lobell, and Ripsman 2009; Ripsman, Taliaferro, and Lobell 2016). International security institutions may assist them in this bargaining process by cloaking the state's policy preferences in a shroud of legitimacy (see Voeten 2005).[5] As David Lake (1992) observes, stakeholders are more likely to support a policy that they oppose if they view the procedure with which it was decided as legitimate. Jean-Marc Blanchard and I (2013, 29–30) have similarly argued that leaders who possess greater legitimacy have an easier time convincing political opponents to support a policy that imposes costs on them. The legitimacy derived from the support of respected international institutions and internationally legitimate procedures should act in a similar fashion, inspiring societal actors to be more willing to sacrifice their personal interests in support of the legitimate policy.[6] Indeed, in the US context, Terrence L. Chapman and Dan Reiter (2004) demonstrate that public support of the US president spikes after the UN Security Council endorses a US use of force, which suggests that it does bolster the legitimacy of military operations.

In this manner President George H. W. Bush coordinated his response to the 1990 Iraqi invasion of Kuwait with the UN not only to influence other states to join the coalition but also to overcome US domestic opposition, particularly within the Senate, to the use of force (Brands 2004, 127). Similarly, President George W. Bush vainly sought UN and later NATO support for his 2003 war against Iraq, in part to mollify an American public and Congress that was split over whether force was warranted (Hook and Spanier 2016). Since the motivation here is less about domestic politics than it is about mobilizing power resources for interstate warfare, it is a quintessentially realist calculation.

3. Generating Domestic Pressure on Other States

Structural realists contend that leaders in an anarchic international system might not care that much about the legitimacy of their policy choices. Since policy mistakes under anarchy could threaten national survival, considerations of legitimacy and morality are subordinate to pragmatic calculations (Kennan 1954; Art and Waltz 1983, 6). Nonetheless, while leaders may not care much, their populations, legislators, and key interest groups might care a great deal about legitimacy. Since, as neoclassical realists acknowledge, not all states possess the autonomy to conduct policy independently of societal actors (Ripsman 2002), the ability to cloak a state's policies in the international legitimacy provided by international institutions may go a long way in untying the hands of less-autonomous allies to support one's policy and generate domestic pressure on those who oppose it. This may explain why the elder President Bush, who secured a UN mandate to wage war against Iraq in 1991, fought alongside a large coalition of states, whereas the younger President Bush, who failed to secure either UN or NATO endorsement in 2003, cobbled together only a small "coalition of the willing."

Conversely, the failure to generate that legitimacy by failing to carry the support of international institutions may reduce international support. In this regard, consider the case of Canada's position toward the 2003 Iraq War. Prime Minister Jean Chretien's government declared in October 2002 that it would support war against Iraq only if the UN authorized the use of force. When the UN failed to do so, amid widespread opposition in Canada—especially in the politically significant province of Quebec—to a war without the UN, the Canadian government remained officially outside the US-led coalition. That a middle power like Canada would shun its most important ally and trade partner—especially after September 11, 2001, when US president George W. Bush declared that states were "either with us or against us"—is testimony to the importance of the domestic legitimacy provided by international institutions (see O'Connor and Vucetic 2010). If the fig leaf of institutional legitimacy can help states augment their power by securing allies, that would be a very realist consideration.

4. Signaling

As neoclassical realists and others point out, the international system does not always provide clear signals to states about constraints, opportunities, and the likely consequences of one's actions (Ripsman, Taliaferro, and Lobell 2016). In the absence of clear signals, unwanted war can occur as a result of misperception and deterrence failure (see Jervis 1988; Stoessinger 2010; Blainey 1988). Furthermore, power politics is not primarily about power, but influence. A great power will employ power resources in an attempt to induce and compel other states to behave in accordance with its interests (see Baldwin 2002; Schmidt and Juneau 2012; Ripsman, Taliaferro, and Lobell 2016).[7] States do not want to squander power unnecessarily in their efforts to influence others, or else their ability to influence others in the future will be undermined. Therefore, it is essential for states to send clear signals to facilitate the indirect use of force, which is much more efficient than the direct use of military power (Schelling 2008; Art 1980; Snyder 2015).

Participation in international institutions allows states to signal their intentions in a public forum, which facilitates interstate influence attempts. Robert

Keohane and Lisa Martin (2010, 56) note, therefore, "States may be as concerned with providing information about themselves—hence bolstering their credibility and therefore the value of their commitments—as they are with acquiring information about others." In the liberal literature, much has been made about the utility of international institutions as a means of sending costly signals of benign intent (see Lipson 2003; Thompson 2006b). Realists, however, are more interested in a different kind of signaling: communicating threats for the purposes of deterrence and signaling resolve to both allies and adversaries. To the extent that membership in an alliance or a public position taken in a multilateral security organization can help send clear signals of intent, states, even great powers, should be eager to use these tools to advance their interests, provided that the cost is manageable. In this manner, for example, US participation in NATO signaled to both the United States' Western European allies and the Soviet Union that the US would resist any Soviet attempts to change the status quo in Europe by force (see Kaplan 1984).

How This Differs from Liberal Institutionalism

Each of the motivations for participation in security institutions discussed previously has as its core purpose the mobilization or projection of power to advance the state's security interests in an anarchic international system. These motivations consequently differ markedly from liberal explanations, which privilege the pursuit of efficiency, economic welfare, or cooperation (e.g., Keohane 1984; Haggard and Simmons 1987; Martin 1993; Stein 2008). In general, liberal institutionalists argue that states embed themselves in international institutions because they mitigate anarchy and its attendant risks of cooperation by providing transparency, monitoring compliance, and detecting cheating (K. Weber 1997; Abbott and Snidal 1998; Fortna 2003). In addition, they reduce the transaction costs associated with cooperation, making it easier and more efficient for states to cooperate (Keohane 1984). This is a substantially different set of explanations from the power- and security-focused neoclassical realist logic I outlined previously.

As I argue elsewhere, liberal approaches to cooperation rest on interests that are at least partially overlapping: the creation of incentives that extend the shadow of the future (Oye 1986) and instrumental trust. In contrast, realist theories view cooperation as episodic, fleeting, and devoid of trust, based instead on short-term calculations of strategic interest (Ripsman 2005; Hoffman 2007; Kydd 2005). Thus, a neoclassical realist theory of cooperation within international institutions rests on a distinct set of assumptions about what motivates states from those that underlie liberal theories.[8] Nonetheless, not all liberal explanations are necessarily incompatible with realism. For example, Keohane's efficiency/transaction cost–reduction model only conflicts with realism if states pursue efficiency for its own sake or for the promotion of welfare. If they do so to conserve resources to preserve power, that would be perfectly consistent with realism. Thus, in principle, a neoclassical realist theory of international institutions could also incorporate elements of liberal insights without departing from a realist framework.[9] Nonetheless, since efficiency and absolute gains underlie the liberal approach to international institutions, liberal theories of international institutions remain analytically separate, and the security-based premises presented in this chapter function as a distinct neoclassical realist logic of international institutions.

Conclusion: A Realist Conception of International Institutions

The puzzle of institutional membership posed by Keohane and Martin *can* be explained within a realist framework. States, even great powers, participate in international institutions because they can make power projection and the use of force more effective, they ease national resource mobilization dilemmas, and they help the state conserve its power resources to enable it to safeguard national security in the future. Failing to use these institutions, therefore, might undermine leaders' other critical goals, such as maintaining power and preserving great power status over the longer term. For these reasons, even the greatest of powers might occasionally feel compelled to adhere to adverse institutional decisions in order to enable themselves to reap the rewards of membership (see Karns and Mingst 1990).

A neoclassical realist perspective—which recognizes that leaders do not necessarily have automatic access to domestic resources, that the way states respond to international pressures depends in part on their unique domestic circumstances, and that states must balance between short-term international exigencies and long-term power requirements—can thus shed more light on the utility of international institutions than structural realism can. In particular, it can explain the anomaly that the attention states devote to international institutions presents for structural realism. This represents a significant step forward for realism and confirms what my colleagues and I argue elsewhere: namely, that neoclassical realism can help explain much of what structural realists merely bracket away, such as international institutions, non-state actors, ideas, and domestic politics (Ripsman, Taliaferro, and Lobell 2016; Kitchen 2010).

Nonetheless, consistent with other branches of realism, neoclassical realism does not expect too much from international institutions. Like other realists, neoclassical realists would not expect states to sacrifice high-level interests to secure the benefits of institutional cooperation. When major conflicts of interest occur between the institutions and the great powers, neoclassical realists too would expect the great powers to go their own way, as the George W. Bush administration did in 2003 or France and Great Britain did in response to Italy's invasion of Abyssinia in the 1930s. Thus, the neoclassical realist position is still grounded in power politics and does not assume that international institutions radically transform international politics, as liberal institutionalists and constructivists do.

Notes

I am grateful for comments on earlier drafts of this paper by Sammy Barkin, Annette Freyberg-Inan, Patrick James, Steven Lobell, T.V. Paul, Paul Poast, Alex Thompson, Anders Wivel, and participants at presentations at the Program on International Politics, Economics, and Security (PIPES) at the University of Chicago, February 2017, and the Dornsife School of International Studies at the University of Southern California, February 2017. I also thank Shoghig Mikaelian and Austin Margulies for their research assistance.

1. For this reason, attempts to explain international institutions from structural realist premises are few and far between. For the argument that a structural realist logic can be applied to explain international institutions, see, e.g., Grieco (1990) and Wivel (2004).

2. Of course, states' predilection for joining institutions could be misguided, but since, as Waltz (1979, 76, 128) observes, states are socialized over time to emulate the successful practices of others while eschewing their less rational behaviors, the persistence of institutional membership makes it a puzzle that realists need to explain.

3. I borrow this metaphor from Baldwin (1985).

4. See also the discussion of the Non-Proliferation Treaty regime in Steven E. Lobell and Brad Nicolson's contribution to this volume.

5. Of course, not all international institutions command legitimacy, nor do all states view the same institutions as being legitimate. Thus, for example, the Israeli public, which views the UN as biased in favor of the Arab world, may be less likely to see the UN as a source of policy legitimacy. For representative Israeli views, see Beker (1988) and Gold (2004).

6. Kenneth Schultz (2003, 117), for example, observes, "The blessing of international bodies serves to make the operation more palatable for public opinion."

7. For other neoclassical realists who use an "elements of national power" approach, see Wohlforth (1993, 6–7) and Schweller (1997, 17–18).

8. Constructivist theories of cooperation within international institutions differ from these materialist explanations in that both realists and liberals expect cooperation only when it is in the national interest (strategic and, for liberals, also economic). In contrast, many constructivists conceive of the possibility of an altruistic trust, in which actors may cooperate with institutional requirements even if it means the state sacrifices national gains (Ripsman 2005; cf. Hoffman 2007; Hoffman 2006; Kydd 2005), while others might explain cooperation as a by-product of identities and practices that have little to do with rationalist interests (e.g., Adler and Pouliot 2011b).

9. Indeed, by its very nature, neoclassical realism seeks to enrich structural realism by drawing on liberal and constructivist insights that can be incorporated into a realist ontology to improve explanatory power without undermining the core realist propositions. To this end, insights about domestic constraints and perceptual limitations help inform the unit- and subunit-level intervening variables that mediate between the systemic constraints and opportunities that drive international politics according to structural realists, on the one hand, and the policy choices states make and international outcomes, on the other (Ripsman, Taliaferro, and Lobell 2016).

CHAPTER 4

Pyrrhic Victory:
A World of Liberal Institutions,
Teeming with Tensions

Georg Sørensen

International institutions (both formal international organizations and less formal sets of rules that govern state action in particular areas; see definition in the introductory chapter of this book) play a key role in the liberal vision of the world. Woodrow Wilson wanted to replace traditional power politics with regulated and peaceful intercourse—the realpolitik of the "Jungle," where dangerous beasts roam and the strong and cunning rule would give way to the orderliness of a kind of "Zoo," where the beasts are put into cages reinforced by the restraints of international organization. According to some more recent liberal thinkers, this view is too optimistic, but present-day liberals continue to emphasize the positive impact of international institutions. Liberals also concede, however, that international institutions are arenas for power politics in which states pursue national interests in competition with other states (see the definition of power politics in the introductory chapter; see also Wivel 2017).

Liberal principles have given rise to several different schools of thought in relation to power and international institutions, some of which are more optimistic than others concerning institutions as vehicles for cooperation. I propose to briefly examine three different strands of liberal thought as a backdrop to an assessment of real-world developments. There have been many different currents in liberal thought since the end of World War II (for an overview, see Jackson and Sørensen 2016, chap. 4); what follows does not give justice to them all. Focus is on major liberal positions in relation to realist thought.[1]

The Cold War: Weak Liberalism

It is perhaps surprising that the Cold War period saw the emergence of an influential liberal analysis that stressed the importance of interdependence and cooperation. This is nonetheless what happened with the contribution by Robert Keohane and Joseph Nye in *Power and Interdependence* (1977). Their argument was that in one part of the international system—the global West of Western Europe, North America, East Asia, and Oceania—the realist system of anarchy, insecurity, and power politics was being replaced by a system of complex interdependence. In this system transnational actors were increasingly important, economic and institutional instruments were more useful than military force, and welfare issues were ranking higher on the agenda than military security. International (Western) institutions played a key role as vehicles for this more cooperative and peaceful order.

Realists were not happy with this account. Kenneth Waltz put realist theory in front with his *Theory of International Politics* (1979). This parsimonious analysis, based on anarchy and the balance of power, squarely focused on unequal state capabilities and placed great power relations, security, and the imminent risk of war on top of the agenda. For Waltz, international institutions were handmaidens for the pursuit of the interests of strong states.

Keohane and Nye had already conceded that even among modern, industrialized countries, an issue could become "a matter of life and death" and then "realist assumptions would again be a reliable guide to events" (Keohane and Nye 1977, 28–29). In the face of realist critique, Keohane maintained that institutions could facilitate cooperation, but only under certain conditions. The most important condition is the existence of common interests among states (Keohane 1993, 277).

These modifications made for a rather weak liberalism: states in anarchy is the starting point, security is a major concern, and state power strongly influences the formation and functioning of international institutions. Realists were quick to point out that this kind of liberalism is merely neorealism "by another name" (Mearsheimer 1995, 85). However, the end of the Cold War helped produce different variants of liberalism that could not be blamed for emulating realism.

The End of the Cold War: Strong Liberalism

Two liberal developments characterized the end of the Cold War: first, a rapid increase in the number of liberal democracies in the world; second, an intensification of economic globalization. For the first time, almost all states were eager to participate in a global economic marketplace. So liberal values, political and economic, were moving forward.

Liberal theory responded with fresh optimism, following the trail blazed by Francis Fukuyama (1989). More recently, Kishore Mahbubani (2014, 55) suggested a "comprehensive theory" of one world, resting on four pillars of convergence (the following draws on Mahbubani [2014, 51–89]):

- *The economic pillar:* There is now a single, global economy, and narrow, national efforts can no longer fix national economies. The march of economic liberalization will continue to strengthen the emerging global economy.
- *The technological pillar:* The advance of technology helps bring about a new global identity. The previous connection to the village, city, or country will be overlapped by new layers of identity, drawn from the connection across borders.
- *The environmental pillar:* Threats to the environment unite the inhabitants of the globe. We need to preserve our one home, yet governance of global issues like the environment is in short supply.
- *The aspirational pillar:* The vast majority of the world's population now shares a common set of material aspirations that help create common interests which override differences in ideology or religion. We are moving toward a one-world dynamic in which our aspirations are greater than our differences.

In short, globalization and integration are pulling us closer in various ways, and power is increasingly dispersed. Government is being replaced by governance in a multilayer and multicentric system (Cerny 2010; Scholte 2010). The most optimistic proponents of strong liberalism look forward to a world where governance above and below the level of the nation-state will be of rapidly increasing importance.

As for international institutions, the inside liberal order that had existed under the structure of bipolar confrontation became the outside order. There was now only one order for the entire world, "bound together by multilateral rules and institutions, a globalizing form of capitalism, and American political leadership" (Ikenberry 2011, 275).

These prospects were questioned from the beginning of the present century. The terrorist attacks of September 11, 2001, emphasized nonconventional security threats to liberal democracies and paved the way for complex wars in Afghanistan and Iraq. The problem of fragile states has remained high on the agenda ever since. The financial crisis of 2008 exposed severe weaknesses in the capitalist economic system, the very foundation of globalization. And both the Brexit vote in the UK and the election of Donald Trump in the US helped launch a "my country first" agenda with little connection to multilateralism and integration; these events reconfirmed that we live in a world of sovereign states

(Campbell and Hall 2015) where international institutions are dominated by the interests of the strongest powers.

Today: Skeptic and Hopeful Liberalism

In the present day, the pendulum has again swung away from the optimistic mood behind strong liberalism. Nevertheless, this current is not a return to the weak liberalism of the Cold War that ended up adopting basic neorealist views. According to liberals, in some parts of the international system, anarchy and the security dilemma have been transcended. Among consolidated liberal democracies, interstate war is out of the question. This dramatic transformation rests on both material and ideational change (Sørensen 2001, 2008) that cannot easily be rolled back to the hostile competition of earlier days. Donald Trump and his policies are intensely disliked in many parts of Europe, but the strong ties of friendship across the Atlantic persist.

Even if China and Russia are not democracies, some liberal factors are at play in relation to them as well. These powers are heavily involved in international institutions, and they are strongly committed to market economies with private property and intensive participation in economic globalization. The commitment to capitalism does create a substantial obligation to the institutions and the common rules and norms that are required for the capitalist system to function. Participation in the global network of production, trade, and finance is now a precondition for growth and prosperity in most countries. The nondemocratic great powers may not be the best friends of the liberal democratic West, but nor are they any longer direct enemies. They are rivals who may become friends but might also revert to become enemies.

Changes in the international system, then, have turned us away from raw anarchy and sharply decreased the risk (and incidence) of interstate war, but it is of course not the liberal nirvana that some looked forward to when the Cold War ended. Progress has happened, and more progress is possible, but progress is not guaranteed and things can go the wrong way as well (Sørensen 2011). The election of Donald Trump signifies that "xenophobic strands of backlash politics have proliferated" (Ikenberry 2018, 7) across the liberal democratic world.

Liberal international relations (IR) thinking today is therefore much more skeptical but remains cautiously optimistic. The sovereign states are again the focal point of analysis because they are the major players in global governance, yet it is also noted that non-state actors are an increasingly important feature of the present world order. These actors are tied in with states, and their efforts do not amount to a new world order. They rather signify a transformation of modern states away from national government and toward complex governance in a more globalized world (Sørensen 2016).

How does this more moderate and skeptical liberalism assess international institutions and power politics? On the one hand, there is a hopeful liberal view; it maintains that the current order is in pretty good shape even if it faces several new challenges. Both China and Russia are deeply integrated in the liberal order; global institutions may not always be perfect, but that is increasingly compensated by networks and partnerships at many different levels, a form of piecemeal global governance that actually amounts to "good enough governance" (Patrick 2014, 73).

On the other hand, the current institutional structure is not adequate or effective in the face of today's serious challenges, and the turn toward nationalism and narrow national interest in some Western countries is a significant move in the wrong direction. We are facing gridlock, "a specific set of conditions and mechanisms that impede global cooperation in the present day" (Hale, Held, and Young 2013, 3), and emphasis is often on the resilience of existing institutions rather than on the construction of new ones. It is probably fair to say that this more sinister mood has dominated recent liberal writing on the subject (Niblett 2017; Nye 2017; Peters 2016; Patrick 2016; Ikenberry 2017, 2018; Colgan and Keohane 2017).

The following sections interrogate the relationship between power politics and international institutions from the vantage point of present-day skeptic and hopeful liberalism. This will include an evaluation of the strengths and shortcomings of the liberal world order (the discussion draws on Sørensen [2016]).

Power in the Present World Order

We need an appropriate way of approaching the relationship between power and institutions in today's world order. The framework suggested here is adapted from Cox and Sinclair (1996). It suggests that a stable and legitimate order is founded on a fit among a power base (Cox emphasizes military and economic capabilities), a common collective image of order expressed in values and norms, and an appropriate set of institutions. Figure 4.1 identifies these requirements for a stable and legitimate world order.

Cox identifies the Pax Americana after 1945 as a successful Western order. The US provided security protection and set up a framework for the economic and social reconstruction of Western Europe and Japan. The order was based on common (liberal democratic) values and an appropriate set of international institutions (the North Atlantic Treaty Organization [NATO], the Bretton Woods, and the United Nations systems).[2] The question is whether such an order is possible today on a world scale.

Let us begin with power. It remains a contested concept; there is no space here for presenting that debate (see Berenskoetter and Williams [2007] for an overview; see also Paul [2016] for an in-depth analysis of rising powers). I focus on what is most commonly seen as the most important (material and nonmaterial) power resources. When we focus on military and economic power, there is no doubt about the continued preponderance of the West in general and the United States in particular:

Figure 4.1 Requirements for a Stable and Legitimate World Order

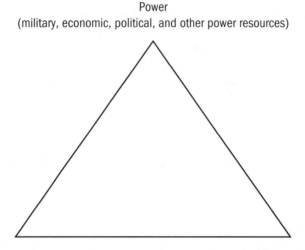

Power
(military, economic, political, and other power resources)

An appropriate set of institutions   Collective image
(values and norms informing world order)

- Military expenditure: Take the fifteen states with the highest military expenditure in 2017. The US share here was 35 percent, China's 13 percent, and Saudi Arabia's 4 percent, while each of the remaining twelve countries accounted for less than 4 percent of the total (Russia was at 3.8 percent in 2018). At the same time, the considerable US expenditure amounted to only 3.1 percent of gross domestic product (GDP), compared to nearly 10 percent during the Vietnam War. This overwhelming military capability is generally agreed to grant the US command of the global commons, that is, the sea, air, and space that "belongs to no one and provide access to much of the globe" (Posen 2003).
- Economic capability: The US share of world GDP in purchasing power parity (PPP) terms was 15.2 percent in 2017. The Chinese share stood at 18.2 percent.[3] In per capita terms, the US stands at US$59,501 and China at US$16,660; that is to say, the Chinese per capita GDP is less than 28 percent of the United States'.

Some skeptics claim that the US/Western lead in military and per capita GDP terms is misleading because current trends point in another direction. Emerging powers, especially China, are catching up fast and will surpass the United States in due course. Twenty-five years ago, the Chinese share of world GDP was 3.81 percent while the US share was more than 25 percent.[4] By 2030 the Chinese economy is expected to be 1.5 times larger than that of the United States.[5] But at the same time, there are serious challenges to the Chinese economy; it is not merely a question of upholding the extreme growth rates of previous decades. In some areas quantitative progress is not matched by qualitative changes; there are environmental and other problems connected to the present model of accumulation.

Further, the connection between material capability and great power status is complex. One aspect of this is whether there are specific kinds of economic strength or military strength that are relatively more important than others. Another aspect concerns the ability to convert economic capacity into actual power across a broad range of issues (Zakaria 1998). In today's world a wide range of power resources, including soft power and institutional power, are needed in order to take the lead. Most observers agree that from this perspective, the United States "will likely remain the world's most powerful country" for some considerable time (Nye 2002; S. Brown 2013, 24).

Meanwhile, the US and West also have problems, even in the face of preponderant material and nonmaterial capabilities. Power is not merely about a variety of resources. It is also about the willingness and ability to make use of these resources in relation to other actors. A nation can be extremely powerful in terms of power resources; at the same time, it can put these resources to use in a way that will undermine rather than enhance its overall power position. That is because we are in a world where even a superpower needs the cooperation of others to achieve its aims, and that requires legitimacy. "The paradox of American power at the end of this millennium," wrote Sebastian Mallaby in 1999, "is that it is too great to be challenged by any other state, yet not great enough to solve problems such as global terrorism and nuclear proliferation. America needs the help and respect of other nations."[6]

In sum, any US or US-Western project of world-order creation faces external challenges from emerging powers, conflict-ridden regions, and human catastrophes in fragile states. It is also constrained, or even driven, by domestic tensions. Reduced social cohesion in the wake of neoliberal globalization, a squeezed middle class, and political polarization and gridlock have created domestic situations in the US and Western liberal democracies that are not conducive to the pursuit of hegemonic projects that will also involve some holding back on the pursuit of narrow national interests for the larger purpose of a stable and effective order.

Overall, the US-Western power position is simultaneously strong and precarious. What are the consequences for international institutions, and what does this mean for the values and norms informing world order? Is a stable and legitimate world order at all possible today? I noted earlier that there is a hopeful liberal view amounting to "good enough governance" and a skeptical view about gridlock. Let me begin with the argument made by the hopefuls.

The Case for Good Enough Governance

The end of the Cold War meant the end of the bipolar confrontation between two superpowers and their respective allies; it was a liberal victory because the forces for economic openness and liberal democracy prevailed. Since the Bretton Woods institutions were open to all countries in principle, rolling out what had been a primarily Western order on a global scale appeared a simple task. But the replacement of bipolarity by unipolarity propelled the United States into an entirely new situation of unconstrained power. Unconstrained power can lead to "we can do whatever we want" policies of unilateralist expansionism or liberal imposition; it can also lead to withdrawal and isolationism (Sørensen 2011, 141–67). After a honeymoon period of moderate multilateralism in the 1990s came the terrorist attacks of September 11, 2001. The George W. Bush presidency turned the United States toward unilateralism aimed at strengthening American power. The United States retreated from international institutions and agreements, rejecting accession to the Kyoto Protocol on global warming, the Biological Weapons Convention, and the International Criminal Court and abandoning the Anti-Ballistic Missile Treaty made with the Soviet Union in 1972. The governance crisis, then, is generated "primarily from choices made by the US government," said G. John Ikenberry in 2006.[7]

According to the optimist view, the good news is that this was not a breakdown of liberal order even if it was a serious crisis. The core values of the order—open and rule-based—remained in place. It was an authority crisis that could be mended by a significant shift of US policies. The content of that shift ought to be clear: "The United States is going to need to invest in re-creating the basic governance institutions of the system—invest in alliances, partnerships, multilateral institutions, special relationships, great-power concerts, cooperative security pacts, and democratic security communities. That is, the United States will need to return to the great tasks of liberal order building" (Ikenberry 2011, 349).

According to the optimist view, exactly such a shift was announced by the Barack Obama presidency in 2008 (Patrick 2014). The Trump administration wants institutional reform as well, but some rather see this as unilateralism, an "onslaught on international law and international institutions."[8] Others consider the "onslaught" to be primarily rhetorical while the substantial policies are pragmatic (Larionova et al. 2017).

There has been no grand institutional reform so far. A reform of the UN has been on the agenda for more than three decades, but old great powers, emerging powers, and developing countries do not agree on the priorities of reform (Weiss and Young 2005), and there are great practical obstacles. A changed composition of the UN Security Council, for example, will require two-thirds approval by the UN General Assembly and domestic ratification by the five permanent members of the council (P5). Apart from limited voting reforms of the World Bank and the International Monetary Fund, the major global institutions retain the ground structures of their creation.

Therefore, the case for "good enough governance" lies elsewhere. The big institutions do remain in place, but they are increasingly supplemented by regional institutions, ad hoc coalitions, global action networks, issue-specific arrangements, and more. In other words, patterns of transnational and transgovernmental relationships have grown and proliferated, giving a new diversity to cooperation across borders. Collective action, according to Stewart Patrick (2014, 62), "is no longer focused solely, or even primarily, on the UN and other universal, treaty-based institutions, or even on a single apex forum such as the G20. Rather, governments have taken to operating in many venues simultaneously, participating in a bewildering array of issue-specific networks and partnerships whose membership varies based on situational interests, shared values, and relevant capabilities." It is not a unified, streamlined structure of governance, but it is getting a lot of things done; it is "good enough governance."

This benign view is discussed in the following sections against the critique of the skeptical view. The latter maintains that the extension of liberal order from a "West-West" context to a global context is no simple matter at all. The Western order was held together by a common enemy, the Soviet Union; tensions between the partners always played out against the background of a larger common threat. Countries participating in the Western order were all liberal democracies, supporting common values of democracy and human rights. In addition, rising great powers—Japan and Germany—restrained themselves as participants in the liberal order. They sought economic and political reconstruction, but not military might or nuclear capacities that could challenge close cooperation. Today, important great powers are autocratic, and they do not accept any restraints in their aspirations for a more prominent place in the global order. They are not animated by a set of common liberal values; it can even be questioned whether Western countries are tied together by such a set of common values today. And the coherence provided by a common enemy is gone. At the same time, the leading liberal state has now turned toward a unilateral "America first" approach.

The skeptics argue that this new situation has already seriously impeded the creation of an effective institutional structure. The lack of common ground among established and emerging powers and the inability of a leading country or coalition of countries to impose solutions make for a world order in which the challenges of global leadership cannot be met; we are in a gridlock in which old institutional solutions are not sufficient and new ones have not been found (Acharya 2016). The next three sections examine the status of governance in three major areas (economy, environment, and security) against the contentions of "good enough governance" and "gridlock."

Good Enough Governance or Gridlock I: The Financial Crisis

Focus in this section is on governance in relation to the financial and economic crisis of 2008, arguably the most serious disruption of the global economy since the Great Depression some eighty-five years ago. The comprehensive crisis had no single cause, but a major contributor were the ways in which banks and other financial institutions were involved in excessive risk taking that led to the near collapse of the entire financial system (for the following points, see Kapoor 2010). The financial system, both in single countries and on a global scale, rewards risk taking. The higher the risk, the greater the prospects for profits (and bonuses). In earlier days, before the deregulation of the financial system, banks in the UK and the US earned the same amount of return on equity as firms in the real economy, about 10 percent. When the crisis hit, bank returns had climbed to 30 percent. Excessive risk taking can take several forms. One is leverage, that is, the more you borrow in order to invest, the higher the leverage. Leverage ratio 1 is when you put up half of your own money and borrow the rest. Around the time of the crisis, leverage ratios for banks such as Deutsche Bank or UBS exceeded 60.

There are three major links between excessive risk taking at the firm level and systemic risk for the financial sector and the general economy. First, a failing financial institution can drag down other financial institutions, as in the case of Lehman Brothers. Second, financial sector breakdown freezes credits and thus halts activity in the real economy. Finally, since real economy meltdown must be avoided, states tend to come to the rescue of the financial sector. Thus, financial institutions always win when risk taking goes well and, because they are bailed out by states, do not lose all that much when it goes wrong. According to the Bank of England, the direct and indirect costs to taxpayers of the financial crisis exceeded $15 trillion, "a sum far greater than any contribution from the financial sector to the real economy" (Kapoor 2010, 38).

In sum, a deregulated financial system provided a host of incentives for excessive risk taking that led to the most severe financial crisis the world had seen since 1929. In fact, the drop in industrial output and world trade was more serious in early 2008 than it was in October 1929. But the economy rebounded much faster after the 2008 crisis than after the earlier stock market crash. Industrial output, world trade volumes, and aggregate economic growth had recovered by 2012, with Europe as a partial exception. This is the basis for the claim that global economic governance worked rather well in responding to the crisis (Drezner 2012).

Both national and international institutions contributed to this result. Central banks cut interest rates, promoted countercyclical lending, and expanded credit facilities. The G20 emerged as a central forum for facilitating coordination and institutional innovation. It created the Financial Stability Board (FSB) with the aim to develop new regulatory standards for financial institutions and made a Basel III agreement with more robust banking standards. To be sure, the G20 is an ad hoc institution with limited powers, but it did achieve something in terms of short-term recovery. In comparison, the World Economic Conference, convened in 1933 to deal with the Great Depression, achieved nothing.

The skeptical view is not impressed by this record. To begin with, in the early phases of the crisis, coordination among central banks was weak and ad hoc, focused on the rich, developed countries. The coordination that emerged in the

G20 lacked both the institutional power and the administrative infrastructure needed for implementation and enforcement of its proposals (Hale, Held, and Young 2013, 170). The FSB, arguably the most ambitious institutional innovation by the G20, faced several serious challenges in developing mechanisms for compliance and promoting effective international financial standards (Helleiner 2010; Kapoor 2010). Basel III rules required an increase in banks' capital reserve requirements; the rules are to be implemented gradually until 2019. But the new requirements are similar to those that applied to US banks before the crisis.[9] Plus, the regulations may incentivize banks to shift assets "off balance sheet" and thus stimulate the creation of a gray-area "shadow banking sector."[10]

At the same time, the G20 has been plagued by disagreement among its members and has not succeeded in transforming itself from a short-term crisis manager to a longer-term steering institution for the global economy. The idea is not to replace or even weaken national regulation systems; they will always be necessary. But the issue of effective supervisory structures at the global level is important because, to address systemic risk, regulators need a system-wide view. The bodies that have been set up so far have limited capacities and little or no statutory powers. That is, there is an intensely globalized financial system, but there is no effective global regulator because the leading countries do not want to surrender the freedom of maneuver that they enjoy under the present system (Kapoor 2010, 99).

The second major problem not addressed by short-term crisis management concerns the "too big to fail" financial institutions, the excessive risk takers that were bailed out by taxpayers at the height of the financial crisis. After six years of deliberations, the FSB presented a proposal in late 2014 aimed at ensuring that the cost of failure would be borne by shareholders, not taxpayers. The proposal requires several "global systemically important banks" to hold a certain amount of cash in order to be able to survive big losses on their own. The proposed requirement was 15–20 percent of the bank's assets, a much bigger cushion than under current rules.

Again, the proposal is a template that must be followed up with specific regulations that take effect by 2019. If eventually successful, critics worry that these regulations will not be enough because the big financial institutions remain too big and too complex to allow for effective supervision, yet the proposal is deemed a step in the right direction.[11]

Finally, there is a set of problems connected with the utterly complex and opaque financial products, high-frequency trading driven by computers and algorithms, a shadow banking system of conduits and money market funds, and the growth of a securitization industry. The common factor behind these problems is the incentive structure in the financial sector that encourages excessive risk taking and short-termism. Nothing much has been done in this area; "the incentive misalignments at the heart of the financial sector are scarcely being addressed" (Kapoor 2010, 99).

In sum, skeptics argue that while short-term crisis management in relation to the 2008 financial meltdown was relatively successful, the substantial measures aimed at reforming the financial system to avoid similar dramatic calamities in the future have been relatively weak, and the multilateral institutional apparatus set in place to tackle these challenges does not have the political clout and the administrative capacity to play more than a limited role when the next crisis comes around. Perceived national interests stand behind this state of affairs. In particular, Western governments are not ready to reform the neoliberal system that has served them well in the past.

Good Enough Governance or Gridlock II: Climate Change

According to several observers, on the issue of climate change, coming years will probably see more results from specific negotiations about particular problems than from global discussions of large-scale agendas. In other words, "good enough governance" can be achieved through a multitude of loosely linked initiatives, what has been called "a regime complex for climate change" (Keohane and Victor 2011). The arguments for and against this view are discussed in what follows.

The hope that a climate change regime complex can do better flows from the relative failure of big multilateral initiatives. One might immediately think that climate change—of all problems—calls for grand, multilateral, concerted action. Many countries, including major countries like Germany and France, have long supported the establishment of a world environmental organization, a strong multilateral institutional anchor for global endeavors for the environment. But the major problem behind the failure of big climate initiatives remains divergent interests among many players, powerful states in particular.

The proudest outcome of the multilateral effort has been the Kyoto Protocol (and its successors), an agreement on reduced emission targets. However, the agreement does not include the two leading greenhouse gas emitters, the United States and China. Nor is the core of the agreement—percentage reduction targets over a certain time span—effective, because governments only partially control emission outcomes and they often evade commitments when those commitments prove too costly (Hale, Held, and Young 2013; Victor 2011). The Kyoto Protocol faced another setback in 2011 when Canada withdrew, citing domestic economic concerns and the fact that the major emitters were not included. Other significant countries, including Russia and Japan, might follow suit.

In the larger scheme then, Kyoto can be considered one element of a diversified regime complex for climate change. One component of the regime is club-making efforts, or "a la carte multilateralism." The most important forums are the Major Economies Forum (MEF)—created by the United States in 2007, with seventeen members (sixteen states and the European Union) responsible for some 80 percent of global emissions—and the G20, which has been preoccupied with the financial crisis but has also taken some time to discuss environmental issues. In addition to these two forums, climate change is on the agenda in several other agencies of the UN system whose primary mandate is something else, including the World Bank, the United Nations Development Program (UNDP), the Global Environment Facility (GEF), and the United Nations Environment Program (UNEP).

The other major component of the regime complex is a variety of bilateral deals. Several countries, including the United States, the United Kingdom, France, and Australia, have created bilateral partnerships with China concerning coal technologies and nuclear power. The United States also collaborates with India about access to nuclear technology. Many countries have signed bilateral deals concerning reduced carbon emissions, including a 2014 deal between China and the United States.[12] Finally, unilateral initiatives abound in several countries, including the US, where individual states such as California have imposed state limits on emissions. Civil society organizations and several firms have also pushed initiatives for controlling emissions.

What is the track record of the climate change regime? Not overly impressive. Emissions have been reduced in several developed countries, but not sufficiently to offset the increases in the developing world. China alone added more than the sum of reductions between 1990 and 2009. Some developed countries contributed to increased emissions too, including Australia, Canada, and Switzerland. The climate regime is therefore "grossly inadequate" when it comes to stabilizing greenhouse gas levels.[13] Current emission growth levels will cause an average rise of global temperatures by a minimum of four degrees Celsius in 2100, instead of the two degrees that is the current ambition.[14]

The monitoring and enforcement mechanisms are weak. Developing countries in particular lack domestic capacity to monitor their own emissions, and there are no precise ways, for example, to measure emissions from deforestation. Several developing countries, including China, resist international monitoring for national sovereignty reasons. Enforcement, meanwhile, is "essentially nonexistent."[15]

Furthermore, there is no adequate financing. The calculation of total cost for a safe climate is of course difficult; the Stern Review put it at 1 percent of global GDP.[16] There is consensus, however, that the cost of doing nothing will be much higher—5 percent of GDP according to the Stern Review. In 2015 the International Energy Agency (IEA) estimated the cost of achieving climate goals by 2020 to be $5 trillion (International Energy Agency 2015). The group of developing countries is scheduled to need $300 billion per year in 2020 to cope with climate change. There is a principled consensus that the developed world will provide $100 billion per year to developing countries from 2020—established at the sixteenth session of the Conference of the Parties (COP-16) in Cancun in 2010—but no substantial framework for financing has been created.

Finally, there is the issue of climate-friendly economic development strategies and the related issue of development and transfer of new technologies. Many small-scale projects are under way in this area. For example, the EU and China created a partnership to develop near-zero emissions coal (NZEC) plants in China using new technologies, and there are several UNEP initiatives on renewable energies focused on biofuels and solar and wind energy. At the same time, however, the "climate-proofing" of larger-scale economic development models is in the early stages, and the larger issue of technology transfer and international property rights remains contested (Wade 2003).

In sum, the climate change regime cannot boast a record of great success. To be sure, the problems related to climate change are intensely connected across borders, but the climate change regime is deeply fragmented. This fragmentation has prompted the call for a "structural change in global governance . . . both inside and outside the UN system" (Biermann et al. 2009, 38). In a sense, a "constitutional moment" has arrived in the governance of climate change because now is the time to do much more if catastrophic damage is to be avoided. Yet the major actors, including states, firms, civil society organizations, and most individuals, do not recognize now as a decisive point in time requiring fundamental change. The Trump administration has moved in the opposite direction by indicating that climate change is a hoax. Moreover, there is no firm guarantee that an integrated and overarching climate regime will produce better results than the currently fragmented sets of institutions. A case can indeed be made that the latter are more flexible and can boast higher adaptability (Keohane and Victor 2011, 15). Unfortunately, these institutions can also be plagued by extreme fragmentation, chaos, and gridlock. At the present time, there is no simple way forward for the climate change regime.

Good Enough Governance or Gridlock III: Security

At UN headquarters a quote from former General Secretary Dag Hammarskjöld is on a wall: "The UN was not created to take humanity to heaven but to save it from hell."[17] The statement was made during the height of the Cold War, and there is no doubt about the meaning of "hell": a devastating war among the great powers. That war never happened, and the UN played a role in that achievement. Cooperation in international institutions matters greatly for the increasing obsolescence of interstate war, but a host of security issues remain on the table. From a human cost perspective, the most important one is domestic conflict in fragile states. The following focuses on the strengths and weaknesses of the regime complex in relation to fragile states.

Unlike the regimes concerned with the economy or the climate, the security regime related to fragile states has a clearly defined center: the United Nations Security Council (UNSC). Council decisions are managed by the UN secretariat's Department of Peacekeeping Operations (DPKO), the Department of Field Support, and the Department of Political Affairs (DPA). Furthermore, in 2005 the UN World Summit adopted a clear formal framework concerning the responsibility to protect (R2P) populations from genocide, war crimes, ethnic cleansing, and crimes against humanity.

The R2P calls on individual states to protect their populations from such crimes and to prevent their incitement. This framework is an important normative development because before 2005 state sovereignty had meant states had the right to conduct their own affairs, free from outside intervention. The R2P, by contrast, invokes state duties and responsibilities in connection with sovereignty. And if these responsibilities are not met, the international community has an explicit responsibility through the UNSC "to help to protect populations . . . in a timely and decisive manner" (United Nations 2005, 138–40).

In other words, there is a well-defined leadership in place and connected bureaucracies to monitor and implement decisions about peace operations in fragile states. Yet grave conflicts continue to emerge in these states, and old conflicts tend to linger on with no clear end in sight. Why has this impressive apparatus not done better?

Most important, serious political discord among the five permanent members of the Security Council has prevented effective action in many cases. Amnesty International's 2014 report speaks of "shameful" inaction in relation to Syrian and Iraqi refugees, ethnic cleansing in the Central African Republic, Boko Haram massacres in Nigeria, atrocities in South Sudan, and the death of children in Palestine from Israeli bombings. The charge is that permanent members have "consistently abused" their veto rights to "promote their political self-interest or geopolitical interest above the interest of protecting civilians."[18]

The Chinese and Russian governments support the principles of R2P but also worry about setting aside the code of sovereignty as freedom from external intervention. This stance has led to an emphasis on prevention of conflict and to operations that have the consent of the affected governments (Teitt 2008). Russia's invocation of the R2P in relation to Ukraine demonstrates how the principle can be twisted to serve national security interests.[19]

France has proposed that the P5 abandon their veto power in cases of genocides, war crimes, and crimes against humanity. This would be a voluntary arrangement, according to the French foreign minister:

> The Charter would not be amended and the change would be implemented through a mutual commitment from the permanent members. In concrete terms, if the Security Council were required to make a decision with regard to a mass crime, the permanent members would agree to suspend their right to veto. The criteria for implementation would be simple: at the request of at least 50 member states, the United Nations Secretary General would be called upon to determine the nature of the crime. . . . To be realistically applicable, this code would exclude cases where the vital national interests of a permanent member of the Council were at stake.[20]

It is quite unusual for a P5 member to suggest a restriction on the veto; the proposal has support from some seventy countries, but it will surely not get very far. The United States, China, and Russia will not support it, even with the caveat of excluding cases that have yet to be defined. In more general terms, reform of the Security Council has been on the agenda for several decades but has not gotten off the ground. Discord concerns not merely China and Russia; the liberal democracies are not in agreement on UNSC reform either.

Gridlock at the Security Council is a major problem but not the only problem in relation to violence in fragile states. First, peace operations are by now a substantial element in UN activities, employing more than 100,000 people with a 2015 budget well over $8 billion.[21] At this magnitude, there is a UN "peace" bureaucracy with its own set of interests. On the one hand, the UN has an incentive to be seen as "doing something" in concrete conflicts; on the other hand, it has an incentive to "pick the winners" and avoid failures. The latter points to a demand that there should be a peace to keep in order for a peace operation to start up, but that would leave people suffering in many places where such conditions are not in place. In any case, the bureaucracy has a primary concern for the UN's reputation and interests (Barnett 1997; Allen and Yuen 2014).

Second, there are financial and personnel constraints. In 2009 General Secretary Ban Ki-moon complained about mounting difficulties in getting sufficient troops, equipment, logistical support, and economic backing.[22] At the same time, the UN Office of Internal Oversight Services has found serious instances of mismanagement, fraud, and corruption in relation to peacekeeping operations (Schaefer 2009).

Finally, there has been much talk among experts and policymakers of conflict-prevention measures, including early warning systems, but achievements in this area have not been impressive. The United Nations does not have a central coordinating unit with primary responsibility for collecting, integrating, and analyzing early warning conflict reports, though some work is done at the DPA. Several regional organizations, including the EU, the Organization for Security and Cooperation in Europe (OSCE), and the African Union (AU), also have early warning and prevention initiatives under way, but the whole area is not very developed or integrated in a framework that includes policy responses.

In sum, the security regime in relation to fragile states is less fragmented than most other regimes in the sense that activities in this area are centrally anchored at the UNSC, which is responsible for deciding, implementing, and overseeing peace operations. But this is not a strong center for resolute responses to mass violence in fragile states, because of disagreements among the P5 and because the UN does not have an effective infrastructure of personnel and equipment to draw on. The UN is dependent on member states and increasingly on regional organizations, including the African Union and the European Union. Thus, acquiring the necessary resources is time-consuming. The UN-AU mission in Darfur, for example, took more than three years to reach full deployment.[23]

At the same time, peace operations are increasingly set up with mandates that include rebuilding efforts so that peace building, state building, and economic development must go together. In institutional terms, this means the involvement of a great many organizations and agencies, including nongovernmental organizations, bilateral donors, multilateral bodies (e.g., the World Bank), regional organizations, and a host of UN agencies. So even with a strong center, there is plenty of room for fragmentation in the conduct of concrete operations.

There is a framework in place for responding to severe humanitarian crisis in fragile states, but it has not been able to formulate and implement effective responses. The case for "governance in pieces" is that the institutions are doing the best they can under difficult circumstances. The objection by many observers is that this is simply not good enough.

Conclusion: Gridlock or Good Enough Governance?

The optimists have a point: a great amount of governance is surely taking place. The immediate problems of the financial crisis were successfully handled by reasonably effective crisis management. A large and diversified climate change regime has taken several initiatives to combat global warming. The complex security challenges posed by fragile states have been responded to by an ambitious R2P regime. At the same time, emerging powers are increasingly integrated into the institutional structure. Overall, this should make room for some considerable liberal optimism: There is a strong institutional order and a respectable track record of promoting economic globalization and other liberal values in the present world order.

Nevertheless, this evidence does not convince the skeptics, and they have a point. The case for gridlock is that the supposedly "good enough governance" emphasized by the optimists amounts to nothing more than inconsistent and fragmented short-termism that provides little more than crisis management, with the next crisis always looming around the corner. There have been no basic initiatives toward reorganizing the financial system; the climate change regime is weak and insufficient; there is no end to serious humanitarian crises in fragile states. In combination, these crises may threaten a more comprehensive breakdown of international institutions.

Emerging powers participate in global governance. Most important, China under Xi Jinping has pushed its regional economic and political influence in Asia but also in other parts of the world. In some ways China attempts to sell itself as "the last liberal great power," but China (or Brazil, Russia, India, or South Africa) is neither willing nor capable of taking the lead in basic reforms of the institutional structure.[24] On the one hand, China and the other emerging economies must focus on significant domestic problems; on the other hand, China is an autocratic state, not a staunch defender of liberal values. At the same time, the rise of Brazil, Russia, India, China, and South Africa (BRICS)—and China in particular—means that the United States and its Western allies will be less dominant than they have been and less capable of constructing a reformed liberal world order. This is happening at a time when the United States is not turning completely away from international institutions but is also not a driving force for effective and legitimate global governance.

In sum, piecemeal governance is taking place, but it is not good enough, because the challenges we face demand more profound reform in order to provide sustainable solutions. Why is this more profound governance not forthcoming? One answer is that we are lacking a "constitutional moment," a crisis that moves important actors and institutions toward unconventional adaptation (Ackerman 1991). The threats and challenges reviewed earlier have not been sufficiently imminent or sufficiently alarming to all major actors to create a constitutional moment.

This situation must be considered in a larger context. First, the threat of great power war has all but disappeared. Recall Tom Daschle's observation that the Cold War exerted "a powerful hold on America," pushing it in the direction of bipartisan internationalism. Even with a renewed Russian nationalism and the crisis in Ukraine, there is little worry of great power war. American international leadership has lost an important incentive for bipartisan cooperation, and therefore such cooperation has not been forthcoming. Moreover, the existence of a common enemy that presented a clear and present danger was an important foundation for Western cooperation during the Cold War. It tied liberal states into a common security arrangement led by the United States, which was an important force for coherence and solidarity, despite discord in particular areas. No such common enemy is a force for coherence today. The "global war on terror" was a candidate after 9/11, and the dangers posed by climate change are a candidate today, but neither greater nor lesser powers have been convinced that they should be compelled to set aside differences and cooperate on those grounds.

Second, states are compelled to look inward to confront their own problems. Decades of neoliberal globalization have decreased the sociopolitical cohesion in the advanced Western states because large sections of the populations have been squeezed in a process leading toward much higher levels of inequality. Political attention is on domestic affairs that present a host of problems in advanced liberal democracies and more so in the emerging powers. In China, for example, rising socioeconomic inequality is a problem, but it competes with other very serious problems, including corruption, social stability, environmental degradation, and the vast task of creating a different model of economic accumulation, less dependent on low wages and exports. Contributing to effective global governance is an item low on the agenda in both advanced and emerging economies.

Third, there is the issue of who has power and how power can be used in the construction of world order. The United States remains supremely powerful, both in material power and in soft power. It is still the leading power by far, but by a smaller margin than it was after World War II. Since the turn of the century,

US power has not been used in constructing an order with public goods for all. American efforts at institutional reform are minimal and focused on a version of the national interest that allows limited space for the production of global public goods. Basic changes in this situation require the emergence of a new dominant political coalition, able and willing to take responsibility for reforming liberal international institutions. At present, other established and emerging great powers can choose to say no to America and pursue their own national interests; that is what they have done. No one has put forward a different plan for better provision of public goods, and it is not clear that any country—or coalition of countries—outside the United States has the power and the willingness to pursue any alternative project. Thus, the world remains stuck with the current provision of piecemeal governance.

Finally, one might ask: Does this matter at all? Is the liberal preoccupation with stable and effective institutions misguided? Could global governance and ultimately world order not merely be based on power, that is, "coalitions of the willing" coming together to solve problems on an ad hoc basis? The liberal answer to this question is that institutions have always played a core role in defining and regulating relationships among states; the institution of sovereignty is even part of what defines a state. After a long phase of intensive globalization, international institutions have become even more important because a host of common problems—including the issue areas discussed in this paper—are really "behind-the-border" difficulties that can only be dealt with effectively if states commit to demanding comprehensive compliance with common norms and rules. Liberals argue that this cooperation can never be accomplished in the absence of strong international institutions. That is why piecemeal governance is bad news for the aspirations of an effective and stable world order.

Notes

1. My summation rests on the premise that liberal theory contains both descriptive and prescriptive elements. For an interesting attempt at a purely positivist liberal theory, see Moravcsik (1997); for a critique of this move toward positivism, see Reus-Smit (2001).

2. In chapter 1 the editors define power politics in international institutions as comprising "power over resources," "power over outcomes," and "agenda-setting power." I agree with this general view even though my analytical approach is slightly different.

3. Statista, "United States' Share of Global Gross Domestic Product (GDP) Adjusted for Purchasing Power Parity (PPP) from 2012 to 2022," 2018, https://www.statista.com/statistics /270267/united-states-share-of-global-gross-domestic-product-gdp/.

4. Quandl, "China Share of World GDP based on PPP, %," 2018, https://www.quandl .com/data/ODA/CHN_PPPSH-China-Share-of-World-GDP-based-on-PPP; and "United States Share of World GDP based on PPP, %," 2018, https://www.quandl.com/data/ODA/USA _PPPSH-United-States-Share-of-World-GDP-based-on-PPP.

5. Investopedia, "U.S. vs. China: Battle to Be the Largest Economy in the World," 2013, https://www.investopedia.com/articles/investing/032013/us-vs-china-battle-be-largest -economy-world.asp.

6. Sebastian Mallaby, "A Mockery in the Eyes of the World," *Washington Post*, January 31, 1999.

7. G. John Ikenberry, "The Global Governance Crisis," *InterDependent* (Spring 2006), https://www.princeton.edu/~slaughtr/Articles/InterDependent.pdf.

8. Jack Goldsmith, "The Trump Onslaught on International Law and Institutions," *Lawfare Blog*, March 17, 2017, https://www.lawfareblog.com/trump-onslaught-international -law-and-institutions.

9. Thomas M. Hoenig, "Get Basel III Right and Avoid Basel IV," *Financial Times*, December 12, 2012, https://www.ft.com/content/99ece1b0-3fa0-11e2-b2ce-00144feabdc0.

10. Angshuman Gooptu, "Will Basel III Help or Hurt?," *Chicago Policy Review*, April 24, 2012, http://chicagopolicyreview.org/2012/04/24/will-basel-iii-help-or-hurt/.

11. M. Stanley and N. Beekarry, "'Too Big To Fail' Impact Assessment," 2014, http:// d5769291.u920.s-gohost.net/2014-governance-and-impact-report/too-big-to-fail-impact-assess ment.html.

12. White House, Office of the Press Secretary, "Fact Sheet: US-China Joint Announce- ment on Climate Change and Clean Energy Cooperation," fact sheet, November 11, 2014, https://obamawhitehouse.archives.gov/the-press-office/2014/11/11/fact-sheet-us-china -joint-announcement-climate-change-and-clean-energy-c.

13. Council on Foreign Relations, "Global Governance Monitor: Climate Change," 2016, https://www.cfr.org/interactives/global-governance-monitor#!/climate-change#issue-brief.

14. Damian Carrington, "Planet Likely to Warm by 4C by 2100, Scientists Warn," *The Guardian*, December 31, 2013, https://www.theguardian.com/environment/2013/dec/31/planet -will-warm-4c-2100-climate.

15. Council on Foreign Relations, "Global Governance Monitor," 13.

16. Nicholas Stern, *Stern Review: The Economics of Climate Change*, October 2006, http:// mudancasclimaticas.cptec.inpe.br/~rmclima/pdfs/destaques/sternreview_report_complete .pdf.

17. Dag Hammarskjöld, address at University of California Convocation, Berkeley, Cal- ifornia, May 13, 1954, https://ask.un.org/loader.php?fid=11125&type=1&key=6bf400a0db 526933d8577cce49f39ad2.

18. Shalil Shetty, Amnesty International general secretary, quoted in BBC, "Amnesty Calls on UN Powers to Lose Veto on Genocide Votes," BBC News, February 25, 2015.

19. Mark Kersten, "Does Russia Have a 'Responsibility to Protect' Ukraine? Don't Buy It," *Globe and Mail*, March 4, 2014, updated May 12, 2018. https://www.theglobeandmail.com /opinion/does-russia-have-a-responsibility-to-protect-ukraine-dont-buy-it/article17271450/.

20. David L. Bosco, "France's Plan to Fix the Veto," *Foreign Policy*, October 4, 2013, https://foreignpolicy.com/2013/10/04/frances-plan-to-fix-the-veto/.

21. Department of Peacekeeping Operations, "How We Are Funded," accessed January 1, 2019, https://peacekeeping.un.org/en/how-we-are-funded.

22. Mariano Aguirre and Joana Abristeka, "Pressing Issues for UN Peacekeeping Opera- tions," Transnational Institute, 2009, https://www.tni.org/en/article/pressing-issues-for-un -peacekeeping-operations. See also Bianca Selway, "Who Pays for Peace?," *Global Observa- tory*, November 4, 2013, http://theglobalobservatory.org/2013/11/who-pays-for-peace/.

23. Department of Peacekeeping Operations, "UNAMID Fact Sheet," accessed January 1, 2019, https://peacekeeping.un.org/en/mission/unamid.

24. Daniel W. Drezner, "Why China Will Be Able to Sell Itself as the Last Liberal Great Power," *Washington Post*, January 24, 2017, https://www.washingtonpost.com/posteverything /wp/2017/01/24/why-china-will-be-able-to-sell-itself-as-the-last-liberal-great-power.

CHAPTER 5

Making Power Politics Great Again? Discursive Institutionalism and the Political Economy of World Politics after Globalization

Ben Rosamond

The intellectual field of international political economy (IPE) has been defined in large part by its concern with the growing institutional complexity of world politics that Wivel and Paul discuss in the opening chapter of this collection. At the same time, IPE scholars have perhaps been most vocal in questioning the continuing primacy of "power politics" as the core mechanism of the global political system. Indeed, some of the primary textbooks used to teach IPE (e.g., Broome 2014; O'Brien and Williams 2016; Ravenhill 2017) use their titles to express an analytical nervousness about the utility or appropriateness of the adjective "international." The latter is held to imply the centrality of state–state interaction. The term "global political economy" carries within it two crucial (and for old school international relations [IR], disruptive) empirical claims: (a) that national governments are no longer the sole or perhaps primary authoritative shapers of domestic economies and (b) that the proliferation of authoritative institutional actors and transnational interests at the global level has transformed the character and logic of political action in world politics (Cerny 1995).

Over the past three decades, much IPE scholarship has revolved around the definition and analysis of "globalization" (Phillips 2005). Typically, the concept of globalization carries a lot of the analytical weight in seeking to describe how and why world politics has moved beyond the phase of "power politics." It sometimes shares the burden with other (potentially overlapping) process concepts such as regionalization, financialization, networkization, and neoliberalization. This is not the place to explore these concepts in depth, other than to note that they together conspire to offer a very distinctive (and complex) ontology of world politics from the version usually associated with standard IR reasoning.[1]

For many IPE scholars, it follows that the proliferation of institutions cannot be reconciled with the continuing centrality of power politics, particularly if the latter is defined in terms of interstate contestation (chapter 1, this volume). This is not to say that institutions and regimes are not the creations of states. They almost always are. The more important question is the extent to which the logics and processes that give rise to institutionalization are the very factors that undermine the capacity of states to exercise autonomy in the first place. In this type of account, institutions become attempts to pool sovereign resources and to recapture control of (usually) economic processes that have gnawed away at the state's capacity to retain internal and external sovereignty. It might be true that states subsequently seek to shape institutional rules to their advantage, but they do so in light of that initial weakness.

There is also a "chicken and egg" quality to these discussions in that institutions may both initiate the types of processes (for example, capital mobility) that weaken state autonomy in the long run and be concrete products of collective state choices. Two things follow. The first is that institutions can become consequential actors in their own right. This is typical in instances when institutional designs involve delegation (such as the International Monetary Fund, the World Trade Organization, the European Commission, and the European Central Bank). State "principals" may deem it useful or appropriate to delegate particular tasks to institutional "agents," but the path-dependent consequence of that moment of rational institutional design may be that the agent acquires long-run autonomy vis-à-vis the principal (Hawkins et al. 2006). The second point is that while states may be the sovereign initiators of institutions, they may do so at the behest of other potentially powerful rule-seeking actors. Thus, the emergence of cross-border economic exchange is likely to prompt those economic agents working in this emergent transnational economic space to demand market rules and perhaps collective policy regimes that optimize their activity. This is a well-established explanation for the emergence and expansion of supranational economic governance in the European Union (Sandholtz and Stone Sweet 1998), a dynamic made more intense by the presence of purposive supranational institutions that seek to augment their competence (Jabko 2006).

In this narrative, states still matter, but world politics has become a multiactor affair involving a variety of meaningful agents—multinational corporations, international and supranational institutions, transnational advocacy organizations, and nongovernmental organizations (NGOs)—as well as states. As a long-standing line of IPE inquiry would have it, the ontology of world politics is no longer international but rather "transnational" (Keohane and Nye 1972). Put another way, (much of) the justification for IPE over (traditional) IR is that the former is a better capture of the nature of world politics than the latter. Of course, to rely on that claim is to accept that IR would become more relevant should the empirics of world politics shift in its favor once again. In other words, it could be that the ontology of world politics could revert to a power politics type should processes such as globalization go into reverse.

The idea that power politics is back in fashion is one that is frequently heard nowadays at the interface of academic and policy discourse. Here there are parallel claims being made about the "return of (great) power politics" and the "end of globalization" / "de-globalization" / the return of "economic nationalism" (Bello 2013; Clift and Woll 2013; Helleiner and Pickel 2005; H. James 2002). These arguments tend to predate the recent populist electoral insurgencies in the rich democracies (what has been called "global Trumpism"), at least analytically.[2] Crudely, debate about the end of globalization emerged most obviously in the wake of the 2008 global financial crisis, while the return of power politics narrative seems to have been heavily stimulated by the Russian annexation of Crimea in 2014. What might be most interesting about Trumpism—impulsive and visceral though it is—is the way it has managed to fashion a narrative that links the breakdown of "globalization" as a structuring principle of world politics to the reassertion of power politics as the appropriate mode of US foreign policy.

This chapter suggests that the issue of power politics versus anarchy need not be an either-or question. It develops an argument, rooted in a broadly constructivist understanding of IPE, to suggest that rather than seeking to settle the matter of whether globalization fundamentally shifted the logic of action in the international system away from power politics (and whether that process has now gone into reverse), we should instead think of globalization and anarchy as rival but coexistent collective understandings, the interaction of which may well be consequential for outcomes in world politics.

IPE, IR, and Power Politics

The general drift of IPE scholarship over recent decades has tended to problematize standard concepts of power and power politics (Guzzini 2000). Of course, the definition of power politics drawn from Goddard and Nexon (2016; as cited in the introduction to this volume) is deliberately non-state-centric, but the term does carry strong realist connotations. The term harbors within itself at least three ways of thinking about "power." The first is a description of the relevant actors (powers) among whom power politics takes place. Any claim about a transformed actor mix simply posits that we can no longer model world politics in terms of the interaction of states as powers. Of particular interest here is the extent to which institutions go beyond their role as facilitators of international transactions to acquire meaningful "actorness" themselves so that, following Barnett and Duvall (2005), they acquire power capacities in relation to resources, outcomes, and agenda setting. This raises the possibility that entities such as giant transnational firms have developed the (state-like) capacity to engage in power-based actions that influence international outcomes (Stopford and Strange

1991) and to become key sites of governance in national and international politics (Crouch 2011).

The second sense is of power as a resource or, put another way, a series of questions about why an entity has power or whether the sources of power influence the mode of behavior of the relevant entity in the relational game of power politics. There are long-established discussions in IR about the extent to which the power of an actor is a function of its access to the means of violence. More recently, some of the literature about the EU's "actorness" has developed some of these themes in ways that are potentially applicable to all relevant actor types. For example, the EU case is said to show that an entity without significant military capacity can possess "market" or "normative" power. The former captures how an actor in possession of authoritative oversight over an integrated economic space is likely to become a major force in the global politics of market regulation, a type of politics that has become a central defining feature of "globalization" (Damro 2012). The latter describes how an actor comes to behave and seek international outcomes in ways that are consistent with its own internal constitutive values (Manners 2002, 2008). Ideal typically, a normative power is strongly constituted by its core values (external behavior reflects its internal value sets), and its modus operandi in world politics involves attempting to shape the prevailing conception of the "normal."[3] There is nothing in principle to deny that market or normative power might be used coercively, but both perspectives open up alternative ways of thinking about power in the third sense: how it is exercised.[4]

The foregoing largely thinks about power politics in relational terms. Indeed, we can get quite a long way via Dahl's (1957) classic formulation of the concept of power ("A has power over B to the extent that he can get B to do something that B would not otherwise do") together with Bachrach and Baratz's (1962) elitist corrective regarding agenda setting and "non-decisions," notwithstanding the various methodological issues these approaches throw up.[5] The IPE reworking of power politics, if we can call it that, would suggest that there are more potential As and Bs in world politics (not just more consequential actors but—as we have seen—consequential actors of different types), that their capacities are resourced in a variety of ways, and that the verb "get" in Dahl's definition can refer to a wide array of actions that range along a continuum from unilateral violence to dialogue among equals.

To this might be added the modifications associated with the so-called structural turn in IR (neo)realism. The latter effectively derives a view of the fundamental rationality (and thus inevitability) of state–state power politics from its assumptive reading of the structure of world politics as anarchic. "Anarchy" places overwhelming emphasis on security in the survivalist sense of the term. When re-presented in structuralist terms and with states thought of as broadly rational (in a utility maximization sense), then interest-driven power politics (in an offensive realist sense) is logical (Mearsheimer 2001), and cooperative institution building to serve anything other than short-term convergent utility functions is irrational.[6] The liberal institutionalist riposte to this last point, largely fashioned in the work of Keohane (e.g., Keohane 1984), is well-known—and significant—not least because this perspective has become (in some scholarly circles at least) more or less coterminous with the "American school" of IPE (see Sell 2016; Cohen 2008). In this view, institutions—as generators of absolute gains—have the effect of mitigating the "power politics" logic of anarchy. Their design is thus functional and rational, particularly in the context of complex interdependence. That institutional persistence serves the self-interest of states helps to explain not only why institutions survive, but also why particular types of economic order emerge and reproduce in the absence of a hegemon (Keohane 1984). From this vantage point IPE is more or less defined as the study of the institutional mitigation of anarchy under conditions of complex interdependence. Its IR roots and its situatedness within prevailing IR debates are obvious. IPE also borrows (not unlike some strains of neorealism) a somewhat reductionist form of reasoning from economics to make deductions about the logics of state behavior (Powell 2002). It follows that this particular version of IPE thus emerges from the concerns of contemporaneous social science as much as it does from the particular set of real-world historical circumstances that accompanied its rise to prominence.

The question of hegemony (or the lack of it) became a central plank of IPE discussions as the field developed through the 1970s and early 1980s. Hegemonic stability theory (HST) maintained that liberal economic orders were dependent on a particular configuration of power in the international system. Put simply, the liberal trading order of the nineteenth century would not have been possible without the key role played by the system's dominant state (Britain) in underwriting that order. In Kindleberger's (1986, 289) classic formulation, a stable liberal order capable of withstanding temporary imbalances and market volatility was possible only if the hegemon was prepared to perform five key tasks: the maintenance of an open market for imports, the provision of countercyclical lending, the supply of exchange-rate stability, the coordination of macroeconomic policy across the system, and willingness to act as a lender of last resort. Even if we accept the simple correlation between a hegemonic power structure and global economic openness, then it follows that the practice of hegemonic stability requires significant institutional innovation if it is to be successful. Thus, exchange-rate stability cannot be enforced through diktat; it requires a mechanism to ensure that parities are fixed and that imbalances in the system can be corrected through domestic adjustment. The gold standard (operating between the 1870s and World War I and later revived in the interwar period) and the Bretton Woods fixed exchange-rate regime, devised in 1944, were institutional expressions of this principle, albeit with quite distinct approaches to domestic policy adjustment. IPE scholarship has long argued about the necessary and sufficient conditions for liberal economic order, which in turn has led to many comparative studies of the nineteenth and late twentieth-/early twenty-first-century "globalization" (O'Rourke and Williamson 1999).

One influential line of argument is associated with a broadly Polanyian reading of global economic ordering. The key point here is to suggest that the survival of open liberal trading orders cannot be solely explained with reference to prevailing distributions of power in the international system. Polanyi's central argument was that liberal economic development tends to subordinate social purpose to the logic of the supposedly self-regulating market. Unrestrained liberal economic orders tend to provoke societal reactions (of varying kinds) that seek to reembed the market within broader social purposes (Polanyi [1944] 2001). Ruggie's (1982) famous capture of this insight led him to suggest that Bretton Woods was an example of "embedded liberalism" in which the degree of international openness was restrained by the systemic commitment of allowing large degrees of domestic macroeconomic policy autonomy in the market democracies. The idea of "embedded liberalism" has become something of a normative article of faith for some scholars since "markets that societies do not recognise as legitimate cannot last" (Abdelal and Ruggie 2009, 152).

Embedded liberalism also connects in interesting ways to the idea of the "impossible trinity," the theorem developed by economists in the 1960s to suggest that domestic monetary policy autonomy would not be possible in a regime characterized by the "goods" of open capital markets and fixed exchange rates (Mundell 1963; Fleming 1962). At face value the impossible trinity idea retells the Bretton Woods era as a classical trade-off in which capital mobility was sacrificed in the interests of preserving national macroeconomic policy agency. The gradual decline of the Bretton Woods formula through the 1960s until the "Nixon shock" of 1971 is often attributed to the unsustainable attempt to maintain broadly Keynesian economic regimes and exchange-rate parities in an era of (re-) emergent de facto capital mobility. Put another way, the Bretton Woods era is frequently seen as a struggle to maintain two ultimately incompatible institutional equilibria, one domestic and the other international. The displacement of national-Keynesian institutional equilibria from the 1970s is then read as a necessary condition for the rise of globalization, which in turn has been made possible and sustained through the construction of a complex post-Westphalian institutional order. The persistence of national variation (despite globalization) is then frequently explained via (new) institutionalist theory. One influential line of argument maintains that the imperatives of a globalized economy play out quite differently in coordinated and uncoordinated market economies (e.g., Swank 2003). In short, institutions matter, not just because there are more of them but also (and most important) because the way in which much comparative and international political economy scholarship apprehends the world is through institutionalist lenses. Institutions are there and seem to matter in part because we are looking for them and expect them to matter.

At the same time, other IPE scholars were seeking to chip away at the robust IR assumptions that sat at the heart of a neoliberal institutionalist perspective.

Strange's (1994a) discussion of the structures of power in the global political economy is perhaps the most obvious starting point since it represents a direct challenge to the idea of the coupling of anarchy's structural logic, on the one hand, with power politics' primacy, on the other. Strange's basic point was to suggest that the global political economy is shaped by the complex interaction of four structures: production, finance, security, and knowledge. This stands in contrast with the realist-informed IPE of Gilpin (2001), in which structures of international security, such as the Cold War, typically play a key role in shaping the parameters of economic order. That the four structures constrained and enabled actor behavior was beyond doubt, but Strange presses the key empirical question in terms of who has control over these structures. Power is not inherent in the structures themselves but rather in those actors that can shape these ever-present structures in temporally specific and value-specific ways. Strange, a vocal critic of regime theory, liberal institutionalist IR, and the orientation to social science that informs them, did not lay out a coherent theory of institutions despite her work being littered with examples of the ways in which institutional forms reflect and shape the operation of structural power across her four dimensions. Perhaps the most important takeaways from Strange's work (at least from the viewpoint of this chapter) are her insistence (a) that structures are malleable, contingent, and historically specific (this foundational point goes quite a long way in explaining her discomfort with general theories of anything); (b) that beliefs and values matter in the global political economy so that, as one close reader of her work puts it, "entire structures reflect dominant value sets" (Germain 2016, 6); and (c) that theory itself plays a potentially performative role in shaping policy choices in the global political economy.[7]

IPE with Constructivist Characteristics

To sum up, so far this chapter has developed two broad points. First, a good deal of political economy scholarship thinks of international and domestic order, the links between them, and key processes of change in terms of institutionalist vocabulary. Only a relatively narrow conception of "institutions" (as creations of rational states and as temporary facilitators of and constraints on state behavior) is even half compatible with traditionalist understandings of power politics (although see Wivel and Paul's chapter on soft balancing in this volume). At the same time, institutionalist approaches are fully compatible with an actor-centered, relational understanding of who gets what, when, and how.

Second, as implied by the brief discussion of parts of Strange's work, it is also helpful to think about structures and structural power in terms of collective understandings and intersubjectivities. Wendt's (1992) constructivist critique of neorealism held that anarchy is best conceived of as a collective construct of actors within the international system. By acting in ways that are consistent with that collective understanding (i.e., practicing power politics), states reproduce a system that seems anarchic. In other words, anarchy is sociological and endogenous rather than objective and exogenous. Structures do not speak for themselves. Thinking about IPE subject matter, Widmaier (2004) follows the broad logic of Wendt's argument in his discussion of the social construction of the "impossible trinity." The theorem is now widely regarded as an article of faith in policy circles so that it is known to be impossible to reconcile the goals of monetary stability, capital mobility, and policy autonomy. But as Widmaier shows, there is strong historical evidence to suggest that market concerns about monetary stability could be assuaged via the coordinated use of income policies, which in turn were compatible with expansionary fiscal policies and the pursuit of domestic full employment. The key ideational shift has been the "neoclassical redefinition of Keynesianism," which has shaped actor expectations decisively away from the idea that the three parts of the trinity could be made to work together.

The point to make here has at least four dimensions. First, the structures of world politics, rather than being material in essence or exogenous to action, are best seen as intersubjective, or rooted in collective understandings that in turn define the parameters of actor behavior in both technical and normative senses (i.e., what is rational to do and what is right or appropriate to do). Second, actor behavior, premised on these broad intersubjectivities, both produces concrete material effects and (through practice) reproduces and reifies the intersubjective structure. Third, a defining feature of intersubjective structures is that they are robust and thus withstand routine technical, normative, or political challenges to their existence. Fourth, intersubjective structures can be made "real" through the design and maintenance of institutions that internalize their logic. To be clear, we are not talking here about the ways in which particular claims about the world come to be adopted, believed in, and acted on by key governing agents. An example of the latter would be the idea that high levels of accumulated public debt and recurrent budget deficits are, without exception, inimical to economic growth. This view, which we might call "deficit fetishism" (Hopkin and Rosamond 2018), has held sway among key national, supranational, and international institutions for much of the period since the 2008 global financial crisis (and its gradual erosion is a subject of great interest), but it falls into a different category than the types of fundamental "structural claims" that are under discussion here.

Indeed, while the likes of "deficit fetishism" may be intersubjective in that they reflect a common basic understanding of how the world works, such ideas are perhaps better understood as secondary to or derivative of deeper discursive structures. To adopt constructivist language, deficit fetishism is something like a causal belief (ongoing certainty about the technical robustness across time and space of an $x \rightarrow y$ relationship) and maybe also a normative belief (the idea that $x \rightarrow y$ is how things *should* be). A constructivist theory of institutional design would hold that institutions are typically expressions of strong causal and normative beliefs across key issue areas. A broader constructivist (or sociological) theory of institutions would read institutions as (a) sites for actor socialization in and around causal and normative beliefs and (b) entities that contribute to fashioning the world in ways that are consistent with those underlying causal and normative beliefs. But at the same time, those causal and normative beliefs (which may equally be captured by the language of "programs" or "paradigms"—see Schmidt [2008]) are situated within a broader worldview (or "philosophy" to borrow again from Schmidt [2008]). It is important to recognize that in this theoretical tradition, labeled "discursive institutionalism" by Schmidt (2008, 2012), institutions are more than simply concrete organizational forms or systems of rules that incentivize, constrain, or enable actor agency. Institutions are "structures and constructs of meaning internal to agents whose 'background ideational abilities' enable them to create (and maintain) institutions while their 'foreground discursive abilities' enable them to communicate critically about them and to change (or maintain) them" (Schmidt 2012, 86).

Anarchy and Globalization

In our discussion so far, the idea of anarchy, from which conventional notions of power politics derive, tends to be both structural (in that it sets imperatives for actor behavior, defines who those actors are, and dictates a logic of action within the system it defines) and ontological (in that it is seen as an inescapable condition of existence for its key actors). As such, anarchy is usefully seen in this sense as a discursive structure or a philosophy or worldview from which a range of behavioral, institutional, and epistemic forms derive. In that respect it resembles "globalization"—a term that has also come to describe a particular set of structural properties with a range of attendant logics. A schematic comparison is set out in table 5.1.

Obviously, anarchy or power politics and globalization represent quite different imaginaries of the world system. One way of reading IPE is as a project

Table 5.1. Schematic Comparison

	Anarchy	Globalization
Key domain of action	Security	Economy
Key actors	States	Multiple actors
Processes	International	Transnational/borderless
Space of competition	Politics among nations	The market
Logic	Power politics	Commerce and competition
State rationality	Security calculus	Competition state
State goals	Security	Competitiveness, global market rules

designed to suggest empirically that the latter has displaced the former as the key foundational truth about world politics. From this reading, IPE is configured to explore—across a range of subdomains (notably production, finance, and trade)—the mechanisms of that displacement. One key way conventional IPE has done this is by examining how globalization has spawned a proliferation of institutions whose purposes have been (a) to deal with the intense collective action problems that accompany the deepening and expansion of transnational or cross-border economic activity and (b) to develop rules and regulatory structures to enhance or manage globalization. In this story globalization amounts to the radical mitigation of anarchy through its undercutting of the primacy of state–state action, its degrading of security imperatives in favor of economic ones, and its transformation of the logic of collective and individual state action (Cerny 2000; Sørensen 2004). It follows that globalization has transformed the primary *raison d'état* of world politics. The delivery of security through whatever means is replaced by the need to ensure competitiveness through the adoption of a suite of policy reforms (i.e., those typically associated with "neoliberalism"— privatization, deregulation, labor market flexibilization, market opening, reduction in corporate tax rates, etc.). Put another way, the logic of globalization posits a form of convergence among states in a world where national boundaries are porous and the actor mix is complex.[8] The struggle for power and survival gives way to the struggle for competitive advantage. In a world defined by an anarchic structure, institutional solutions to collective action problems are ephemeral and fleeting. They are structurally destined to yield relative gains. Under globalization, institutional logics of absolute gains are congruent, it is argued, with the overall rationality of a global liberal order in which Ricardian exploitations of comparative advantage are rewarded with greater prosperity.[9]

Needless to say, the foregoing relies on a benign, much contested, and probably highly simplistic understanding of globalization. The presentation without nuance was deliberate because "globalization" has also been a powerful discursive frame from which particular claims about the technical and normative propriety of particular policy choices follow (Hay and Rosamond 2002). As indicated previously, like other claims about the defining structures of world politics, "globalization" is an intersubjective construction, underwritten by behaviors, policies, and institutional forms that affirm its structural or existential character. This is not to say that the effects or effectiveness of globalization discourse have been uniform or homogenous. Aside from being contested in multiple sites, research has consistently shown significant variation in the ways in which the concept of "globalization" has been understood, internalized, and acted on in different national settings (Antoniades 2007). But even taking this variation into account, the very idea of globalization relies on an imaginary of the past in which economic space was bordered and national governments were sovereign.

Indeed, the idea of the national economy of the past is a central discursive prop of the very idea of globalization that in turn has become a key feature of the generation of intellectual knowledge about globalization and the corporate and policy discourse in which the concept first emerged (Cameron and Palan 2004). This brings forth two points of note. First, the generation of academic knowledge about the structural properties of the world is potentially implicated in the reproduction through discourse of those structural properties. This is a more or less uncontroversial claim among sociologists of knowledge, but it is worth restating that how we know and understand a social object (how we create science about it) is a central facet of the "thingness" of that social object (Brown 2003; Strandsbjerg 2010). To take a couple of examples, the notions that "climate" can be the object of a global governance regime or that "finance" should be governable are heavily dependent on prior intellectual work that effectively "scientized" both of these concepts as respectively a "geophysical system" and a domain susceptible to stability-instability dynamics (Allan 2017; Dumouchel 2018). As Cameron and Palan (2004) note, the intellectual trajectory of "globalization" is distinctive in that the academic world (or significant parts of it) tended to internalize the corporate and policy logic of the concept (the redundancy of economic borders, the dominance of the market, the replacement of authority hierarchies with networks, etc.) and to work with these as axioms on which subsequent analyses could be built. There is also a notably close relationship between some of the more prominent academic attempts to theorize a form of globalization with a social purpose and periodically fashionable policy doctrines of "managed globalization" (Abdelal and Meunier 2010).

Second, while the tendency in discourses of globalization has been toward naturalizing the concept of globalization so that its imperatives are irresistible, and the range of policy choice is heavily circumscribed, there has always been—within that discourse—the possibility, or the expectation, that the inevitable could be rendered contingent. The fact that globalization is discussed in terms of a transformation, novelty, and the emergence of new ordering principles means that the discourse carries within itself an implicit theory of history. Post–Cold War narratives of the triumphant march of markets and liberal democracy (which by definition were teleological) have some ties with the (then-)emergent idea of globalization, but this linkage of globalization to the "end of history" now has little purchase, particularly as the period since the end of the Cold War has been punctuated by a series of crises *of* globalization.[10] In short, in a discursive environment where some actors seek to render the contingent necessary or to defend the contingent as normatively preferable, it becomes possible to imagine alternatives to "globalization."

It follows that while "globalization" and "anarchy" can be seen as rival discourses of the structuring principles of world politics, there is one key important difference. As argued in the preceding paragraph, the architecture of globalization discourse contains within it the imagination of "nonglobalization." Anarchy, on the other hand, is a discourse that cannot, by definition, imagine its nonexistence. It is a perpetual condition in which the derivative logic of power politics is the inevitably "tragic" by-product. The political, behavioral, and policy logics of globalization are equally "obvious," but their performance comes to be seen as essential to the reproduction of the system. The globalized system depends on their enactment; it does not simply force actors into particular modes of behavior. Ultimately, they have an alternative, and a lot of rhetorical energy is expended on ensuring that relevant actors do the right thing.[11] At the same time, the rigidly ontological claims about anarchy have arguably made it easier to refute its existence empirically and to posit that the world has changed (cf. Strange 1994b).[12] This is how the standard IPE claims enumerated previously have been able to gain such traction and why in some regional subsystems, notably the European Union, realist analytics have had such a hard time in finding any purchase (Collard-Wexler 2006; although see Wivel 2004).

Conclusions

The foregoing points to an unacknowledged discursive relationship between globalization and anarchy. This is certainly worthy of greater examination, and there is interesting work to be done by taking a sociology of knowledge approach. The conjecture here is that the study of anarchy–power politics, on the one hand, and the political economy of globalization, on the other, has been undertaken by more or less discrete scholarly communities. Thus, at the level of "high scholarship"—the point where academics have relatively narrow research foci and where a variety of institutional forms (subfield configurations, journals, professional associations, commonly held narratives of a field's history, etc.) help to shape and define the acceptable parameters of scholarly fields—anarchy would be the background common sense of some defined clusters of scholarship, but definitely not for others, where globalization would perform the equivalent function. For example, one common story told about IPE is that it is a relatively new field founded in the early 1970s amid the collapse of Bretton Woods and the recognition that the world was more and more characterized by "complex interdependence."[13] This myth of foundation does, of course, stand up to some empirical scrutiny, but it also self-defines IPE as post–power politics in focus and sets tight exclusionary parameters for what work—past or present—could be properly considered as IPE (Clift and Rosamond 2009). Equally (perhaps more) interesting is the way in which newcomers to the study of international relations come to understand the place of the rival structural narratives of anarchy and globalization within the field or discipline as a whole. To what extent are they perceived as sequential or rival or coexistent or (in combination) emergent structuring logics of world politics? To what extent are textbooks and syllabi silent on the relationship between these two apparently incommensurable ideas?

It might be said that anarchy and globalization are perfectly capable of existing concurrently as rival but ultimately complementary scholarly projects and in the minds of real-world actors in world politics. In the former sense, it could be argued that there is no need for IPE to vanquish IR and security studies with its more empirically astute grasp of the international system or indeed for proponents of anarchy to suppose that substantive political-economic changes could tilt the balance back in their favor. Put another way, globalization and anarchy could be thought of as coexistent and overlapping, with the power politics of the overlap being of particular interest. Equally, it would also be fruitful to think about globalization and anarchy as not just rival policy narratives that end up shaping the world one way or another in their images. It might be a mistake to simply regard their intersubjective status as unproblematically bifurcated, where some actors (mostly foreign policy elites, say) conceive of their structural locus as anarchic, whereas (say) the CEOs of transnational firms have internalized causal and normative beliefs associated with globalization. What is also interesting to think about is the extent to which collective understandings themselves appreciate that action in world politics is structured, enabled, and constrained by the prevailing logics of anarchy and globalization. For example, the assumption of anarchy might shape a state's approach to the realization of its foreign policy goals. Alternatively, foreign policy goals may themselves be inextricably entwined with shifting understandings of globalization and the ways in which globalization shapes problem and solution sets.

This raises important questions about the capacity of crises (or perhaps more interestingly, the way in which crises are constructed and understood; see Hay 1996; Widmaier, Blyth, and Seabrooke 2007) to disturb settled structural narratives or perhaps to recalibrate the relationship between them. These articulations, problematizations, and contestations of crises and of what crises must and should mean represent crucial sites of contemporary power politics. Indeed, there is certainly a clear discursive linkage between two supposed shifts in the "America first" worldview espoused by President Trump. One of the key features, it seems, of "America first" Trumpism is its willingness to speak offensively (in both senses of the term) in world politics in terms of foreign and security policy and to float the national interest as the referent object in economics, thereby directly challenging the neoliberal emphasis on the convergence of national interest and the promotion of open markets. Needless to say, this type of claims making is both challenging to the existing cobweb of institutional and normative ordering principles of world politics and potentially constrained by it.

Notes

1. The question of whether IPE is or should be regarded as a subfield of IR is somewhat more than a moot point but is beyond the scope of this piece (see Clift 2014; Clift and Rosamond 2009; M. Watson 2005). There is, of course, a version of IPE that retains the general orientation of IR while insisting that economic and security logics are key determinants of the nature and conduct of world politics.

2. Mark Blyth, "Global Trumpism: Why Trump's Victory Was 30 Years in the Making and Why It Won't Stop Here." *Foreign Affairs*, November 15, 2016, https://www.foreignaffairs .com/articles/2016-11-15/global-trumpism.

3. Again, an ideal type normative power would seek to propagate conceptions of normal world politics that are broadly post-Westphalian and in which civic liberal universal values prevailed. While the explicit normativity of the normative power approach is often neglected, it is worth pointing out that the analytical core of the approach is consistent with a wide range of constitutive principles, which in turn may contradict one another (see Rosamond 2014).

4. Damro (2012) is explicit that coercion is a characteristic feature of market power, while Manners (2008) insists that the use of normative power properly understood would be dialogic rather than coercive in nature.

5. Among these problems are (a) capturing the counterfactual that is implied in the account of B's behavior, (b) isolating the independent effect of A's action on B, and (c) dealing with the implication that we can capture the exercise of power only if we have access to the real preferences of both A and B.

6. The place of the rationality postulate within structural realism is a complex issue. See Alan Shadunts, "The Rational Actor Assumption in Structural Realism," E-International Relations, October 28, 2016, http://www.e-ir.info/2016/10/28/the-rational-actor-assumption -in-structural-realism/.

7. She did not use the word "performative," of course, but Germain's reading shows how interested Strange was in intersubjective beliefs and values and the processes that they unleash. The relationship between theory and values forms the subject matter of chapter 1 of *States and Markets* (Strange 1994a). Strange pushed the idea much more explicitly in an incomplete paper drafted at the end of her life (Strange 1998) in which she suggested that bad theories could be constitutive (again, not her word) of bad policy practice.

8. A premise, it should be said, that is widely contested in much comparative political economy literature, not least that associated with the "varieties of capitalism" approach (Hall and Soskice 2001).

9. As is obvious from this brief exegesis, Ricardian comparative advantage does quite a bit of (unacknowledged) work within a standard liberal IPE framing of globalization. For an important critique, see M. Watson (2017).

10. See, for example, Francis Fukuyama's take on these issues: "Francis Fukuyama: The Future of Globalization," World Affairs, February 16, 2017, video, 3:05, https://www.youtube .com/watch?v=HLEYK1sz-eI.

11. Of course, this is more or less the same point that Wendt (1992) makes about anarchy. My comment is not about the sociological reality of power politics but rather about the discourse that surrounds it.

12. The term "empirical refutation" is being used in a rather cavalier fashion here. What is meant is certainly not falsification in the Popperian sense but rather the ways in which (a) the anarchic imaginary of the world (and derivatives or close relatives of it) has been challenged by a transformationist policy discourse since the mid- to late 1980s and (b) academic knowledge production has traded more and more in subfield and conceptual vocabulary that in its mere utterance is a denial of the primacy of anarchy–power politics.

13. In this narrative IPE is often described as a subfield of IR.

Part III

The Processes of Power Politics and International Institutions

Maximizing Security through International Institutions: Soft-Balancing Strategies Reconsidered

Anders Wivel and T.V. Paul

As the institutionalization of the international realm has increased, so has the use of soft balancing as a security strategy. Discussions and analyses of soft balancing often mention the use of institutions as an integral part of soft-balancing strategies, but so far the logics of institutional soft balancing remain relatively unexplored.

This is a problem for three reasons. First, scholars working on soft balancing tend to view the use of international institutions as an important tool of statecraft. They argue that soft-balancing strategies rely "on informal alignments, international institutions and economic sanctions to restrain threatening powers" (Paul 2018, 2). Therefore, exploring the logic and use of institutional soft balancing will help us advance our understanding of soft balancing in theory and practice. Second, and related, one of the most serious points of criticism raised against the concept of soft balancing has been that it is underspecified and therefore difficult to distinguish from diplomacy in general. In the words of Lieber and Alexander, a fundamental flaw of soft balancing is that it does not "offer effective means for distinguishing soft balancing from routine diplomatic friction between countries" (2005, 125). Our chapter seeks to counter this criticism by specifying one particular soft-balancing strategy: institutional soft balancing.

Finally, institutional soft balancing is here to stay, and it is likely to become even more important in the future. As argued in the introductory chapter to this volume, despite the current challenges, the international institutional order is "more comprehensive, more complex, and more robust" than at any time in world history. Consequently, international institutions—defined as "*associational clusters among states with some bureaucratic structures that create and manage self-imposed and other-imposed constraints on state policies and behaviors"*—not only constrain and enable individual states but also contribute to changing the fabric of world politics. This development underpins the use of soft-balancing strategies over hard military balancing under certain strategic conditions (Paul 2018, 24–26).

This chapter explores why, when, and how states use international institutions in soft-balancing strategies and discusses whether this is an effective way to restrain power and aggression. Although we acknowledge that institutions may affect the actions of states and other actors in many and complex ways, we here focus exclusively on institutions as means of soft balancing, that is, we examine how states use international institutions to balance the power and influence of other states (He 2008). Our argument proceeds in six steps. First, we define what we mean by institutional soft balancing and unpack how soft balancing differs from traditional hard military balancing. Given this understanding of institutional soft balancing, the following three sections explore why, when, and how states use institutions for soft balancing, before we discuss whether institutional soft balancing is effective. We end the chapter with a discussion of the future of institutional soft balancing.

What Is Institutional Soft Balancing?

Balance of power gained prominence as a foreign policy strategy among the Italian city-states in fifteenth-century Europe and as a fundamental principle of diplomacy in the 1713 Treaty of Utrecht, which prescribed that no state should be able to dominate others.[1] Intrinsically linked to the birth of the modern states system and the developing thought on its constituent mechanisms by early realists such as Niccoló Machiavelli ([1532] 2003; Sullivan 1973), balance of power was soon regarded as the primary instrument for preserving state survival and systemic stability by use of arms buildup, coalition building, and preventive war (Donnelly 2000; Gulick 1955; Little 2007). Some believe balancing occurs automatically as a law of politics (Waltz 1979; Mearsheimer 2014), while others think of it as a conscious manual strategy (Levy 2004; Morgenthau 1967).

Recent scholarship has pointed to the absence of traditional balancing since the end of the Cold War (Brooks and Wohlforth 2016; Hansen, Toft, and Wivel 2009; He 2012; Kapstein and Mastanduno 1999; Monteiro 2014; Paul, Wirtz, and Fortmann 2004; Paul 2005, 2018; Walt 2005; Pape 2005; Schweller 2004; Wivel 2008; Wivel and Wæver 2018; Wohlforth 1999, 2009). This is true at the global level, where no coalition has formed against the US unipole, and at the regional level, where Russia and China have increasingly played a hegemonic role in their respective regions with little evidence of intense balancing by rival great powers or smaller states. Even if we modify the balance of power proposition by arguing that states tend to balance threat rather than power (Walt 1987), there is little evidence of balancing. For instance, neither the US intervention in Iraq in 2003 nor the Russian interventions in Georgia in 2008 and in Ukraine since 2014 have provoked other states to pursue a balancing strategy. In contrast, despite sustained "naming and shaming" by US policymakers and North Atlantic Treaty Organization (NATO) officials, most European NATO member states have continued to allocate defense budgets well below the 2 percent of GDP threshold that they have all agreed to, even after the events in Georgia and Ukraine.[2] China's forays into the South China Sea and threatening actions toward Japan have raised some balancing activity by the US, such as the Obama administration's "pivot to Asia," but none yet to the level the theory would have predicted. China is actually making steady inroads into the Pacific without a strong counterpush by the US.[3] Before these instances the NATO bombardment of Serbia in 1999 and the US-led invasion of Iraq in 2003 also produced no active balancing coalitions despite intense opposition expressed by other great powers such as Russia and China and, in the latter instance, even European states such as Germany and France.

The apparent lack of balancing has spurred some scholars to question the prominence of power balancing in world history altogether (Buzan and Little 1996; Wohlforth et al. 2007). Others have argued that rather than the absence of balancing, we are witnessing a new type of balancing via increasing the cost of conquest and military aggression by diplomatic, economic, and institutional means (e.g., Pape 2005; Paul 2005, 2018). This type of balancing, soft balancing, can be defined as "restraining the power or aggressive policies of a state through international institutions, concerted diplomacy via limited, informal ententes, and economic sanctions in order to make its aggressive actions less legitimate in the eyes of the world and hence its strategic goals more difficult to obtain" (Paul 2018, 20). Thus, soft balancing encompasses strategies based on "coalition building and diplomatic bargaining within international institutions, short of formal bilateral and multilateral alliances" (Pape 2005, 58; Paul 2004, 3, 14). Whereas the primary aim of hard balancing is to increase the cost of aggression by military means—that is, through formal alliances and arms buildups—the primary aim of soft balancing is to increase the cost of aggression by nonmilitary means. One of these means, which has grown increasingly important since the end of World War II, is international institutions. We understand institutional soft balancing as a coercive strategy, in which states use international institutions instrumentally to reduce other states' profit from noncompliance, to increase the marginal costs of noncompliant behavior, and to undermine the legitimacy of noncompliant actions and signal the potential use of hard balancing if soft balancing turns out to be unsuccessful.[4]

Why Do States Use Institutions for Soft Balancing?

States use formal international institutions for soft balancing for three reasons. First, institutions are important sources of international legitimacy. They convey an intersubjective understanding of moral appropriateness (Weitsman 2014, 42).

Speaking in the name of an international institution lifts the argument (at least rhetorically) outside the realm of narrow self-interest because it expresses the opinion of a larger collective of states and sometimes even international society. International institutions are effective instruments for doing this because they are characterized by at least some measure of independence from member states, that is, "the authority to act with a degree of autonomy, and often with neutrality, in defined spheres" (Abbott and Snidal 1998, 9). Consequently, they may be used to shame the aggressor by portraying the aggression as the pursuit of narrow self-interest at the expense of international society or at least a part of it. This shaming effect is most effective when the aggressor itself is a member of the institution as it points to the hypocrisy of violating rules that the aggressor agreed to previously. At the very least, it incurs the cost on the aggressor of justifying why it broke the rules (or typically trying to argue why this is not a case of breaking the rules at all). In addition, the institution will have provisions for sanctions against rule breakers that may increase the costs of aggression further (Neumann and Gstöhl 2006, 19–21). Thus, acting through international institutions serves the double purpose of delegitimizing the actions of the aggressor and legitimating the actions of the soft balancers themselves who speak on behalf of a larger group of states, sometimes even international society, and point to the violation of previously agreed rules and norms by the aggressor. As noted by Thompson, "reputation costs are highest when states act in defiance of formal legal commitments and IOs [international organizations]" (2009, 19).

Second, institutional soft balancing is often more cost-effective than soft balancing outside institutions. Institutions provide a diplomatic infrastructure with previously agreed rules and norms of negotiation and decision making, and institutions typically have a civil service providing information and administrative assistance. This all makes the startup costs of forging soft-balancing coalitions through international institutions lower than coalition building outside the institution. Thus, international institutions facilitate collective action because they are "transaction cost economizing" (Abbott and Snidal 1998, 9). In addition, the potential costs of retaliation from the aggressor are smaller when a state acts through an institution. The aggressor is less likely to retaliate against an institutionalized collective because the likelihood of breaking up the coalition is smaller and the potential costs of retaliation are bigger. International institutions cast shadows of past and future because of their durability. They are the expression of a previously negotiated order in which states have already identified their nonnegotiable bastions and collectively defined the red lines not to be crossed in interstate relations. Consequently, international institutions provide an already negotiated starting point for action. This facilitates negotiations among states and helps to legitimize the actions taken to domestic actors within the negotiating states. At the same time, an important message of continuity is sent to the aggressor state: we have a stable institutionalized coalition and our position is unlikely to change in the future.

Third, institutional soft balancing typically offers opportunities for a "flexible response" to aggression. Official statements of shaming and condemnation may be formulated on a scale from the mere expression of disagreement to accusation of violation of basic principles of international law, and economic sanctions may be directed against sectors of more or less vital importance to the aggressor state. Eventually, the institution might signal the resolve to add hard balancing to soft balancing. Thus, through institutions, soft balancing may be initiated relatively quickly and at minimal costs while at the same time providing opportunities for escalation (Pape 2005, 17). In that sense, critics are right to point out that soft balancing may be seen as "diplomatic friction" (Lieber and Alexander 2005, 109) but wrong to assume that this friction is "the inadvertent side-effect of usual diplomatic interaction." Institutional soft balancing is better understood as a "method" for signaling resolve and incurring costs on aggressor states and at the same time avoiding costly hard-balancing strategies (Saltzman 2012, 133). It is not just diplomatic friction or random activity as critics have charged but involves concrete policy postures on a continuous basis in response to a particular threatening behavior by a power and is backed by institutional disapproval, delegitimation, and in some instances, sanctions.

When Do States Use Institutional Soft Balancing?

The extensive use of soft balancing in contemporary international relations and the alleged indistinguishability of soft balancing from diplomacy in general (discussed previously) have led critics to view soft balancing as "unipolar politics as usual" (Brooks and Wohlforth 2008, 71). However, institutional soft balancing is not a recent phenomenon. The great powers reduced each other's action space by institutional measures in the nineteenth-century Concert of Europe, and in the first half of the twentieth century, the Allied states attempted to curb the aggressive policies of Germany, Italy, and Japan thorough the League of Nations (Paul 2018, chap. 3). During the Cold War, the Group of 77 (G77) served as a platform for developing states soft-balancing the industrialized states within the UN, and the small Nordic welfare states sought to soft-balance both East and West through an agenda emphasizing peaceful conflict resolution, human rights, and global equality. Beginning in the 1970s, the Conference on Security and Cooperation in Europe (CSCE), initially a joint East-West initiative on détente, was used by Western policymakers as an instrument for soft-balancing the Soviet Union by providing a platform for Soviet bloc dissident groups.

Still, the evolution of international society, since the end of the Second World War in particular, has been conducive to soft-balancing strategies in general and institutional soft balancing in particular. At the global and regional levels, this development refers to a change in the fabric of international relations. This change is the combined effect of economic globalization, changes in the offensive-defensive balance favoring the defensive and deterrent (in particular as a consequence of nuclear weapons), and increasingly institutionalized and universally accepted norms against military conquest resulting in increased costs and diminishing benefits from territorial expansion (Paul 2018, 15–19). Consequently, over time, hard balancing has become less salient as a state strategy for balancing threats and power, and soft balancing has become more important, because there are fewer incidents of military conquest and because, even when territorial expansion does happen, balancing states have strong incentives to solve the dispute through diplomacy and institutions before taking military action. This development is conducive to the use of institutional soft-balancing strategies in particular. Economic and military interdependence and an increase in the "interaction capacity" of the international system have created a growing need to coordinate among states leading to a growth of formal international intergovernmental organizations (IGOs) from the establishment of commissions for governing the traffic on the Elbe (1821) and the Rhine (1831) to the more than 250 IGOs today.[5] Most issue areas that become venues for international disagreement and conflict already have an established institutional infrastructure offering a cost-effective route to signaling intent, incurring costs on violators and defectors, and signaling political bastions, thereby offering states ever more opportunities to pursue institutional soft balancing.

At the interstate level, states use institutional soft balancing when at least one of four conditions is fulfilled. First, states use institutional soft balancing to counter violations of the rules of the game in international relations, in particular when these violations are committed by great powers. Rules of the game include, most fundamentally, codes of conduct for when and how war is a legitimate political instrument and norms of state sovereignty. These rules of the game constitute the basic normative structure of international society and serve the interests of weaker powers by increasing the predictability and stability of international affairs. They function as a cushioning against brute great power politics in international anarchy. Institutional soft balancing offers the opportunity to signal that a red line has been crossed and thereby show that this red line still exists and is important to international society or a significant caucus within international society without engaging in a military conflict over the violation. Institutional soft balancing may appear at various stages before the actual violation of the rules of the game and after the violation. States may take advantage of existing international institutions to soft-balance, for example, by coordinating and acting fast when they face the threat of a violation and by taking advantage of institutional mechanisms for speaking out against the violation. They may also take the opportunity to institutionalize relations among one another in order to signal their concern over the violation and their intention to cooperate more closely in the future. The 1999 Kosovo air campaign and the 2003 Iraq War exemplify these mechanisms.[6]

Neither the Kosovo air campaign nor the Iraq War was based on a direct mandate from the UN or consensus among the five permanent members of the

UN Security Council (P5). Both operations were offensive military interventions seen by critics as violating the sovereignty norm as well as codes of conduct for great power consultation. Yet in both cases, the response was institutional rather than military. The US-led NATO offensive in Kosovo in 1999, in support of the Kosovo Albanians against President Slobodan Milošević's Serbian regime, upset China and Russia, who interpreted it as a clear violation of the sovereignty norm, setting a potential precedent for future interventions. In response, China and Russia successfully blocked UN approval of the intervention. Russia suspended its participation in the Partnership of Peace Program and in the Russia NATO Founding Act, thereby using institutional nonparticipation to signal its concern and attempting to undermine the legitimacy of the intervention. While these actions were unsuccessful in preventing NATO bombings of Serbia, Russia successfully took advantage of its G8 membership to make this the primary institution for great power dialogue on the conflict and the adoption of a protocol for negotiating its end. Subsequently, in 2001 China, Russia, and four Central Asian states announced the formation on the Shanghai Cooperation Organization (SCO), an institution largely focused at curbing US influence in Central Asia (Ferguson 2012). The invasion of Iraq in March 2003 by a US-led coalition of the willing followed an unsuccessful six-month effort by the US administration to secure a mandate from the UN Security Council. The UN mandate was denied not only by Russia and China but also by US NATO allies Germany and France, who also used NATO and EU declarations to signal their concern for the long-term consequences for international stability and peace if the US invaded Iraq rather than accept additional weapons inspections and attempts at peaceful disarmament. Thus, Germany and France used the EU and NATO to undermine the legitimacy of the invasion and thereby increase its political costs to the United States. At the same time, using institutional soft balancing to focus specifically on the challenge from Iraq allowed the European countries to continue their close cooperation with the United States on other issues (Wivel 2008, 295). These issues included, for example, reforming international trade through the World Trade Organization and even cooperating closely on security issues in Afghanistan. Subsequently, the European Security Strategy adopted by the European Council in December 2003 signaled the willingness of EU member states to act independently of the United States. It explicitly stressed the importance of "an international order based on effective multilateralism" (European Council 2003, 9) and the ambition to "contribute to an effective multilateral system leading to a fairer, safer and more united world" (14).

Second, states use institutional soft balancing in cases of threats and violations of the territorial integrity of friendly states and coalition partners. Here institutional soft balancing offers an opportunity for political support to the state under threat or attack and at the same time avoids military confrontation with the aggressor. One example is the EU's use of restrictive measures against Russia as a response to Russia's 2014 annexation of Crimea and subsequent attempts to destabilize Ukraine. In 2014 EU member states decided to cancel the EU-Russia summit and supported the suspension of talks with Russia over joining the Organization for Economic Cooperation and Development (OECD) and the International Energy Agency (IEA). Thus, member states used the EU to deny Russia membership of international institutions and thereby to curb Russian influence. Also, the EU institutional soft-balancing toolkit against Russia includes asset freezing and travel bans against selected entities and individuals, restrictions on economic relations with Crimea and Sevastopol, and sanctions against Russia in selected economic sectors.[7]

Third, institutional soft balancing may be used when there is no smoking gun pointing to one particular aggressor—for example, in the case of terrorism or a cyberattack—but there are strong indications who the aggressor is. In this case, member states of an institution can condemn the actions or seek protection against future actions without directly confronting the likely aggressor. An example of this type of institutional soft balancing is Estonia's response to comprehensive cyberattacks on Estonian government agencies, banks, and media outlets in April and May 2007. While attacks came from Russian IP addresses, there was no solid evidence of the Russian government's involvement. As summed up by one cybersecurity official at the Estonian Ministry of Defense, "It was a great security test. We just don't know who to send the bill to."[8] The Estonian government responded by pursuing a high profile in NATO cybersecurity policy in close cooperation with its Western allies. This has included hosting the NATO Cooperative Cyber Defence Center of Excellence (CCDCEO) since 2008. The CCDCEO subsequently funded the first and second Tallinn manuals, aiming to apply international law and norms to cyber warfare and attacks (Mälksoo 2013). Thus, by using the nonmilitary aspects of NATO, Estonia and its allies were able to signal their concern and develop measures against future cyberattacks without engaging in a direct confrontation with Russia. A parallel development can be observed in the Euro-Atlantic area more generally with EU member states enhancing cybersecurity cooperation and EU and NATO holding coordinated exercises on how to respond to attacks (European Commission 2017).[9]

Finally, institutional soft balancing may be the response to hegemonic agenda setting. Like Minded Developing Countries (LMDC) serves as a platform for developing states soft-balancing the West within the UN in, for example, human rights and environmental policy, just as the G77 aimed to balance the industrialized states during the Cold War. In both cases the aim was to balance the political and ideological hegemony of the West and the North. The continuous attempts by EU member states since 1990 to strengthen the EU as a security actor may be interpreted as an effort to soft-balance US hegemony in Euro-Atlantic security affairs without provoking abandonment from the American security provider (Hansen, Toft, and Wivel 2009, 72–75).

In all four cases, international institutions offered member states a platform for increasing costs and decreasing benefits of what was perceived as other states' noncompliant behavior by speaking on behalf of a collective, ideally the international community, and at the same time, the institutions functioned as shields against retaliation from the targeted state(s).

How Do States Use Institutional Soft Balancing?

A useful distinction can be made between institutional soft balancing against states that are members of the same international institution as the balancer and institutional soft balancing targeted at states outside the institution (He 2015). The Council of Europe and the United Nations are important, if sometimes ineffective, instruments for soft institutional balancing targeting member states. States acting through the UN have the opportunity of a flexible response against a member state resulting ultimately in a military intervention if the aggressor state does not comply. Thus, states are likely to put much effort into battles over the design of decision-making procedures and principles for action as these mechanisms will define the action space for and effectiveness of balancing. Institutions with more limited membership, such as the EU or SCO, are less likely to be used as vehicles for institutional soft balancing against member states. They are more likely to be used as instruments for institutional soft balancing against nonmembers. However, in the rare event that they are used for soft balancing against member states, they are likely to have an effect because the aggressor state is being balanced by its closest allies and is unlikely to find alternatives. For instance, in the immediate aftermath of the 2008 Russo-Georgian War, the SCO stressed the sanctity of borders, and China refused to comment on Russia's allegations that the United States had orchestrated the conflict. This was a warning to Russia that SCO members China, Kazakhstan, Kyrgyzstan, Tajikistan, and Uzbekistan were not going to spend any political capital on supporting Russia and a signal that they would not support Russian intervention in Central Asia and were willing to restrain Russian influence by undermining the legitimacy of Russian actions (Mouritzen and Wivel 2012, 175–80). Institutions may also be used as instruments for soft balancing against nonmembers. The EU, the Association of Southeast Asian Nations Plus Three (APT), and the Regional Comprehensive Economic Partnership (RCEP) are examples of international institutions used by their member states as instruments for soft-balancing economic pressures from the United States (He 2015; Wivel 2004).

A third use of institutional soft balancing is regulating access to membership. This gatekeeping function may be directed against applicants for membership or may be used to undermine the power and influence of nonmembers by denying them access to potential allies. The post–Cold War enlargements of the EU offered former Soviet bloc states in Central and Eastern Europe membership in the union, but membership came at a price. It required the former Communist states to adapt to the political and economic demands of the EU in return for membership, and at the same time, EU membership restricted Russia's ability to exercise power and influence over these states (Mouritzen and Wivel 2005). Thus, institutional soft balancing helps to explain why Russia continues to view the United States, Europe, the EU, and NATO as one bloc and why it has responded aggressively to EU policies in Ukraine.

Is Institutional Soft Balancing Effective?

Is soft institutional balancing an effective means for maximizing state interests in the face of aggression? The question may be answered in absolute or relative terms. In absolute terms, we may ask: Did institutional soft balancing get the job done, that is, prevent the aggressor from pursuing policies threatening the interests of the soft-balancing states? There are two reasons why the answer may be no. First, the aggressor may respond negatively or not at all to soft balancing because the costs incurred by shaming or sanctions are assessed as lower than the benefits of continued aggression. If institutional soft-balancing strategies are to be effective, they need to be directed at key domestic groups in the aggressor state—for example, incurring costs on a particular strong economic interest group or incurring costs on the regime by calling attention to the aggression (cf. Moravcsik 1995). Even if this is the case (and sometimes because this is the case), soft balancing may confirm the aggressor's perception that it is the soft balancers who are behaving aggressively by interfering in what is considered internal affairs or actions in a legitimate sphere of interest. As a result, the soft balancers may experience a particularly unfortunate version of the security spiral. The aggressor state may step up military action in response to the soft balancing, which can lead to intensified institutional activity in the form of declarations and sanctions from the soft balancers and an even harder military response from the aggressor state. If the soft balancers do not have the political will or military capability to back up sanctions and declarations with military power, the aggressor state may ultimately call their bluff by intensifying the conflict and leaving them with little choice other than accepting the revised state of affairs. One example of this dynamic is the 2008 Russian-Georgian War, which was the first military invasion by Russia since the collapse of the Soviet Union. Even though the invasion was strongly condemned by the West, the EU ended up brokering a peace agreement between the two countries, accepting most Russian demands and leaving Russia with little incentive to leave Georgian soil.

Second, soft balancing is prone to being hijacked by domestic interest groups and sectoral interests. Which sanctions are to be decided, and how are they to be implemented? The answer to these questions may be of vital importance to strong economic interests in the domestic societies of the soft balancers. This risk increases if soft balancing takes place through international institutions because many of the interest groups of domestic society have strong networks and competencies for lobbying the institution's civil service and political representatives. Also, the media framing of soft-balancing policies may make it more or less costly for a state to soft balance.

Measuring the success of institutional soft balancing in relative terms, we may ask: Effective compared to what? For instance, NATO and EU policies condemning the actions of Russia in Georgia and Ukraine have been failures if measured against the goal of stopping Russian aggression against these two countries. But at the same time, they may have worked better than the alternatives: either a military buildup against Russia, increasing the risk of war, or each member state left to fend for itself, leaving the Baltic States in particular in a vulnerable position. Institutional soft balancing is far from perfect, but sometimes it is as good as it gets. In an increasingly globalized and interdependent world, it may well be the most appropriate policy choice to avoid costly rivalries, arms races, and economic isolation.

What Is the Future of Institutional Soft Balancing?

Institutional soft balancing is likely to remain important in the future. Populist leaders challenge globalization, but they have few means at their disposal to reverse it without undermining their own economies and ultimately the security of the state they represent and the livelihood of the voters who elected them. For an increasing number of states, the most cost-effective way of pursing the national interest is strategic use of the institutional infrastructure of international relations. In this effort, institutional soft balancing is a key tool allowing states to take advantage of the flexibility and legitimacy of an institutional response to challenges.

The semiretirement of the United States as the primary guarantor of a globalized, institutionalized order is at the same time challenging the robustness of this order and creating strong incentives for institutional soft balancing. While the institutional trade order in the first two decades after the Cold War was aptly captured by the metaphor of a spaghetti bowl with multiple overlapping agreements (Alter and Meunier 2009), it is increasingly resembling a jigsaw puzzle of regionally based trading agreements (Menon 2014). The US withdrawal from the Trans-Pacific Partnership (TPP) did not result in the institution's collapse but in Japan's taking leadership and the signing of the Comprehensive and Progressive Agreement for Trans-Pacific Partnership (CPTTP). Likewise, US reluctance to commit to the Transatlantic Trade and Investment Partnership (TTIP) did not stop the EU from concluding trade agreements with Canada and Mexico. As noted by Sampanis (2012, 98), the cost of defiance against great powers is reduced if secondary states can offer lucrative consumer markets, and the CCTTP and the EU offer useful institutional frameworks for regional powers such as Germany, France, and Japan to soft-balance the United States and China in the future.

American retrenchment is not just about a change in policy but more fundamentally about a weakening of US relative power and the widespread perception of a coming power transition. American power is based not only on the material capabilities of the United States but also on the institutional order that the United States built during the Cold War and expanded afterward (Ikenberry 2011). Power transition is usually accompanied by institutional transformation. The decline of US power is likely to trigger not only hard balancing but also intensified soft institutional balancing, including, for example, the establishment of new international institutions intended to replace old institutions (He 2018). In a highly institutionalized international system, institutional soft balancing is likely to take a prominent role in the fight over future regional and global orders.

Notes

1. The definition and use of the balance of power varies widely among authors. As early as 1953, Ernst Haas identified eight different meanings of the concept used by scholars and policymakers, and its meaning has varied over time from a rational instrument for preserving the survival of individual states to a fundamental mechanism for maintaining systemic stability and a normative ideal (Little 2007). We focus here on balancing as a strategy.

2. Ian Johnston, "NATO to 'Name and Shame' Countries Which Fail to Meet Defence Budget Target," *Independent*, June 14, 2015, https://www.independent.co.uk/news/world/politics/nato-to-name-and-shame-countries-which-fail-to-meet-defence-budget-target-10319596.html.

3. Simon Winchester, "China's Pacific Overtures," *New York Times*, November 6, 2015, https://www.nytimes.com/2015/11/07/opinion/chinas-pacific-overtures.html.

4. See Paul (2018, 23) for the general soft-balancing argument from which this is adapted.

5. Interaction capacity is here understood as the level of communication, transportation, and organization capability in the international system. See Buzan, Jones, and Little (1993). For an empirical application of the concept of interaction capacity, see Lobell and Nicholson's contribution to this volume.

6. For a more detailed account of soft balancing in the Kosovo and Iraq conflicts, see Paul (2018, chap. 5).

7. European Council, "EU Restrictive Measures in Response to the Crisis in Ukraine," last modified December 17, 2018, http://www.consilium.europa.eu/en/policies/sanctions/ukraine-crisis/.

8. Damien McGuinness, "How a Cyber Attack Transformed Estonia," BBC News, April 27, 2017, https://www.bbc.com/news/39655415.

9. See also European External Action Service, "EU Drives International Cooperation on Cybersecurity; Tests Ability to Respond to Threats," September 14, 2017, https://eeas.europa.eu/headquarters/headquarters-homepage/32160/eu-drives-international-cooperation-cybersecurity-tests-ability-respond-threats_en.

CHAPTER 7

The Power in Opacity: Rethinking Information in International Organizations

Austin Carson and Alexander Thompson

Following years of debate over the importance of international institutions, especially the extent to which power politics undermine their influence, there is a promising trend among international relations (IR) scholars to move beyond categorical claims in favor of more nuanced arguments. The result is an emerging middle ground, where scholars explore and even embrace the role of power to help explain the creation, design, and impact of institutions. We contribute to this theoretical terrain through a novel focus on the relationship between power and information in the context of international organizations (IOs). The information function of IOs is often touted as a key source of efficiency gains, promoting cooperation and compliance among states (Keohane 1984; Mitchell 1998; Donno 2010). In practice, however, IO activities and decision making are often quite opaque. This point has been made most forcefully in the context of the "democratic deficit" debate, in which critics emphasize the lack of transparency and accountability vis-à-vis publics and civil society groups, leaving them with little influence over IOs.[1]

Building on these concerns, we ask: In what ways is information, as an unevenly distributed resource, a potential source of power within IOs? We analyze how the informational demands that emerge from participating in a complex organization can affect relative influence within it. In doing so, this chapter addresses several of the important theoretical issues raised in the framework chapter by Wivel and Paul, especially questions on how international institutions, as a form of political context, shape power politics. We focus on various dimensions of the institutional setting within IOs that translate into information advantages and disadvantages, with consequences for how power is understood and exercised.

We make three main claims. First, states themselves often lack information when it comes to IO activities, even when they are members of the IO in question. Opacity matters for governments inside of IOs, not just for private actors on the outside. Second, the information supplied by IOs is not distributed or consumed evenly across states. We argue that power advantages due to information are the result of the interaction between information provision (an institutional variable) and information-processing capacity (a state-level variable). In effect, then, a given IO has different degrees of transparency: it could be open from the perspective of some states but relatively opaque for others. Finally, states with information advantages are empowered relative to their peers. We discuss some mechanisms by which advantaged states can exercise information-based influence in multilateral settings.

As Wivel and Paul (in this volume) note, power politics and international institutions have always coexisted in practice, suggesting a need for theoretical approaches that integrate these two important features of international politics. By taking both state power and the role of IOs seriously, we contribute to this integration and depart from the realist-institutionalist debates that often exaggerate the divide. We agree with realists that some states have disproportionate influence on and within IOs, but we diverge from realism by focusing on a subtler power dynamic, one that may not correlate with a state's material capabilities, as traditionally defined, and that derives from the design and practice of IOs themselves. Similarly, we agree with institutionalists that IOs have independent effects and that information production by institutions alters state behavior under anarchy; however, we depart by exploring how this information might create perverse effects by differentially empowering member states.

Our focus on information contributes to a more complex view of how power works within institutions. A key theme of this volume is that "power politics" should be understood broadly.[2] It can include both active, intentional measures and more passive, structural forms of influence or advantage, and it can include both material and nonmaterial sources of power. Our focus on information dynamics highlights the importance of this varied conception. For example, our chapter suggests that some institutional features, like reporting requirements or technical complexity, can produce information dynamics that have unintended—and even undiagnosed—impacts on relative state influence. However, we also find examples of member states diagnosing the information-power nexus within a given institution and exploiting it to drive agendas and influence decisions. We believe both are important aspects of influence within institutions. Moreover, although we discuss the importance of a state's material capacity, our focus on information also draws attention to the "softer" sources of power emphasized in the liberal tradition (Nye 2011; Lobell, in this volume) and to the distinct ways that power is derived and exercised within IOs.[3]

Our chapter proceeds as follows. The next section reviews the theoretical literature to set the stage for our analysis of the power in opacity. We then build on work in IR and the study of organizations in other domains to develop propositions on how information can translate into power within IOs. Using examples from a range of IOs, we note variation in the degree and uniformity of *access* to decision making and *reporting* on the organization's activities and explain how these features can empower some states relative to others. We also discuss the important role of state *capacity* in determining which governments can take full advantage of IO transparency and which are hurt most by opacity. A concluding section highlights some important theoretical implications, both positive and normative, and raises questions for future research on information as a source of power in global governance.

Power and Institutions in Theory

For decades, scholars in the realist tradition doubted the efficacy and even the relevance of international institutions.[4] For most realists, institutions matter only when they support the interests of materially powerful states (Schweller 2001; Goldsmith 2003). As Wivel and Paul (in this volume) note, this perspective offers little insight into the expanding and complex role of IOs in international affairs. At the same time, institutionalists focused most of their attention on the efficiency gains made possible by institutions and largely overlooked power considerations (Keohane 1984; Koremenos, Lipson, and Snidal 2001).[5] To be sure, these mostly rationalist scholars often recognized that power politics matters; however, they tended to treat the role of power as an alternative explanation rather than integrate it into their theoretical frameworks.[6]

Fortunately, a growing body of scholarship seizes a middle ground that takes both international institutions and the role of power politics seriously. There are several fertile lines of research. Various studies have analyzed how large states influence the negotiations that produce institutions and international rule making, with important distributive consequences (Krasner 1991; Gruber 2000; Steinberg 2002; Drezner 2008). Scholars of institutional design have also explored the role of power and drawn several interesting conclusions. For example, powerful states seem to eschew institutions that entail high levels of legalization and delegation, although power asymmetries and anticipated shifts in relative power can be partly accommodated with institutional features such as flexibility and informality (Koremenos 2002; Vabulas and Snidal 2013).[7] In the domain of security affairs, an important literature shows that powerful states drive institutional outcomes but are nevertheless constrained by those same institutions, often in ways that place significant limits on the exercise of power politics (Ikenberry 2001; Lake 1999; Voeten 2001). Obtaining the burden sharing and political benefits that stem from engaging IOs, for example, requires even great powers to accept constraints and forgo their most ambitious goals (Weitsman 2014; Thompson 2009; Kreps 2011). Finally, power dynamics have been used to explain voting and other aspects of IO behavior in areas as diverse as

International Monetary Fund (IMF) lending and UN peacekeeping (Stone 2004; Dreher, Sturm, and Vreeland 2009; Copelovitch 2010; Lim and Vreeland 2013; Allen and Yuen 2014).

These studies have expanded our understanding of power and IOs, however they have done so while maintaining a fairly traditional and narrow conception of state power based on such factors as economic size and military capabilities.[8] Most of the emphasis is on how states use external sources and applications of power to influence activities within IOs, with less attention to how internal factors—institutional rules, structures, and practices—shape power dynamics. An important exception is Stone's (2011) work on informal IO rules that allow powerful states to exercise extraordinary influence in certain situations. A literature on how states use formal and informal leadership positions within IOs paints an even more complex picture of how power operates and shows that external material capabilities are not the only source of power in IOs.[9] Indeed, Kaya (2015) argues that the distribution of power across states does not translate directly into influence within IOs but is instead mediated through its rules and conventions. This suggests that we should look beyond directed power—the ability of A to influence B—to consider institutional sources of power that privilege some states over others and have the potential to produce systematically biased outcomes (Barnett and Duvall 2005).

In this spirit, and consistent with calls to broaden our understanding of "power politics" (Goddard and Nexon 2015; Avant and Westerwinter 2016; Wivel and Paul, in this volume), we believe there are significant advantages to expanding the conceptual aperture to include another medium of power: information. Rather than treat information solely as an engine of cooperation, we explore its power dimension. We ask to what extent differential access to information and capacity to use information is a source of power within IOs.

We draw initial guidance from the field of organization studies, which has wrestled with versions of this question in the context of firm behavior and bureaucratic performance. The central insight of this research is that information and power are intimately linked within organizations. Two key themes emerge about the specific ways in which information can create (dis)advantages for different actors. One set of findings focuses on *information supply*. An organization's hierarchical design and reporting systems distribute information in ways that can systematically enhance the role of certain subunits (Bariff and Galbraith 1978; Mechanic 1962; Pettigrew 1972). Moreover, particularly influential actors can tap into and control multiple sources of both practical and more political information within a given organizational structure (Pettigrew 1973, 28; Bacharach and Lawler 1980), a finding that is echoed in network theory's focus on "brokers."[10] A second set of findings focuses on the role of *information consumption*. Organizations and subunits vary in their capacity to assimilate, integrate, learn from, and use available information—what this literature refers to as "absorptive capacity."[11] Variation in this capacity influences performance and adaptability to new situations.[12] Informational supply is, therefore, only half the story. Meaningful differences in the capacity to act and adapt flow from differences in the ability of actors to access, integrate, and act on new information.

These studies of organizations in other domains suggest the plausibility of our intuition about two sides of an information-power coin. In the next section, we apply and extend these insights to show that some states might experience a more opaque existence within an IO and to argue that information operates as a source of power in this context. In some cases, this may augment the influence of already powerful states, but it can also make it possible for relatively weak states to leverage information-power dynamics to "punch above their weight-class."[13]

Information and Power within IOs

As suppliers of information, IOs benefit some states more than others. We focus on how access, reporting, and capacity create information advantages and disadvantages, which we then link to relative state influence within an institution.

We are not the first to note the relationship between information and power in IR. Outside the context of IOs, one set of scholars has identified strategic information advantages that originate among domestic-level institutions. Milner's (1997) work on domestic politics and international cooperation, for example, argues that executives often benefit from an information advantage over legislatures, which allows the former to shape the contours of cooperative agreements in their preferred direction. With respect to the exercise of interstate power, Reiter and Stam (2008, 23–24) argue that democracies "are better at forecasting war outcomes and associated costs" and that "authoritarian militaries in particular provide lower quality information to their leaderships than do their democratic counterparts." This information advantage allows leaders of democracies to make better decisions about whether and how to fight wars. Schultz (2001) argues that the transparency of democratic political processes provides other states with more information about resolve, making democracies more effective when they issue coercive threats. In various ways, then, information is possessed unevenly across actors, with consequences for their relative power.

Of particular relevance to this volume, other scholars have linked information to power in the context of global governance, although they typically emphasize non-state actors as the beneficiaries. Keck and Sikkink's (1998) research on transnational advocacy networks, for example, identifies information advantages as a source of power that allows non-state groups to pressure and persuade state leaders. Indeed, Nye (2011, 120) notes that globalization and the "information revolution" have augmented the role of private actors and "greatly enhanced their soft power." A substantial literature on IO secretariats notes that they often possess informational advantages that allow them to develop autonomy and evade control efforts by their member-state principals (Hawkins et al.

2006a; Barnett and Finnemore 2004; Graham 2014; Johnson 2014). A specific claim that parallels some of our later points is that IO bureaucracies are empowered by technical complexity and insider knowledge that further breeds information advantages and sources of influence, even vis-à-vis powerful states (Hawkins et al. 2006b, 14, 31; Johnson 2014, 31–33).

We build on these insights and innovate in three ways. First, we focus on relative power advantages *among states* rather than focusing on how information endows private actors and IO staff with additional influence. Second, we specify the sources of variation in information advantage, taking the properties of both IOs and states seriously. Third, we add consideration of information processing capacity alongside information availability. Most prior work has focused on how different actors derive some influence advantage from their greater access to information about technical issues, agreements, or preferences. We observe this as well. However, we also note that technical complexity breeds information advantages and suggest that states vary significantly in their ability to *absorb* information and convert it to various currencies of influence.

We identify three features of IO governance that can render states unequally informed and thus relatively advantaged or disadvantaged. The first two features, access and reporting, are the primary determinants of an IO's transparency and correspond to the supply side of information in organizations, as discussed in the previous section. The third feature adapts the concept of "absorptive capacity" to reflect on states' varying ability to process information. This corresponds to the issue of information consumption raised in organization studies. As we explain, although these information effects are largely the product of formal IO design, they are also influenced by the informal practices of IOs and the capabilities of states themselves. Table 7.1 summarizes these key dimensions and notes examples that we discuss in the following sections.

To be clear, our purpose is not to advance a fully specified theory. Rather, our goal is to provide a starting point for analyzing information and power together within IOs in a novel way. We do so by developing a theoretical framework that focuses analytical attention on the interaction between information provision as a function of institutions and information-processing capacity as a feature of states.

Access

The formal and informal features of IOs create differences in *access* to information. Although IOs offer forums for states to meet, deliberate, and share ideas, states vary in the degree to which they have access to these activities. States most clearly lack access when membership is restricted; regional IOs, alliances, and like-minded clubs like the OECD explicitly exclude certain states. However, some IOs limit access even for their own members, especially when politically sensitive information is involved. Sensitive information arises most often in

Table 7.1. Three Dimensions of the Power in Opacity

Dimension	Description	Example(s)
Access	Variation in member state access to formal and informal negotiations, deliberations, and IO-related data	• Information sharing under the Iran nuclear deal and in the IAEA • UN Security Council meetings and deliberations
Reporting	Variation in quality, quantity, and comprehensiveness of IO-produced reports on institutional processes	• Reports on member activities in the UN Human Rights Council versus the OPCW
Capacity	Variation in member states' ability to absorb, process, and act on IO-related information	• Varied legal and diplomatic capacity among WTO members • Development lending and the technical know-how of recipient states

security institutions like the International Atomic Energy Agency (IAEA). When it comes to implementing the 2015 nuclear deal with Iran, for example, IAEA members have different levels of access to information. In some cases, only Iran is involved in information sharing with IAEA staff; in other cases, the other members of the Joint Commission (the US, the UK, Russia, China, France, Germany, and the EU) are privy to information and responsible for reviewing it; and in yet other cases, the entire Board of Governors (a subset of thirty-five states) is kept in the loop.[14]

For some IOs, differential access results from explicit institutional structures. Although the meetings of the UN Security Council are formally open, the consultations and bargaining that take place behind the scenes—where deals are struck and the frankest discussions take place—are private and confined largely to its fifteen members (Grigorescu 2010, 30). The Security Council is, in other words, an "inner circle" when it comes to deliberations (Johnstone 2003). The executive boards of most multilateral development banks, which typically make the most important decisions and oversee the staff, clearly privilege certain members. While the largest donors are directly represented by their own executive directors on these boards, the vast majority of members are represented indirectly through groups.

Beyond the formal structures and procedures of IOs, there are other obstacles to equitable participation and access. Consensus decision making, the de jure approach in many IOs, might seem inclusive on paper but often breeds informal practices that are in fact exclusionary. At recent UN climate change conferences, progress has been slowed by the need to gain consensus across the almost 200 countries that attend. In practice, a relatively small number of delegations—often the largest developed and developing country emitters of greenhouse gases—tends to meet behind closed doors to work out the details on the most controversial issues. In 2009 a small number of developing countries blocked the adoption of the Copenhagen Accord, complaining of an "untransparent" and "undemocratic" negotiating process (International Institute for Sustainable Development 2009, 1). The "green room" procedure during multilateral negotiations for the General Agreement on Tariffs and Trade (GATT) and World Trade Organization (WTO) is another example of an informal (though quite institutionalized) practice that generates opacity. When progress needs to be made on important issues during the negotiations, a small number of delegations meets behind the scenes to bargain over the details. In a similar vein, the Security Council often relies on the "Arria formula," the convening of ad hoc meetings with selectively invited nonmember participants (both states and civil society representatives) who can supply information on important issues. This increases access overall; however, these meetings are confidential, leaving all nonparticipants in the dark.

In addition, intelligence collection and intelligence products might give some states access advantages within IOs. First, states may target IOs for intelligence collection, monitoring IO-hosted discussions, acquiring IO-generated reports, or tracking behavior by the IO secretariat (Lefebvre 2003). Although rarely acknowledged, intelligence monitoring has long been suspected at larger institutions like the UN (Bosco 2009). This monitoring can give some governments privileged insights into negotiations and sensitive conclusions of an IO. States with large intelligence bureaucracies are the most obvious beneficiaries of this dynamic, but others—such as the governments that host IO secretariats—may also have advantages. Second, intelligence products developed at home, such as intelligence-based conclusions about noncompliance, can generate access advantages. The United States, for example, may share details derived from sensitive intelligence sources with the IAEA secretariat and a subset of governments with whom it is friendly. The wider body of member states in the IAEA, however, will lack access to potentially important details like the location of a reprocessing facility or weapon designs on a laptop.[15] Although the IAEA safeguards staff ultimately report their conclusions about compliance to the entire body, equalizing access in one sense, the details regarding sourcing can remain opaque (Carnegie and Carson 2018).

Access privileges provide exclusive benefits over time. The concept of "boundary persons" from organization studies suggests unique sources of influence for states and delegates that can access a wide range of regime forums. "Insider" delegations that participate more broadly can gain superior knowledge across the range of governance issues and serve as brokers. States and delegations that lack broad-ranging access simply cannot compete on informational terms.[16] When Robert Dahl (1999) complains that IOs appear undemocratic because they rely on opaque "bureaucratic bargaining systems" that prevent direct participation by citizens, this is also true for some states.

Reporting

IOs also vary in terms of the extent and quality of *reporting* about their activities. The reporting practices in an IO function as its "information system," determining what IO activities are summarized and assessed and how that information is shared. The stark contrast between the United Nations Human Rights Council (HRC) and the Organization for the Prohibition of Chemical Weapons (OPCW) illustrates reporting variation. A central function of the Human Rights Council is a universal periodic review in which the human rights record of every UN member is surveyed on a regular basis. As part of the review process, the HRC receives self-reports from member states, information from other UN human rights entities, and civil society documents. The council then holds a session reviewing the documentation and offers recommendations for human rights improvements. All this information is made fully available. The document inputs, statements, and even audio or video recordings of the review sessions are available to the public and any other interested party through the UN website.[17]

Not surprisingly, much more opacity exists regarding information on chemical weapons stockpiles received and gathered by the OPCW under the terms of the Chemical Weapons Convention. Indeed, the sensitivity of the issue area led states to equip the IO with safeguards for sensitive information. The convention text stipulates that the OPCW "shall take every precaution to protect the confidentiality of information on civil and military activities and facilities coming to its knowledge."[18] A treaty annex is devoted to "General Principles for the Handling of Confidential Information" and requires the head of the OPCW to develop "a stringent regime governing the handling of confidential information by the Technical Secretariat" and to ensure personnel employed by the OPCW do not disclose confidential information.[19] These confidentiality provisions serve a clear political purpose in reassuring members that sensitive disclosures will not endanger their security or embarrass them domestically. However, the trade-off is creating information silos reminiscent of those produced by national security classification systems at the national level. Robust reporting on OPCW activities is sacrificed in favor of national security concerns.

Exogenous factors, such as the state of information technology and innovations like the digital revolution, can also influence the feasibility of more equitable IO reporting. On one end of the spectrum, efforts to widely publish the meetings of the League of Nations in the 1920s and 1930s became prohibitively expensive owing to the costliness of printing (Grigorescu 2015, 142). In contrast, IOs now regularly create websites to facilitate public access to documents. For example, panel reports resolving trade disputes from the WTO can be posted to the website for a fraction of the cost of printed records. The original panel report for the Boeing-Airbus dispute, for example, runs 1,049 pages, excluding appendixes.[20] In general, the digitization of records now allows those IOs that embrace transparency to report their activities cheaply and easily (Mason 2008, 9).

The two components of IO transparency—access and reporting—interact. Regular, robust, and widely circulated reporting tends to level the information playing field and can offset problems posed by limited access. In contrast, a lack of reporting can serve to exacerbate the effects of uneven access. For example, the closed nature of meetings for which minutes are not circulated is even more consequential and can render many states poorly informed (e.g., see Clegg 2013, 386). In these relatively opaque settings, well-positioned states may be able to glean confidential information through informal channels or, in the case of security issues, their own national technical means.[21] Confidentiality therefore breeds added opportunities for information advantages.

Capacity

Finally, adapting the concept of "absorptive capacity" in organization studies, it is important to consider variation in the *information processing capacity* of states, which affects the ability of governments to benefit from access and reporting. Information processing capacity refers to a state's ability to internally share, integrate, and act on information in a way that permits meaningful participation and political influence. In the context of IOs, it is a function of delegation size and, more generally, government expertise and resources. Such capacity helps across a range of processes, including negotiating agreements, understanding rules and coming into compliance, making effective use of any dispute resolution procedures, and taking advantage of IO-administered projects.

Even when information is supplied in theory, some governments are not able to participate effectively (or at all) or to gather and process information with appropriate expertise. At the WTO, with its myriad councils, committees, and working groups, many countries are not able to participate robustly and effectively. As Woods (2001) notes, "Even if all meetings were open to them, most developing countries do not have the personnel and resources to cover the plethora of meetings and issues going on at any one time." This includes the less formal consultations associated with the "green room" procedure (Zweifel 2006, 121). One report by the WTO secretariat notes that trade disputes have grown in complexity and will continue to do so as the dispute settlement system matures (WTO 2015). The report identifies a threefold growth in the number of technical exhibits submitted by states during panel disputes and the need to hire more staff to handle the elevated workload. Indeed, lack of legal expertise and capacity is a major concern for developing-country representatives to the WTO (Busch, Reinhardt, and Schaffer 2009).

Across IOs more generally, the "negotiating load" has increased substantially with issues and meetings proliferating around the globe (Kaul et al. 2003, 30).[22] The increasing complexity of issues and overlapping agendas of many international institutions further exacerbate this problem; they make the quantity but also the *quality* of representation crucial. Effective decision makers and negotiators must possess appropriate expertise and experience, endowments that vary dramatically across countries (Held 2004, 370). The representatives of some smaller countries may receive low-quality guidance from their capitals and sometimes rely on nongovernmental organizations (NGOs) and other inputs to understand issues and formulate policies and negotiation strategies (Chasek and Rajamani 2003).

Information processing capacity requires that a member state possess both technical and practical expertise. On the technical side, environment and trade are issue areas that now demand significant scientific and legal expertise for a state's delegation to consume and act on information effectively. On the practical side, the development sector features lending agencies with laborious procedures for developing project proposals and accessing funding, including strict fiduciary standards and monitoring and reporting requirements. These are sensible: donors want to know that their money is being put to good use. But they do come with a downside. Only some countries are familiar with the procedures and know-how to play the game, and some lack the capacity to navigate the process. One evaluation report of the Global Environment Facility (GEF) warns that, as a result of the complex and specific requirements for securing a GEF grant, "the understanding of the GEF and its unique requirements has not spread to most development participants." Most recipients are merely "indirect participants," the report notes, because they rely on the World Bank, the United Nations Development Program (UNDP), and other implementing agencies to represent them during the process (GEF 1999, 2). These smaller and more inexperienced countries become dependent on IO staff to advise them on project development and the design of loan programs and to monitor outcomes following implementation. In effect, they are information outsiders in their own organizations.

One counterintuitive implication is that some of the reforms associated with greater IO accountability could have perverse effects. For low-capacity governments, increased reporting, information flows, and meetings intensify the divide between them and other governments—and even some NGOs—with the resources to participate fully and to absorb and analyze more information. Designing an IO to equitably distribute information among members requires that it be *actively* informative, not only making information available but reaching out to supply it to disadvantaged parties.

Theoretical Implications and Research Questions

The three information-related dimensions we identify—access, reporting, and state capacity—can create meaningful information privileges for certain states, which can translate into greater control and influence over IO outcomes. Despite a growing interest in the role of information and in IO-state relationships, scholars have not devoted enough attention to these power dynamics.[23] One critical implication of this discussion is that, while IOs are often described as being more or less informative or transparent, it is more useful to think of these qualities in *relational* terms.[24] The question is not so much whether an IO provides information-based benefits but to whom this information is supplied and which states are most able to take advantage of it. It is because of these distributive effects that there is *power* in IO opacity.

Our discussion raises many questions for future theoretical development and research at the intersection of power politics and institutions, with direct relevance to the agenda laid out in this volume. First, how exactly are information advantages used to produce favorable outcomes? The empirical examples cited previously suggest that states can translate regime-specific knowledge, of issues and of other actors' preferences, into greater bargaining power in multilateral settings. To the extent that information advantages render arguments more credible and legitimate, they could lend states increased authority to set negotiating agendas and could be used for more effective strategizing and persuasion in the conduct of bargaining. States with information advantages, especially technical and procedural knowledge, are also well placed to make more effective use of IO services like dispute resolution and project development, which often require specific know-how and experience to navigate effectively. Finally, states might use their information to strategically and more credibly "name and shame" their counterparts or label them as noncompliant with IO rules, thereby shaping their behavior or reputations.[25]

Second, what features of IOs affect the supply and distribution of information? Beyond the differences in access and reporting we have discussed, other institutional features can indirectly contribute to information asymmetries. In IOs with a large and diverse membership, for example, we may see greater disparities across states. The issues addressed by an IO, and the related legal and scientific complexity of IO rules, could also exacerbate these differences. Some IOs respond by providing technical assistance and capacity building for information outsiders, or by allowing more access to civil society, which could temper these asymmetries. Addressing these issues would help us develop and assess reform proposals aimed at making IOs more fair and effective.

Third, which states are most likely to have information-based power, and how might this change over time? Theorizing and gathering data on member state "absorptive capacity" is important to shed light on the information consumption and processing side of the equation. Recent constructivist research into diplomatic practice and the importance of professional competence in multilateral diplomacy raises the possibility of further cross-paradigmatic inquiry. Specifically, future research could assess how diplomatic practitioner competence mediates between formal information access and member state influence, shedding additional light on the information-power nexus.[26] Moreover, exogenous changes, such as the rise of cyber technology, have likely influenced access, reporting, and capacity dynamics in global governance in interesting ways. At the state-to-state level, governments like Russia, China, and North Korea have made headlines using cyber technology to gain an advantage in espionage. Future research could unpack the effects of new technology, including the ways cyber technology both eases equitable reporting by IOs *and* allows some governments disproportionate access via intelligence collection.

More generally, we should explore instances in which the power effects of information appear to be decoupled from more traditional sources of power (e.g., economic and military capabilities).[27] Smaller countries can devote disproportionate resources toward certain regimes and issue areas, allowing them to participate, gain experience, and tilt the information playing field in their favor. The areas of trade and environment appear to include examples of small states gaining disproportionate influence through specialization and the use of information.[28] An interesting question is whether this phenomenon is observed as often in security affairs.[29]

Unpacking the relationship between information and power in IOs has interesting theoretical implications. Consistent with realism, we argue that power disparities matter in the context of IOs. States may use this advantage instrumentally to drive favorable outcomes within IOs and to steer new issues toward IOs in which they are privileged. Thus, like some other contributors to this volume (see the chapters by Ripsman and by Barkin and Weitsman), we contribute to efforts to understand how states use IOs instrumentally to advance their interests. However, our arguments about information and power extend well beyond traditional realist concerns. First, to understand the role played by information inequalities, we have to take institutions—their design and their practices—as seriously as we take state power. Information is a source of power that is distinct from traditional measures based on material capabilities. Second, we do not assume that power based on information advantages must be exercised instrumentally or coercively to matter. Some states are simply advantaged on a routine basis without exercising this power intentionally. Indeed, we have suggested some ways in which IO reform that is intended to help weaker states, such as greater legalization and transparency, may in fact exacerbate information inequalities. Finally, although our chapter challenges the view that IOs are an unmitigated good when it comes to the provision of information, we do not fundamentally challenge the notion, central to liberalism, that IOs produce beneficial outcomes overall. We do suggest that these benefits may not be shared equally.

This exercise has potentially important normative implications as well. As international policy is increasingly conducted at the multilateral level, the importance of power and inequality within IOs is enhanced and growing. While governments and other observers will always be concerned about overt imbalances and the role of power politics in IOs, information inequalities provide a subtler and indirect means for exercising power that is less likely to elicit an explicit challenge. In international affairs disproportionate access to information and knowledge is a powerful tool. Those with more information are often able to make more authoritative arguments that allow them to define events to their advantage and to drive policy outcomes accordingly (Barnett and Finnemore 2004; Krebs and Lobasz 2007). Even when IOs supply more information overall and are Pareto-improving, we should still strive to understand the distribution of these benefits.

When it comes to the issue of IO transparency, overwhelmingly the focus of concern has been on NGOs and other civil society actors. Complaints about the democratic deficit of IOs, and their lack of accountability, have focused on these outsiders, not on the member states themselves. If we are right that some states are left in the dark, at least relative to others, then these normative concerns about IO accountability and legitimacy should extend to the intergovernmental realm as well.

Notes

For helpful comments on earlier drafts, we thank Ron Krebs, Helen Milner, Julia Gray, Jane Vaynman, Annette Freyberg-Inan, T.V. Paul, Anders Wivel, and workshop participants at Princeton's Niehaus Center and the University of Copenhagen.

1. For various perspectives on this debate, see Held and Koenig-Archibugi (2005).

2. For similarly broad conceptualizations of power and power politics, see Barnett and Duvall (2005) and Goddard and Nexon (2016).

3. For other examples of how power is exercised in unique ways within IOs, see Martin-Brûlé, Pingeot, and Pouliot (in this volume).

4. Classic statements of this position include Mearsheimer (1994) and Waltz (1979).

5. For a more general critique of this perspective on institutions, see Moe (2005).

6. For examples of institutionalists treating power as an alternative explanation, see Thompson and Verdier (2014) and Koremenos (2005).

7. Hawkins et al. (2006b) emphasizes that powerful states are reluctant to delegate authority to an IO unless its rules match the distribution of power. J. M. Smith (2000) finds that economically powerful states are less likely to support legalized dispute settlement mechanisms in trade agreements.

8. Exceptions include Büthe and Mattli (2011), which identifies domestic institutions as a source of international agenda-setting power.

9. The most developed arguments along these lines are in the context of the EU. See Tallberg (2003) and Kleine (2013).

10. Informational "gatekeepers" and "boundary persons" are noted in more recent research, such as Manev and Stevenson (2001) and Tortoriello, Reagans, and McEvily (2012). On the power of brokers in international networks, see Hafner-Burton, Kahler, and Montgomery (2009) and Goddard (2009a).

11. The original statement is Cohen and Levinthal (1990). See also the sources reviewed in Zahra and George (2002).

12. On variation see Lane and Lubatkin (1998).

13. On this possibility in the context of the EU, see Grøn and Wivel (2011).

14. See IAEA (2015, 4) and, in particular, Annex IV of the Joint Comprehensive Plan of Action (JCPOA).

15. According to an account of one episode, "Senior American intelligence officials called the leaders of the international atomic inspection agency to the top of a skyscraper overlooking the Danube in Vienna and unveiled the contents of what they said was a stolen Iranian laptop computer." William J. Broad and David E. Sanger, "Relying on Computer, U.S. Seeks to Prove Iran's Nuclear Aims," *New York Times*, November 13, 2005, https://www.nytimes.com/2005/11/13/world/middleeast/relying-on-computer-us-seeks-to-prove-irans-nuclear-aims.html.

16. Access and brokering potential are partly a function of state capacity, a point we develop later in the chapter.

17. The website is http://www.ohchr.org/EN/HRBodies/UPR/Pages/UPRMain.aspx.

18. See Article VIII of the Chemical Weapons Convention.

19. Annex on the Protection of Confidential Information, Chemical Weapons Convention.

20. *European Communities and Certain Member States—Measures Affecting Trade in Large Civil Aircraft*, DS 316, 30 June 2010.

21. Stone (2011, 57) discusses the ability of US representatives to gather information through informal channels in the IMF.

22. For an effort to quantify the negotiation burden on governments across environmental IOs, see Muñoz, Thrasher, and Najam (2009).

23. Scholars using principal-agent theory also emphasize the importance of information to understand the control of principals (usually member states) over agents (the IO staff). See Hawkins et al. (2006a); Pollack (2003, 26–27); and Johnson (2014). Importantly, such work has not yet analyzed the differential access among state principals to such information and variation in their information processing capacity.

24. Grigorescu (2007, 627) makes a similar point. In this respect our understanding of IO transparency is consistent with calls to focus on the relations and interactions between actors in the study of international politics. See, e.g., Jackson and Nexon (1999).

25. For examples of how the United States uses this strategy, see Kelley (2017).

26. On the practice of international diplomacy, see Adler and Pouliot (2011a) and Pouliot (2016).

27. This is consistent with the focus on institutions as "structural modifiers," as discussed by Lobell and Nicholson (in this volume).

28. In the area of trade and the WTO, see Davis and Bermeo (2009) and Kim (2008). On climate change and the role of small island states, see Betzold (2010). On these dynamics in the EU context, see Grøn and Wivel (2011) and Panke (2012).

29. For an example, see the unusually strong influence of Nordic states in European Union security affairs that is described in Jakobsen (2009).

CHAPTER 8

Revisionists, Networks, and the Liberal Institutional Order

Stacie Goddard

Since the end of World War II, the United States has engaged in what John Ikenberry calls "the most ambitious and far-reaching liberal order building" in history (2011, xi). This liberal institutional order, a "far flung system of multilateral arrangements, multilateral institutions, alliances, trade agreements, and political partnerships," is designed to strengthen liberal political and economic norms, undercut geopolitical competition, and, as a result, ensure stability in world politics (e.g., Ikenberry 2011; Glaser 2010; Johnston 2008). Yet while at the end of the Cold War these liberal institutions appeared an order triumphant, in the last decade the liberal international order has come under increased revisionist fire, with states seemingly poised to challenge and even overturn existing political, economic, and security institutions. China contests the legitimacy of US security institutions in the Asia-Pacific, arguing the established territorial status quo is illegitimate and unsustainable. Other states, notably Russia and Iran, overtly challenge established norms of territorial integrity and weapons proliferation, arguing that such norms are mere reflections of US arrogance, hypocrisy, and dominance. In the wake of such challenges, the once-robust international order seems vulnerable.

For some scholars, these challenges come as no surprise. Institutional orders are inherently ephemeral: whether it is to increase military security, augment economic gains, or spread a new ideology, revisionist states will seek to upend existing institutional orders (see, e.g., Organski and Kugler 1980, 23; Gilpin 1981). In contrast, institutionalists argue that the future is not so grim, that contemporary institutions will largely restrain revisionist challenges. The current institutional order creates states that are not only likely but eager to play by the rules of the game. The status quo provides all states with increased security and economic wealth, and revisionism is unlikely in a system "easy to join, and hard to overturn." If states do attempt revisionism, these efforts will be swiftly contained, as institutions give status quo states "the capacities, partnerships, and principles to confront today's great-power spoilers and revisionists" (Ikenberry 2014).

This raises the question, to what extent do institutions shape revisionist behavior? Prediction in the social sciences is difficult business under any conditions, but predicting the future course of the liberal international order is made even more problematic by a lack of theory about how revisionist states challenge institutions in international relations.[1] Much of the field remains bifurcated into those who argue that liberal institutions prevent revisionist challenges and those who see institutions as epiphenomenal to state behavior and revisionism in international politics. This chapter, in contrast, argues that we need to build better theories about how states practice revisionist politics *within* institutions— how it is that institutions might provide states with the instruments to challenge the institutional order. I argue that current institutional theory makes at least four problematic assumptions about revisionism and international orders: that revisionist states remain "outside" institutions; that integrating revisionist states constrains challenges to the status quo; that institutions augment, rather than detract from, status quo powers; and that revisionists can overturn the status quo only through the use of force. Using a network approach, I argue that international relations theorists might be better able to conceptualize how revisionist states are positioned with an institutional order, which states are likely to engage in revisionist behavior, and what instruments revisionists are likely to deploy in pursuing revisionist aims.

The chapter proceeds as follows. I begin with a definition of revisionist powers and an overview of the current literature on revisionism and international orders. I then turn to a discussion of network theory, explaining how a network approach can productively illuminate the relationship between institutional structures and revisionist power politics.

International Orders and Revisionist States: An Overview

Scholars have long argued that the international system, far from being anarchic, is marked by patterns of institutional order. These institutional orders, as defined by Ikenberry (2011), are "manifest in the settled rules and arrangements between states that define and guide their interaction." These institutions are established and maintained by "states at the top of the system's hierarchy" that "take advantage of their elite status and establish rules, institutions and privileges that primarily benefit themselves" (Rapkin and Thompson 2003, 317). These great powers are most likely to establish institutions in the wake of major conflict. As F. H. Hinsley argues, "At the end of every war since the end of the eighteenth century, the leading states made a concerted effort . . . to reconstruct the system on lines that would enable them, or so they believed, to avoid a further war" (1982, 4).

But while institutions provide stability and order, they are not eternal. Echoing Gilpin, Ikenberry notes, "In every era, great powers have risen up to build rules and institutions of relations between states, only to see those ordering arrangements eventually break down or transform" (2011, 11). Whereas the "status quo" powers at the top of the system will work to preserve institutions, revisionists, dissatisfied with their subordinate position, hope to "redraft the rules by which relations among nations work" (Organski and Kugler 1980, 23). New powers seek institutions that distribute goods more in line with the changing balance of power. Others seek institutional change for ideological reasons, demanding that institutional norms and rules reflect a cultural image at home.

In general, we can identify states as revisionists based on two characteristics. The first is the capacity to "redraft the rules" of the international system. Many states may dislike the status quo, but for our purposes here, we are interested only in those states that present a plausible challenge to an existing international order. Second, revisionism is also a matter of intent: rising powers need not be revisionist states. We are thus looking for those rising powers that have stated their interest in challenging the rules and norms of the international system. Using this definition, I identify a universe of revisionist states from 1815 onward (see table 8.1).

Table 8.1. Revisionist States and Aims in the International System

State	Revisionist aims
Russia, 1820s–50s	Modify territorial boundaries in Near East
Prussia, 1840s–71	Unify Germany; overturn Concert of Europe diplomacy for claims based on conservative nationalism
France, 1850–71	Reformulate concert treaties; create a European settlement along nationalist lines
Germany, 1890s–1914	Modify distribution of colonies among great powers.
United States, 1815–present	1815–23: Territorially expand at the expense of European empires; challenge colonial claims in Western Hemisphere 1870–98: Modify territorial settlements in South America, Latin America, and Asia. 1945–present: Replace UK imperial order with US "liberal" order
Germany, 1930s	Conquest of Europe; establish regional/global hegemony
Japan, 1930s	Remake territorial boundaries in Asia; establish exclusive economic sphere
Soviet Union, 1920–89	Remake boundaries in Eastern Europe; establish global communist system

As table 8.1 shows, not all revisionist politics are created equal. While some revisionists, such as Russia in the 1820s, sought minor revisions within the existing order, others, such as Nazi Germany, pursued hegemonic ambitions. Scholars often attribute this variation to a revisionist's intentions and, in particular, whether a revisionist harbors "limited" or "revolutionary" aims. Whereas limited-aims revisionist states will seek modest reform, revolutionaries will demand far-reaching changes to international institutions, even if this change leads to catastrophic war (Schweller 1999, 19; see also Gilpin 1988; Kydd 1997).

In contrast, liberal institutionalists argue that the appearance and intensity of revisionist politics depends as much on the institutional order as it does on a state's interest.[2] Integration thus ensures the continuity of the international system (Gilpin 1981). Four mechanisms in particular constrain potential revisionism. The first two are rationalist mechanisms: institutions both create incentives to cooperate and increase the costs of defection. On the one hand, when a revisionist power is integrated into an institution, this creates incentives for rising powers to embrace rules and eschew revisionist behavior. In the contemporary world, for example, potential revisionists can easily join liberal institutions and reap benefits from free trade and collective security guarantees. At the same time, these institutions can punish defectors, making them difficult to overturn (Ikenberry 2011, 91–117; see also Keohane 1993). Once states enter institutions, there are material costs for rejecting the rules. Both Russia and Iran, for example, have suffered substantial economic costs for violating institutional rules. Revisionist states might incur serious reputational costs as well.

Third, institutions have binding effects as well. While some scholars have treated binding as another way to express the costs of cooperation and defection, others describe binding as a specific mechanism to decrease revisionist behavior. When revisionists are bound to an institution, they link states' capacity for collective action and thus curtail a revisionist's ability to mobilize against an institution. Joseph Grieco argues that France, for example, sought to "bind" Germany to its interests by embedding it in the European Coal and Steel Community. In doing so, France ensured that it had a voice in Germany's affairs and that any attempt by Germany to increase its power must proceed through institutional pathways. Likewise, when a great power "binds" its military mobilization to a revisionist state—via concrete acts such as permanent alliances or joint military exercises—it ensures that any military mobilization must occur jointly and thus disrupts the ability of a state to act autonomously (Grieco 1995, 331–34).[3]

Fourth, institutions can *socialize* revisionist powers. Constructivists, in particular, argue that when states are integrated into institutions, the institutions' rules and norms will shape the boundaries of appropriate behavior (see, e.g., Wendt 1999; Checkel 2005, 801–26; Finnemore and Sikkink 1998; Johnston

2003). Through processes of persuasion, mimicry, and even coercion, revisionist states learn to modify their behavior. They may, for example, come to eschew violence as an "illegitimate" strategy of power politics. At a deeper level, participation in institutions can change the interests and identities of revisionist states.

Through each of these mechanisms, institutions constrain revisionist behavior, either by preventing powers from challenging existing rules and institutions or by inducing restraint within the revisionist power itself. The more revisionists participate in international institutions, the fewer challenges we should see to the existing international order: institutions should remain stable in their rules and norms, membership in institutions should remain consistent over time, and when revisionists are integrated into institutions, violence should be minimal. The argument that institutions shape revisionist politics is plausible. This raises the question: To what extent have institutions constrained revisionist behavior? Table 8.2 provides an overview of the universe of revisionist states in the international system from 1815 onward. I classified revisionists in six periods of institutional order: the Concert of Europe period (1815–56), the post-Crimean Concert of Europe period (1856–71), the imperial order (1872–1914), the interwar period (1918–38), the Cold War (1947–91), and the post–Cold War liberal order (1991–present).

In each of the institutional orders identified in table 8.2, revisionist states have challenged some aspect of the existing order. Indeed, at first glance, there seems to be little connection between a state's integration into dominant institutions and its attempts to upend the status quo. Revisionists that seemed integrated into the institutional order—such as Prussia in the 1860s and Japan in the 1930s—have mounted far-reaching, revolutionary, and sometimes violent challenges to the rules and norms of the existing system. Even in the cases where revisionist states appear restrained, such as Russia under the Concert of Europe and Germany in the post–Cold War period, significant revisionist behavior persisted.

For some, especially realists, this overview of cases might call into question institutionalist arguments altogether, suggesting that institutions have little to no effect on revisionist states (Mearsheimer 1994). For these theorists, institutions have never been anything more than reflections of the distribution of power in international politics. It is hardly surprising then that whether a state is integrated into institutions has little effect on revisionist behavior. But this approach, I argue, is misguided. It is not that institutions are epiphenomenal to power politics; it is that institutions both enable and constrain power politics. By neglecting to explain how institutions might facilitate revisionist behavior, institutionalists have overpredicted the constraining effects of institutional orders. To develop a theory of revisionists and institutional orders, I turn to a network approach to world politics.

Table 8.2. Revisionists, 1815–2015

Revisionist state	Integrated into system?	Outcome
Russia (1817–56)	Yes. Core member of all institutions. (Concert of Europe, Holy Alliance, Quintuple Alliance)	Little to no revisionism
United States (1815)	No. No alliances.	Exit. Built ties within Western Hemisphere.
Prussia (1856–71)	Yes. Core member of all institutions. (Concert of Europe, post-Crimea)	Rule-based revolution. Produced a massive transformation in boundaries; institutionalization of nationalism as source of sovereignty claims, with limited violence and with preservation of institutions.
France (1856–71)	Yes. Core member of all institutions. (Concert of Europe, post-Crimea)	Rule-based revolution until 1864.
Germany (1871–1914)	Yes. Core member of bilateral alliances and trade networks.	Unilateral force. Pursued colonial revision in North Africa and Asia; revisionist use of force on the Continent.
Germany (interwar, Europe)	Yes. Versailles system, League of Nations, Locarno system.	Unilateral force, World War II.
Italy (interwar, Europe)	Yes. Versailles System, League of Nations.	Mixed. Restrained through 1939.
Soviet Union (interwar, Europe)	Mixed. Isolated, entered League of Nations in 1934.	Exit.
Japan (interwar, Global)	Yes. League of Nations, Washington system.	Unilateral force. Attempted territorial conquest throughout East and Southeast Asia.
USSR (Cold War)	Mixed. UN Security Council. Sought initial role in Bretton Woods.	Exit. Created alternative institutions. China isolated.
Germany and Japan (Cold War)	Yes. UN system; bilateral alliances; NATO, trade system.	Limited or no revisionism.
China (post Cold War)	Mixed. Russia and China new members of economic institutions; both excluded from security institutions.	Mixed.
Russia (post Cold War)	Mixed. UN, Washington Consensus system (WTO, IMF, World Bank), NATO	Some unilateral force.

Networks, Institutions, and Revisionist Politics: An Overview

In the introduction to this volume, Wivel and Paul define institutions as "*associational clusters among states with some bureaucratic structures that create and manage self-imposed and other-imposed constraints on state policies and behaviors.*" It is this associational approach to institutions that informs the theory here: institutions are not simply static organizational structures; they are a series of institutionalized networks among states. By networks I mean the regular ties among actors, or the "continuing series of transactions to which participants attach shared understandings, memories, forecasts, rights, and obligations" (Tilly 1998, 456). Drawing from this definition, there are myriad types of institutionalized networks in international relations. Alliances, both permanent and temporary, are networks: they are a continuing series of transactions centered on the provision of security. Trade relationships and financial transactions are also networks, a set of regular economic transactions among actors. We can also conceive of diplomatic exchanges as a series of more or less institutionalized networks (see, e.g., Renshon 2016).

Who the "actors" are within any network is defined empirically; depending on the subject being researched, they may be individuals, coalitions, institutions, or states. In this chapter, I am primarily concerned with network ties among states. In some ways, this approach departs from much of network analysis in international relations theory, in which scholars adopt a network approach precisely so that they may move away from state-centric models and conceptualize alternative ways of organizing collective action and exercising agency in international politics. Keck and Sikkink (1998), for example, argue that transnational activist networks are key actors, ones that can exercise power beyond the boundaries of the state (see also Carpenter 2011). Likewise, scholars suggest that networks of terrorists and organized criminals challenge the state's monopoly on violence and order, calling into question the utility of state-centric theory. But there is no inherent reason why network theory should exclude the study of ties between states.

As Hafner-Burton, Kahler, and Montgomery argue in their excellent review article, network analysis provides ideal tools to both conceptualize and measure institutionalized orders in international politics. Networks, they argue, "form structures, which in turn may constrain and enable agents" (Hafner-Burton, Kahler, and Montgomery 2009, 560). For decades, "structure" has often been reduced to the neorealist conception of the term, in which states are positioned in relation to one another solely according to their material capabilities (e.g., Waltz 1979). A network approach, in contrast, suggests that structures can be more broadly conceived as "emergent properties of persistent patterns of relations among agents [states] that can define, enable, and constrain those agents" (Hafner-Burton, Kahler, and Montgomery 2009, 561).

Conceiving of governance as a series of networks requires mapping both the *form* and the *content* of networks or, put another way, mapping both the social and cultural elements of networks (Nexon 2009b; Hafner-Burton, Kahler, and Montgomery 2009, 573). On the one hand, institutionalized networks form patterned material structures. Recent literature draws attention to the way in which institutional governance and specifically a hegemon's relations are structurally patterned (Ikenberry 2011; Nexon 2009b; Nexon and Wright 2007). Nexon and Wright (2007), for example, argue that imperial structures typically take the form of a "'hub and spoke' system of authority, where cores are connected to peripheries but peripheries themselves are disconnected—or segmented—from one another." Ikenberry (2011) perhaps provides the most developed network model of governance (although he does not explicitly conceive of these institutions as a series of networks). According to Ikenberry, at any given point the international system can range from being relatively "flat" or oligarchic—that is to say, dominated by a select group of great powers—to being hierarchical, managed by a single hegemon or empire. A typical example of oligarchic institutional governance would be international order under the Concert of Europe. Within hierarchies, two forms tend to dominate: the imperial-hierarchical form articulated by Nexon and others and a "liberal hegemonic" form in which, instead of relying on hub-and-spoke systems, the hegemon becomes embedded in a series of reciprocal relationships with lesser powers. The US-led governance system during the Cold War and after has represented a mix of these ideal-typical forms, with the US preferring a hub-and-spoke system in the governance of East Asia, while relying on a liberal hegemonic form in Western Europe.

When we speak of mapping the content of networks of international governance, we are primarily talking about the rules and norms that govern "legitimate" conduct in the international system. Gilpin (1981, 42–43), for example, argues that ideology is integral to hegemonic orders. Organski, too, draws our attention to the cultural content of international systems, that hegemons rule over states that "abide by the same rules of trade, diplomacy and war" and thus the order "is legitimized by an ideology and rooted in the power differential of the groups that compose it" (1968, 361, 364). The specific content of these rules varies across time and space. The networks established by the Concert of Europe, for example, mandated diplomacy in line with an established "balance of power," defined not only as the automatic pursuit of state interest but as a collective equilibrium among European states (Schroeder 1994; Mitzen 2014). Scholars have written extensively on the content of the American-led hegemonic system, stressing the predominance of "liberal" norms of trade, diplomacy, human rights, and multilateralism (see, e.g., Ikenberry 2001).

Indeed, much of the analysis of institutional orders is already congruent with a network approach. What then are the benefits of making these foundations more explicit? I argue that treating institutions as networks corrects three problematic assumptions in institutional theory and its treatment of revisionist power politics. First, a network approach allows scholars to better conceptualize the relationship of revisionist powers to an existing international order. Most analyses of governance systems focus on the hegemon's position or, at best, the position of the hegemon and those status quo secondary powers that support the system. As described earlier, this descriptive move ends up oversimplifying the relationship of revisionist powers to existing international institutions, portraying revisionists as either being "inside" or "outside" the international order. Second, focusing on network position allows us to think more carefully about the constraining and *enabling* effects of positions. This opens up space for thinking about how revisionists might benefit from their position within an institutional order. Finally, focusing on a revisionist's access to networked resources—military, economic, and social—allows us to move beyond the argument that revisionist challenges are necessarily violent.

The Inside/Outside Assumption, Revisionists, and Network Position

To begin with, most studies of international order employ a strict "inside/outside" assumption. Revisionist states are on the "outside" of international orders: they fail to join organizations, vociferously challenge existing norms, and ultimately remain isolated from the status quo system. Those states that join or come "inside" institutions, in contrast, are viewed as joining the ranks of the status quo. These "integrated" powers are seen as accepting status quo institutions. Once inside, they are unlikely to pose a challenge to global governance.[4] Whether or not a state is inside or outside an institutional order, furthermore, is measured by its membership within the order's key institutions. So, for example, some argue that China is now clearly more "inside" the international order because it has joined key liberal institutions like the World Trade Organization. Unlike the Soviet Union, which remained isolated from institutions, after the Cold War Russia came "inside" the institutional order.

To be clear, some scholars suggest that the inside/outside dichotomy is not so simple and that revisionists' positions within institutions might be somewhat more complex. Ikenberry, for example, argues that "countries like Russia and China are not fully embedded in the international order," suggesting that some states take on liminal roles in status quo institutions (2011, 9). Alistair Johnston, in his sophisticated analysis of China's relationship to existing institutions, notes that measuring the level of integration into the international system is problematic and that states might "participate in these international institutions" without accepting "the norms of the community" (2003, 11). But even in these accounts, the inside/outside distinction remains critical: states inside institutions, which reap the benefits of membership, are unlikely to engage in revisionist behavior; states outside the institutional order, in contrast, may seek to revise the order.

As argued previously, however, the empirical record casts doubt on this relationship: states inside institutional orders can act as revisionists. This is not to say that institutionalists are wrong; rather, the theory needs a more robust conceptualization of institutional position. Liberal institutionalists have adopted a relatively thin model of state's position, focused primarily on whether a state is inside or outside institutional structures. From a network perspective, a liberal model does not capture the wide variety of network positions within any given institutional structure. For example, ties—transactions among actors—may be weak (occasional, informal) or strong (frequent and institutionalized). They may be symmetrical (equal in strength across all actors) or asymmetrical (weaker in some areas, stronger in others).

Here a network theory is useful. Network theory more carefully elucidates how a series of institutionalized transactions create a network position. A network position is simply a description of an actor's relative ties within a given network, its position within the network structures described previously. Drawing from Hafner-Burton, Montgomery, and Kahler (2009), I suggest two types of network position are critical in revisionist behavior: access and "between-ness," or what I will call brokerage positions.[5] By *access*, I mean the number of strong ties a state has with other states in a network (Hafner-Burton and Montgomery 2006, 2). In a simple network model, State A is a more central node in the network than State B. Actors within a network can be centrally positioned in several ways. States can possess high or low *degree centrality*, defined simply as the number of ties a state has with other states in the system. States can also possess high *prestige centrality*, which we can define as the number of ties a state has with states that also have several strong ties within the system (in other words, a state can have ties to other well-positioned states). Centrality, in essence, measures the degree to which a state is integrated into a specific network subgroup. States with strong ties to most of the subgroup's members are deeply embedded within relevant institutions.

It may seem that "access" is equivalent to institutionalist's "integration." Yet thinking of a state's position in terms of access allows theorists to move beyond measurements like "organizational membership" to better conceptualize how a state is positioned within an institutional order. For one, access is a relative, not an absolute, measure of institutional position. If we use simple measures of "inside" and "outside," then it appears that interwar Japan was inside the post–World War I institutional order. Japan was among the five great powers (with Britain, the United States, France, and Italy) that set the agenda for the Paris Peace Conference in 1919; it joined the League of Nations in 1920 as a charter member and was one of the four members of the League Council. It was a core actor in the Washington system, working with Britain, the United States, France, and Italy to limit its naval procurements, settle disputes in the Pacific through consultation, and affirm China's sovereignty and territorial integrity (Asada

2007, 84–105; Iriye 1990, 17–27). Throughout the 1920s, Japan integrated into global economic networks as well. But from a relative perspective, in each of these networks described previously, asymmetry dominated. At Versailles, for example, Japan found that the "big three"—the United States, Britain, and France—controlled interactions. In the Washington system, Japan was a mere junior partner compared to Britain and the United States (see, e.g., Hosoya 1982, 8; Beasley 1987, 167–69). Its economic ties were asymmetric, with Japan far more dependent on imports than the great powers depended on Japan's exports. Scholars also suggest that the racial content of ties excluded Japan from dominant institutions (Búzás 2013; Ward 2013; cf. Dickinson 1999, 236). Japan believed there was "an Anglo-American conspiracy to isolate Japan" in an "attempt to oppress the non-Anglo-Saxon races, especially the coloured races, by the two English-speaking countries, Britain and the United States" (Beasley 1987, 167).

Second, using network theory, we can also conceive of actors as being *between* institutional orders as well, what network theorists call bridging or brokerage positions. Within the international system, there is often one dominant institutional order, the network structure containing the most great powers in the international system. Many of these institutional ties are built in the wake of major conflict "to reconstruct the system on lines that would enable them, or so they believed, to avoid a further war" (Hinsley 1982, 4). These relations become institutionalized in alliances, legal economic agreements, and official diplomatic relations. While there may be one dominant order in the international system, network structures are not homogenous. Alongside this dominant network structure are subgroups composed of networks representing regional alliances, local economic agreements, or sociocultural ties that cross state boundaries.[6] At the intersection of the dominant network and subgroups are brokers, which bridge the structural holes between "cliques" in the international system (that is to say, a broker is an actor with ties with two cohesive subgroups in the international system). In economics a broker might be an actor with ties to different firms. In politics a broker might be an actor who maintains ties with rival coalitions, domestic or international.[7]

Conceptualizing institutional position in network terms is useful in thinking about contemporary revisionist politics. As noted previously, in the wake of the Cold War, Russia sought access to liberal institutions and became a member of the World Trade Organization and the G8. But even at the height of cooperation, Russia had relatively little access to these organizations. Within economic networks, Russia's position was always asymmetric. With Russia's dependence on oil and gas as its sole sources of income, its trade networks were vulnerable compared to those of Western states. Russia's extraordinarily weak property rights and volatile domestic politics left its financial relations uneven and unpredictable (Logvinenko 2017). Russia has very little access to security institutions, remaining not only isolated from but antagonistic to the North Atlantic Treaty

Organization (NATO). Even as Russia's membership in core institutions increased then, its overall network position was marginal, and as described later, it was more likely to be drawn toward certain patterns of revisionist behavior.

China's position, too, becomes more complicated when viewed with network measures. On the one hand, institutionalists are correct that China has become far more integrated into the international institutional order. In 1966 China belonged to one intergovernmental organization (IGO); by 2003 it belonged to forty-six IGOs. It increasingly oriented its foreign policy toward the norms of the liberal international order. But especially in the last decade, China also appears to be building ties outside the dominant institutional order. The Asian Infrastructure Investment Bank (AIIB) places China at the core of new financial networks. With "One Belt, One Road," China is strengthening its bilateral networks in South Asia and beyond. These networks put China in an emerging "brokerage" position between a Western-oriented institutional order and nascent economic structures.

Overall, then, a network approach allows theorists to develop a more robust conception of the position of revisionist states. But of course the point here is not simply to describe actors' positions but to explain how they causally affect the practice of revisionist politics under institutional structures. Here, network concepts of position might help scholars better explain *under what conditions* institutions exert effects on state behavior and how this influences the pursuit of revisionism in world politics.

Institutions as Enabling and Constraining Revisionist Behavior

A second assumption, related to the previous inside/outside discussion, is that once inside an international institution, revisionist powers are likely to be constrained. As argued earlier, liberal institutionalists suggest that it is through integration that revisionism is decreased, if not eliminated entirely (Organski 1968; Gilpin 1981). The previous quick overview suggested that this argument is problematic and that even integrated states are likely to pursue revisionist aims. From a conventional institutionalist perspective, this revisionism may seem surprising; from a network perspective, it is not: network structures "define, *enable*, and constrain those agents" (Hafner-Burton, Kahler, and Montgomery 2009, 561). Network structures are not merely constraints on revisionist behavior; because they contain resources—alliances, economic assets, and social power—they also give revisionists the tools to practice power politics within an institutional order.

This suggests that whether mechanisms of constraint operate depends on variation in network positions. For example, states with high access might be more inclined to behave the way in which institutionalists suggest and largely forgo revisionist behavior. Revisionists with access are likely to reap significant benefits from the existing international order; challenging the system thus carries serious costs. States with a high degree of access experience more binding effects as they become increasingly dependent on institutions to maintain their power in international relations. States with more access are more likely to be socialized within that system as they interact frequently with other states in the system and are also deeply embedded in the system's norms and rules. As a result, they are more likely than other states to embrace a system's norms as well as to see them as structure-inhibiting actions within the international system.

The more access a state has, the more likely that state has power within an existing institutional structure. An actor's material ties, for example, allow it to mobilize alliances during a conflict. States with access are also more likely to have access to social capital or cultural resources that give states greater authority to make demands in the international system. Because of this, these states can "set agendas, frame debates," and generally set the rules of the game in the international system (Beckfield 2003, 404). Access can confer coercive power as well. As Hafner-Burton and Montgomery argue, actors with a high degree of centrality can withhold social benefits such as membership and recognition or enact social sanctions such as marginalization as a method of coercion (2006, 11). All of this suggests that states with access are likely to pursue power politics within institutional structures rather than challenge them outright.

Germany is a good example of a state with extremely high access. It is at the core of Western economic, security, and social relations. Even as German power grew during the Cold War, it was hardly inclined to turn that power toward revisionist ends. At the same time, Germany has not entirely forgone revisionist ends; arguably it has used its high access to affect revisionist strategies within Europe. It has reshaped the economic policies of peripheral states, reorienting them around its own interests. It has leveraged its position to push for social and diplomatic policies, most recently on issues of financial austerity. From a network perspective, Germany has used its access to pursue its aims within institutions.

Increased brokerage, in contrast, loosens the constraints on revisionist behavior. When states have brokerage positions, liberal institutionalist mechanisms are less likely to operate. When a state holds a brokerage position, it has the capacity to mobilize resources outside the dominant institutional structure and revise institutions in significant ways. Ties outside the institutional order gives these revisionists access to new allies, alternative economic ties, and diverse cultural resources, all of which the revisionist can mobilize in support of its transformative aims. Moreover, it is not simply that brokering positions give states that already have revisionist aims freedom to pursue their goals. Bridging structural holes has significant feedback effects that can push even conservative states toward a revisionist agenda—in other words, institutional position can create revisionism. Brokerage positions lower the costs, indeed may increase the benefits, of challenging the institutional order. Brokerage positions open up new opportunities for mobilization outside the system. Efforts to bind a bridging revisionist will prove difficult, as these states can mobilize alternative networks to slip the leash of existing institutions (see, e.g., Walt 2009, 107).

For this reason, institutionalists have likely overstated the constraining effects liberal institutions will have on China's position. While institutionalists have been quick to identify the constraining effects of integration, they have not discussed the enabling effects of this new position: that is, the fact that institutional integration gives China increased centrality with which to press its claims in international politics. It may be precisely because of that centrality that China proved able to pull states like France and Britain into the orbit of the AIIB; it has the authority to speak on behalf of financial institutions. China, moreover, is an emerging broker, with its ties in the Shanghai Cooperation Organization and increasing relations with the Association of Southeast Asian Nations (ASEAN). This suggests a flexibility that might belie Ikenberry's claim that Western institutions are difficult to overturn through revisionist strategies.

Revising the Institutional Order Is Violent

Finally, many studies of revisionist states seem to assume that serious challenges to the international system are violent ones. Certainly, for foundational authors in the power transition literature—Gilpin, Organski, and Kugler among them—a true revisionist challenge comes in the form of a major-power or hegemonic war. No doubt there are cases of hegemonic revisionism. Napoleon attempted to overturn the eighteenth-century balance-of-power system through hegemonic war; Hitler and Japan ultimately pressed their revisionist claims through force. In contrast, negotiation within the rules is treated as acceptance of the status quo system—rising powers are agreeing to play by the rules and accept the existing structure.

At the same time, other cases suggest the violence-negotiation dichotomy is not so simple. Yes, Prussia united Germany through the limited application of force, but it also accomplished its revisionist program through diplomacy, using negotiations to hold off a European-wide coalition against its revisionist challenge (see, e.g., Goddard 2009a). Scholars often treat the US-Britain power transition as evidence that the US was a status quo power, willing to accept the British system of free trade and colonial rule, but ignore the extent to which the US negotiated radical territorial changes in the Southern Hemisphere and East Asia. Even when massive violence erupted, revisionist states often began by pressing their claims through negotiation. Germany and Japan in the 1920s and early 1930s are prime examples.

For this reason, a network approach pushes scholars to go beyond treating revisionism as a necessary violent attempt to challenge and overturn the institutional order. As argued previously, revisionists have adopted a wide range of strategies to reform and revolutionize institutions. Rather than conceive of revisionism as violence then, it is more useful to think of revisionism as any attempt by a state to mobilize all the network resources at its disposal to transform the institutional order. All power politics—revisionist politics included—involve "efforts to collectively mobilize in the pursuit of influence or to interfere with the ability of targets to pursue joint-action" (Goddard and Nexon 2016). Here in particular, the focus is on how states use the resources given to them by the networks *within* the institutional order in order to pursue transformation of that institutional order.

Following from this, theorists suggest that a state's network position shapes which instruments—military, economic, or social power—a state can mobilize in pursuit of its revisionist aims. A state with dense economic networks, for example, is likely to draw from those resources to challenge an institutional order. During the nineteenth century, for example, Prussia maintained exclusive relations with German states through the Zollverein, a German customs union formed in 1834 to manage tariffs among the German states. As Prussia began to pursue revisionist aims, the Zollverein provided economic ties that linked the power to the German states. Indeed, these networks also gave Prussia social power, forging a *Kleindeutsch* ideology legitimating Prussian leadership over the German Confederation.

Social and political networks give revisionists leverage as well. The Soviet Union lacked access to most Western institutions but, during both the interwar and postwar periods, invested in the Communist International—the Comintern—which eventually evolved into a "machine of huge dimensions, which for over a decade extended its activity and its tentacles over a geopolitical scenario that was more or less global" (Pons 2014, 85). The links between the Soviet government and local communist parties were often contentious at best, yet the Comintern formalized Soviet relations with communist parties in Eastern and Western Europe, Asia, and even Latin America, creating a vast network of communist emissaries that could be mobilized to counter the growing Western order (Pons 2015, 68–90). The point is not only that revisionists have alternatives to military power. Rather, it is to say that the form of a revisionist challenge—the instruments that a revisionist is likely to use to challenge the institutional order—is likely to depend on a state's position within networks. It makes no sense to reduce "power politics" or "revisionist strategies" to military challenges. Indeed, outright military attacks on institutional orders may be strategies of last resort rather than effective revisionist politics.

Thinking of revisionist strategies as attempts to mobilize networks sheds light on contemporary power politics within the liberal international order. Much has been written about Russia's military power, or lack thereof, and its aggressive attacks on the institutional order in Crimea, Ukraine, and Syria. Yet for all the focus on Russia's mobilization of its military power, its use of its position within economic (energy) and, more important, social-ideological networks has proved the greater challenge to the institutional order. Even before the 2016 US election, Vladimir Putin was relying on ideological appeals and economic aid to mobilize political parties of all ideological stripes in an effort to split apart the European Union and NATO (Goddard and Nexon 2016; Maness and Valeriano 2015).

Likewise, the focus on China's efforts at military modernization, and its increased assertiveness in the South China Seas, may be distracting scholars from the real power politics at play. China has forged new economic and political ties through institutions like the Shanghai Cooperation Organization, the Belt and Road Initiative, and the AIIB. Scholars are right that these ties do not necessarily signal revisionist aims. They were largely formed in response to specific demands, not as a means to challenge the liberal order. But over time, these ties will shape instruments China can use to challenge the institutional order.

Conclusion

In 2014 some began to warn of a return to global power politics, as revisionists seemingly began to challenge the institutional order. "Whether it is Russian forces seizing Crimea, China making aggressive claims in its coastal waters, Japan responding with an increasingly assertive strategy of its own, or Iran trying to use its alliances with Syria and Hezbollah to dominate the Middle East, old-fashioned power plays are back in international relations" (Mead 2014). Others rebutted these arguments, claiming that this alarmism was "based on a colossal misreading of modern power realities. It is a misreading of the logic and character of the existing world order. . . . Russia and, especially, China are deeply integrated into the world economy and its governing institutions" (Ikenberry 2014). Those institutions would continue to restrain revisionism and power politics.

This chapter suggests that both approaches to revisionism are misguided. Revisionism is not limited to aggressive attacks on the institutional order. Institutions cannot supplant global power politics. Rather, what we should be asking is how revisionist politics play out in specific institutional settings. How is it that the institutional order, and states' positions within that order, shape the outcomes of revisionist challenges? Using a network approach, I've argued that conceiving of institutions as networks allows scholars to compare the dynamics of revisionism in different institutional orders. It allows scholars to theorize how relative position might affect revisionists' ambitions and strategies. And it pushes us to see power politics, not only as the use of military power, but as the mobilization of all forms of power to collectively challenge the institutional order.

Notes

1. As Alastair I. Johnston argues, "For a concept at the core of international relations theorizing, it is disturbing how little thought . . . has gone into determining whether a state

is status quo or revisionist." For some exceptions, see Gilpin 1981; Schweller 1997; Organski and Kugler 1980; Rapkin and Thompson 2003.

2. The mechanisms described in this chapter are drawn from three varieties of liberal institutionalism: rational institutionalism (e.g., Keohane 1993), historical institutionalism (e.g., Ikenberry 2011), and sociological or constructivist liberal institutionalism (Barnett and Finnemore 1999).

3. On economic tools, see Germann 2014. On military alliances and binding, see Weitsman 2004, esp. 23; Deudney 1996, esp. 213–16.

4. On the integration of revisionist states, see Ikenberry 2011; Johnston 2003; Rapkin and Thompson 2003; Gilpin 1981.

5. In much of network analysis, "between-ness centrality" is another measure of access within a clique, and those actors with more "between-ness" are considered more central to the clique. Here I am interested in actors that bridge cliques, and they may or may not be central within a particular network subgroup.

6. I define the dominant network as the largest group of closely connected major powers that constitutes the institutional order. Subgroups are composed of other institutionalized networks that contain either a subset of major powers or a significant number of minor powers. I thank the reviewers for this definition.

7. On structural holes in international relations, see Nexon 2009b.

Part IV

The Power Politics of Global and Regional Institutions

CHAPTER 9

Structural Modifiers, the Non-Proliferation Treaty Regime, and Fostering a Less Competitive International Environment

Steven E. Lobell and Brad Nicholson

For many realists international regimes are epiphenomenal.[1] They reflect the distribution of power in the international system (Gilpin 1987, 34). They are created by the hegemon to facilitate its rule (Brooks and Wohlforth 2008, 148–70; Organski 1968, 361–66).[2] They mirror its security, economic, and foreign policy priorities and interests. Ikenberry, Mastanduno, and Wohlforth argue that the unipole creates regimes because it "benefits disproportionately from promoting systemwide outcomes that reflect its values and interests" (2009, 14). The hegemon, as the greatest power, enforces the rules it codifies; it is not the rules themselves that constrain and condition inter-state behavior. Rather, as John Mearsheimer reminds us, institutions "are based on the self-interested calculations of the great power," and norms and institutions are "reflections of the distribution of power in the world" (Mearsheimer 1994, 7; Grieco 1990, 36–49). Thus, international institutions are merely a consequence of state behavior and not the cause of it.[3]

This edited volume on international institutions and power politics explores how power politics influences (and is influenced by) the institutionalization of world politics. In this chapter, we explore how institutions limit the pursuit of power and influence in an anarchic system. We focus on how and why the Non-Proliferation Treaty (NPT) regime, including the NPT and the International Atomic Energy Agency (IAEA), has contributed to restraint in the proliferation of nuclear weapons and weapons technology since 1945 (Walsh 2005; Müller 1997).[4] Specifically, we ask, given the expectations of widespread nuclear proliferation in the 1950s and 1960s, and again following the end of the Cold War, let alone instances when states have abandoned or dismantled nuclear weapon programs (e.g., Brazil, Argentina, Taiwan, South Africa, South Korea, Libya, Ukraine, Kazakhstan, and Belarus), why hasn't there been more proliferation?

International relations (IR) scholars characterize the invention of the atomic bomb as a "nuclear revolution." It had a transformative effect on interstate warfare (Mearsheimer 2001, 128–33; Powell 1990; Freedman 1989; Jervis 1989; Waltz 1981, 3–7).[5] Nuclear weapons allow states to protect their territorial sovereignty and autonomy through deterrence rather than more traditional security strategies, including defense, power projection, and compellence (Sechser and Furhmann 2013, 175–78). IR realist scholars argue that nuclear weapons, along with the bipolar distribution of power, contributed to the "long peace," or the absence of major war among the great powers since World War II (Sagan 1996; Sagan and Waltz 1995; Mearsheimer 1990; Kennedy 1987; Gaddis 1986). The stabilizing effect of nuclear weapons is attributed to a secure second-strike capability or a mutually assured retaliatory capability; an initiator is deterred from attacking because enough of the target state's nuclear weapons will survive the initial strike and thereby allow it to massively retaliate and destroy the initiator.[6] Lacking a secure second-strike capability, however, nuclear states are locked into a dangerous cult-of-the-offensive or use-them-or-lose-them preemptive environment.[7]

Kenneth Waltz (1979, 74–77) argues that states emulate the best practices of the successful states or risk falling behind.[8] The practice of emulating success raises an important question. If nuclear weapons are an excellent deterrent for states (i.e., states with a survivable retaliatory nuclear capability) and if more nuclear weapons "may be better," why wasn't there a lot more proliferation of nuclear weapons by major and middle powers during the Cold War and after the Cold War (Monteiro 2014, 49–52, 90–98; Gavin 2010; Frankel 1993; Van Evera 1990; Waltz 1981)? The rate of nuclear proliferation peaked in the 1960s (Brown et al. 2010). In 1963 President John Kennedy admitted that he was "haunted by the feeling that by 1970, unless we are successful, there may be 10 nuclear powers instead of 4, and by 1975, 15 or 20."[9]

There are some real barriers to nuclear proliferation (Monteiro and Debs 2014; Sagan 1996). The United States required immense resources to develop the first nuclear weapons (Schwartz 1998). In the decade following World War II, most of the great powers were still recovering both physically and financially from the devastation of war. The Soviet Union's post-war superpower status was essential to its acquiring nuclear weapons because its power was heightened and not diminished following the war (Burns and Siracusa 2013). Developing nuclear weapons and sustaining a deterrent force that includes a viable second-strike capability diverts massive resources away from other economic, political, and military priorities and requires technological expertise. Exceptions such as Pakistan and North Korea suggest the barriers have been lowered enough that a determined state can mobilize the required assets, including financial and knowledge-based, no matter how resource deficient. The limited arsenals of nuclear weapons possessed by Pakistan and North Korea do not fully provide an overwhelming deterrent in the traditional sense (i.e., second strike) as during the Cold War between the superpowers. Even the existence of nascent nuclear weapon capabilities, however, appears to play some role in modifying or amplifying perceptions of power.

Several non-resource-material factors also limit proliferation. They include the role of nuclear taboos, American hegemony and the extension of its nuclear umbrella to overseas allies in Europe and Asia, the success of the IAEA and NPT in blocking the proliferation of nuclear technology to non-nuclear powers (through bilateral export controls and the Nuclear Suppliers Group NSG), the role of superpower pressure in discouraging proliferation (and incentives and threats of punishment for remaining non-nuclear), the special peace among liberal states and respect for international law and norms, and the obsolescence of war as a social institution (Solingen 2012; Paul 2009; Tannenwald 2005; Thayer 1995; Mueller 1988). Liberal institutionalists emphasize the strengthening of the NPT inspection authority in 1995. This effort resulted in the Comprehensive Test Ban Treaty (CTBT), a separate initiative from the NPT itself, which introduced new inspection techniques, including verification instruments that have become more effective over time (Bunn 2003).

However, the CTBT never came into force. Following the 1996 opening of the treaty for signature, seven conferences were organized between 1999 and 2013 by the ratifying states. Article XIV of the CTBT states that the treaty will enter into force after ratification by all forty-four states listed in Annex 2 of the treaty.[10] Notably, among the treaty's eight non-signatory states was the United States. Its failure to ratify the CTBT, despite President Bill Clinton's role in negotiating the treaty among the NPT signatory states, seemed to indicate the ascendancy of interests in issues related to proliferation. For example, even the strengthened institution was unable to stop India and Pakistan from exploding nuclear weapons in 1998. Neither of these states, along with Israel, Egypt, Iran, North Korea, China, and the United States, were signatories to Article XIV of the treaty.

The nuclear Non-Proliferation Treaty was signed in 1968. It went into force in 1970. In 1995 the Non-Proliferation Treaty was extended indefinitely when the CTBT was negotiated, despite the CTBT's failure to enter into force. The NPT recognized five states as nuclear-weapon powers—US, Russia, the United Kingdom, France, and China—and committed them to eventually eliminate their nuclear arsenals. According to George Bunn (2003), "The IAEA has the dual responsibility of helping countries that do not have nuclear weapons to engage in peaceful nuclear programs while ensuring that they do not make nuclear weapons." The renegotiation of the NPT also committed the nuclear states to an eventual goal of disarmament. In 1997 additional protocols were enacted in response to Iraq's ability to hide its nuclear program from inspectors before the 1991 Gulf War. However, a fundamental difference between the earlier NPT and the new protocols was that each party negotiated with the IAEA individual safeguards and inspection criteria. The development of the CTBT actually weakened the NPT constraints. One of the primary reasons the US did not ratify the CTBT was because of the need to modernize the American nuclear arsenal. This highlights some of the paradoxes associated with balancing individual state interests and supporting multilateral enforcement regimes.

We contend that the NPT regime plays a role in mitigating the proliferation of nuclear weapons.[11] It dampens the competitiveness of the international environment. Specifically, international institutions constitute non-material structural modifiers, similar to the role played by geography and technology.[12] Though not structural themselves, as modifiers, these international institutions can affect the international system. They do so by affecting the system's interaction capacity, socialization of the units, and competition among the units (Wivel 2004). We argue that most states conform to and emulate non-proliferation norms. States conform because the norms are the most successful of the practices at the time and, therefore, nuclear proliferators risk being left behind (Weber 1990). A change in what is the most successful practice, though, could unleash a wave of nuclear proliferation.

The contrasting cases of Iraq and South Africa at the end of the Cold War highlight the NPT's influence on state behavior. South Africa dismantled its nuclear arsenal and fully accounted for all its nuclear materials to the IAEA. The international community's negative response to Iraq's nuclear program, which was viewed as violating the NPT, contributed to its dismantling its nuclear arsenal (Stumpf 1995). Ultimately, South Africa was fully integrated into the broader international community. Integration would have been impossible had South Africa maintained a weaponized nuclear program owing to the politics of non-proliferation.

Iraq, on the other hand, maintained deliberate ambiguity regarding the status of its nuclear program. Following the 1991 Gulf War and its military defeat, Iraq engaged in subterfuge. To deter domestic and external threats, the regime maintained the appearance of some level of nuclear capacity. The resulting twenty-year sanctions regime, enacted largely because Iraq's nuclear aspirations were unclear, only ended with the 2003 invasion of Iraq.

One unintended and inadvertent consequence of the NPT regime is the spread of enrichment and reprocessing technologies around the globe (Stulberg and Fuhrmann 2013, 203). Rather than violate the NPT and become a pariah state, withdraw from it (North Korea), or not sign it (India, Pakistan, Israel), some states have selected to acquire enrichment and reprocessing technologies that "could enable a short sprint to the bomb" legally (Walsh 2005, 20). In the face of such challenges, controlling the proliferation of nuclear weapon–related technologies, such as complex guidance systems, becomes almost as important as the nuclear materials themselves. Completely separating nuclear weapon–related technology from nuclear weapon proliferation, though, is not possible. As the North Korea and Pakistan nuclear examples demonstrate, a highly industrialized economy is not a prerequisite for achieving nuclear weapon status. While there is considerable international concern regarding proliferation among developing countries, the real risk to proliferation norms may lie with powerful industrialized economies. Members of the G20 have both the industrial base and technological capacity to develop or acquire advanced conventional weapon systems, such as air-, sea-, or ground-launched ballistic missiles, which leverage high-technology guidance systems and delivery platforms. These capabilities are what make nuclear weapons the penultimate deterrent.

System and Structure

Kenneth Waltz relegates norms and institutions, and most other variables, to the unit level of analysis. For Waltz, a system is composed of (1) structure and (2) inter-acting parts or units (Waltz 1979, 80).[13] The three characteristics or features that determine a system's structure are (1) the principles by which the parts are arranged (anarchy), (2) the characteristics of the units (functionally undifferentiated), and (3) the distribution of capabilities across the units (as the distribution of capabilities change so does the system's structure).

For Waltz, the structure of the international system does not act on the units directly. It affects their behavior through the twin processes of competition among states and socialization or learned behavior (Waltz 1979, 74; Thies 2010). Both processes encourage emulation, sameness, and similarities in states' behavior.[14] Competitors emulate the successful states, or they risk "fall[ing] by the wayside" and losing their position in the international system (Waltz 1979, 118; Resende-Santos 2007, 47–62). Similarly, according to João Resende-Santos, "States emulate successful innovations of others out of fear of the disadvantage of being less competitively organized and equipped" (1996, 196).

For Waltz (1979, 74–77), for a system to exist, there must be at least a minimum level of interaction among its units. As Robert Jervis reminds us, systems vary in "how interconnected they are" (1979, 215). If interaction is non-existent or too low, the processes of socialization and competition cannot function to reward or penalize state behavior (Buzan, Jones, and Little 1993, 78). Interaction, therefore, is a necessary attribute of a system. It is the interaction of states that affects the socialization of the actors and the competition among them (Waltz 1979, 74–77).

Structural Modifiers: Interaction Capacity, Socialization, and Competition

Waltz's structural realism is too sparse. "Only in rare circumstances," Norrin Ripsman, Jeffrey Taliaferro, and Steven Lobell argue, "does the international system provide clear information to states about the external constraints and opportunities they face" (2016, 2). Similarly, defensive realists maintain that the international system alone provides few incentives for expansion. They argue that expansion is often the product of non-structural domestic or unit-level political pathologies, such as parochial interest groups, strategic culture, log-rolled coalitions, and misperceptions (Glaser 1994; Van Evera 1998; Jervis 1978).

To address this shortcoming, several realists highlight the role of non-structural and yet non-unit-level forces (Lobell 2018). They are capable of modifying the system's structure including anarchy, the functionally undifferentiated units, and its polarity (Lobell, Ripsman, and Taliaferro 2009; Rose 1998; Buzan, Jones, and Little 1993).[15] At play are non-structural and yet not national-domestic level variables. For instance, for Glenn Snyder, structural modifiers or process variables have several common characteristics: (1) they are "system-wide influences that are structural in their inherent nature but not potent enough internationally to warrant that designation"; (2) they "modify the effects of the more basic structural elements on the interaction process"; and (3) they "affect the behavior of all actors more or less evenly" (1996, 169). Non-proliferation regimes, as process variables, affect states that possess nuclear weapons, states that do not possess nuclear weapons, and especially those that desire to possess nuclear weapons.

Similarly, Stephen Van Evera introduces the concept of the *fine-grained* structure of power. Van Evera's more granular types of power include the distinction between offensive and defensive power, the power of first strike versus retaliatory power, and rising and declining power (Van Evera 1999, 7–11). These forces are not structure. They can, though, modify the effects of anarchy and polarity and thus inter-state behavior. Van Evera argues these fine-grained modifiers have more influence on the likelihood of international conflict or cooperation than the gross or aggregate distribution of power alone. The distinctions inherent in describing the fine-grained structure of power facilitate a state's ability to forecast and discern other actors' intent within the international system and improve the state's chances of survival. The resulting additional information assists states in navigating the imperfect information environment described by Waltz's sparse structural realism.

Two structural modifiers help us to understand how the NPT regime limited and restrained nuclear proliferation during the Cold War and post–Cold War periods: (1) interaction capacity and (2) the process of competition and socialization. Like technology and geography, international institutions can modify the structure of the international system; shared norms and organizations affect the system's interaction capacity, its competition, and its socialization. Thus, they modify the international structure itself by either dampening or exacerbating its competitiveness. Moreover, such shared institutions can change over time. They reflect emerging or fading behavior trends among actors or groups of actors in the international system. Unlike technology and geography, though, shared norms and organizations are a non-material force.

For instance, the economically and politically integrated nature of the industrialized world prevented greater proliferation. States are socialized into a system in which the NPT reinforces the norm of non-proliferation. The Brazilian and Argentinian nuclear programs provide an interesting example. Both states had independent nuclear programs and willingly submitted to the IAEA and NPT protocols in 1990 after a long history of non-participation (Reiss 1988). Their primary motivation for eventually joining the NPT was to obtain the benefits made demonstrably available to the states emulating the successful practices of the NPT signatories. They valued the greater information acquisition from further integration. Specifically, as NPT holdouts and pariah states, they would have been excluded from access to information regarding the fine-grained nature of power. They risked falling behind regional, sub-systemic, and global rivals.

Interaction Capacity

Some level of interaction among the units must occur for a system to exist. According to Buzan, Jones, and Little, interaction capacity "affect[s] the ability and willingness of units to interact, but also determine[s] what types and levels of interaction are possible and desired" (1993, 69). Where interaction is nonexistent or too low, there is no system or structure. Without some level of interaction, hierarchy, rather than anarchy among the units, would occur. Moreover, according to Buzan, Jones, and Little (1993, 73–74), throughout most of human history, modest technological capability translated into low levels of interaction among the units. Functional differentiation and specialization, rather than functionally similar states, was common.

Norms and institutions play an important role in facilitating communication between the units. They affect the interaction capacity of the system (Nye 1988, 250). Institutions also serve as a set of rules for interaction, a forum for resolving disputes, a fire alarm for catching cheaters, and a means to create efficiency in exchanges. However, critics of regimes are correct that institutions, and particularly security institutions, often lack enforcement provisions and have weak verification capability (Scribner, Ralston, and Metz 1985). Enforcement and verification, however, are not their only purposes or sole roles. Institutions affect the interaction capacity of a system and its level of competitiveness. The interaction capacity of a system with few shared norms is much lower than one in which significant norms and practices are shared widely among the major actors.

Interaction capacity can make for a less competitive environment (Buzan, Little, and Jones 1993, 72–74). When Belarus, Kazakhstan, and Ukraine surrendered their nuclear arsenals and became signatories to the NPT, it highlighted the influence of interaction capacity on state decision making. The high interactivity of the post–Cold War system reinforced the valuation of the NPT norms.

During the Cold War, the bipolar international system aligned secondary and minor states to one or another of the superpowers. Particularly in key strategic areas, like the Middle East, Europe, and Northeast Asia, extension of the super-power nuclear umbrella served states' security interests. Following the collapse of the bipolar order, there was not widespread proliferation of technologies leading to development of nuclear weapons to replace previous security guarantees by the superpowers. Additionally, nuclear disarmament occurred in certain instances. The voluntary surrender of nuclear weapons by countries as diverse as Ukraine and South Africa contributed further to the belief in the best practice of not proliferating nuclear weapons. These norms are underwritten by power relation-ships between states, in which the actions of the most powerful actors in the system apply conforming pressure to the comprising units.

Competition among Actors and Socialization of Actors

Competition and socialization are processes (Waltz 1979, 74–77). They cause states to produce sameness and similarities in their behavior. As Steve Weber notes, "When a system undergoes structural change, actors within the system may adapt their behavior only slowly, and they may do so by a number of paths" (1990, 56). Socialization and competition condition the choices of states; they narrow the range of possible outcomes. Specifically, states are encouraged to emulate and conform to the best practices of the most successful states.

Socialization and security competition, which drive emulation, are modified by nonstructural and non-unit-level forces. These include geography, technology, and norms and institutions (Thies 2010). Technology can modify a system's structure. When technology favors the defense over the offense, Jervis main-tains, it will "render international anarchy relatively unimportant" (1978, 187). Similarly, Steve Weber (1990) argues that nuclear weapons modify anarchy "by inhibiting aggression and ameliorating the security dilemma" and by creating superpower "joint custodianship" over the international system.

Norms and institutions, like geography and technology, do not change the fact of anarchy. The NPT and its protocols, particularly the CTBT, serve to reinforce the established superpower "custodianship" and bring states into nuclear non-proliferation conformity. The regime implicitly protects the status of the great powers as the preeminent nuclear-armed states. It is an extension of the distribution of power. The non-proliferation institutions also emphasize the centrality of the major nuclear powers as the primary norms makers on all nuclear technology–related issues, including the spread of nuclear technologies to other states in the system. Thus, nuclear proliferators are ostracized; they select to return to the fold and abandon their nuclear programs or suffer further isolation.

As structural modifiers, norms and institutions affect the process and pace of socialization and the competition among states. They make anarchy more opaque. As Waltz notes, "Socialization brings members of a group into conformity with its norms" (1979, 75–76, 127). Socialization, as a process, "limits and molds behavior" of states and "encourages similarities of attributes and behavior." The import of IOs on nuclear proliferation is threefold: (1) states emulate norms and institutions, contributing to behavior that can result in a less competitive environment rather than a more competitive one; (2) successful practices are determined by the structure of the system itself and not by individual leaders, their regime type, or their beliefs and ideas; (3) a hegemon or leader might not be necessary to create and enforce the rules or provide the public good of international stability (Russett and Oneal 2001, 161–69). States conform to and emulate common international norms, including the norm of non-proliferation, because preventing the spread of nuclear weapons and technology is the most successful of the practices among states. Proliferators, especially middle or weak powers, risk falling behind regional rivals if they are branded as rogue or pariah states for cheating or breaking these norms. Certain states engage in nuclear proliferation despite existing norms and others do not because not all states respond in the same ways to similar structural modifiers (Ripsman, Taliaferro, and Lobell 2016, 41).

Socialization provides incentives for secondary and middle states to adhere and conform to the NPT. The decisions by Poland, Czechoslovakia, Australia, and South Korea not to develop nuclear weapons can be interpreted as emulation of the superpowers' own adherence to the NPT as the established best practice for states. Additionally, proliferation activities by secondary states could induce granular and targeted balancing by more powerful states focused specifically on countering proliferation-related behaviors (Lobell 2018, 6). One example of the NPT structural modifiers' influence is the exhaustive sanctions regime imposed on Iran. While major powers did not view Iran's aggregate power as a threat requiring balance, Iran's intent to possess nuclear weapons provoked a strong response targeted at forcing an adherence to the NPT's norms. As Waltz notes: "Competition spurs the actors to accommodate their ways to the socially most acceptable and successful practices" (1979, 77). Most states, specifically those that have the ability to do so, have not weaponized nuclear technology, suggesting the protocols and norms associated with the NPT limit the spread of nuclear weapons and associated technologies by influencing state behavior.

Undesired and Unintended Consequence

One undesired and unintended consequence of the NPT regime is the spread of enrichment and reprocessing technologies.[16] To remain in good standing and part of the nonnuclear club, and to not openly violate the NPT or withdraw from it, states have acquired enrichment and reprocessing technologies legally. These technologies enable a short nuclear breakout time line. States have acquired these technologies under the guise of reprocessing and enrichment for civilian purposes (Fuhrmann 2012; Kroenig 2010). This tendency will likely only continue to present a challenge to counter-proliferation regimes. One response is bilateral export controls and the establishment of the NSG (McGoldrick 2011). Beginning with just seven members in 1974, the NSG now has forty-eight countries, including all the declared nuclear powers and most major industrialized states. These are the states that could relatively easily develop nuclear weapons. Following the failure of NPT inspection regimes to detect Iraq's development of a nuclear weapon program before the first Gulf War, the NSG focused on tracking "dual use" technologies. Technological mobility and information portability will continue to pose a significant challenge to anti-proliferation protocols and regimes (Evan and Hays 2006). History demonstrates that containing the spread of knowledge and know-how is difficult at best, if not nearly impossible.

Conclusion

NPT regimes contribute to limiting the spread of nuclear weapons. We argue that interaction capacity and socialization, together with the established NPT regime, modify the structure and state behavior. They push states to dismantle weapons, abandon research programs, and forgo pursuing nuclear weapons.

These modifiers cannot, however, change the structural fact of anarchy and polarity. Jack Donnelly argues that norms and institutions are "*in principle* structural at the international, no less than the national, level" (2000, 127). Glenn Snyder argues, "If international institutions develop sufficient independent power and authority, at some point they would cease being structural modifiers and become a defining characteristic of structure itself" (1996, 171). We disagree. Despite the existence of strong constraints like the NPT, some states develop nuclear weapons. The NPT incentivizes emulation but cannot override structural constraints.

Notes

1. There is debate among realists about the future of US grand strategy and whether it should "lean forward" and maintain its global and deep-engagement position (Brooks, Ikenberry, and Wohlforth 2013) or "pull back" and pursue a more restrained approach (Posen 2014). One issue in this debate is whether the US can afford to continue to unilaterally provide many of the global public goods that support the liberal institutional order vis-à-vis international regimes and whether it is necessary to do so.

2. Levy and Thompson (2010, 17) differentiate between maritime and continental systems. For Levy and Thompson, only the former creates international regimes "to protect and expand trade" and, in doing so, to "protect their positions of economic and naval dominance." The latter seeks "territorial hegemony over land and people and economic hegemony over markets." In contrast, see Monteiro (2012, 20–21), who argues that a unipole could pursue an offensive dominance strategy.

3. In contrast, see Barkin (this volume), Finnemore (2009), and Schweller and Priess (1997).

4. Especially among states that have the economic, technological, and scientific capacity to develop a nuclear weapons program.

5. For a criticism of the deterring assumption of nuclear weapons against conventional attack for secondary states, see Narang (2014).

6. On nuclear weapons as coercive tools of statecraft, see Pape (1996, 35–38).

7. On the cult of the offensive, see Van Evera (1984).

8. For instance, Eric Labs notes, "Successful expanders learn from past mistakes and they try to go about expanding in a manner that draws the least attention of the other great powers" (1997, 13).

9. John F. Kennedy, news conference, March 21, 1963, accessed December 27, 2018, https://www.presidency.ucsb.edu/documents/the-presidents-news-conference-169.

10. For a complete listing of Article XIV signatories and abstainers, see United Nations Office for Disarmament Affairs, "Comprehensive Nuclear Test Ban Treaty," https://www.un.org/disarmament/wmd/nuclear/ctbt/.

11. Our argument is at variance with recent work on proliferation, including Narang (2014) and Monteiro and Debs (2014). They emphasize the specific historical context and the strategic context in which nuclear weapons were acquired and deployed.

12. On modifiers, see Ripsman, Taliaferro, and Lobell (2016, 38–43).

13. For an alternative understanding of the international system, see Jervis (1997).

14. Taliaferro suggests that the willingness and the ability of states to emulate the successful military technologies and practices of the great powers (a form of internal balancing) are a function of levels of external vulnerability as mediated through the extractive and mobilization capacity of existing state institutions (Taliaferro 2009, 194–226).

15. Mearsheimer (2001, 114–19) also introduces several structural modifiers, including the stopping power of water and other geographical factors, such as insular and contiguous states, that affect the system's war proneness.

16. On undesired consequences, see Jervis (1979, 216–19).

CHAPTER 10

The Power Politics of United Nations Peace Operations

Sarah-Myriam Martin-Brûlé, Lou Pingeot, and Vincent Pouliot

In this volume's introduction, Wivel and Paul invite us to revisit the multifaceted connections between the struggle for influence among states and the pervasive role played by international organizations (IOs) in contemporary world politics. This call is in line with a 2015 piece by Goddard and Nexon (2015, 1), who argue that power politics, "the struggle for influence among political communities, broadly understood," is not the preserve of realism in international relations (IR) theory. Focusing on the variety of resources and modalities of power that actors deploy on the world stage in their contestation for influence, the authors expand the scope of power politics to any instance of collective mobilization. To broaden the analytical category of power politics, Goddard and Nexon call for more attention to be paid to the different contexts in which these political dynamics take place.

In this chapter we focus on IOs as a particular form that international institutions may take. Our specific locus of power politics is United Nations peace operations. Through this case, we address both key questions raised by the editors: First, how do states use international institutions to maximize influence? And second, how does the institutional setting affect how power is understood and exercised? As we move from New York City to actual theaters of intervention, we show how peace operations are not only sites but also tools of power politics. Great powers, troop contributors, regional actors, and host states make use of this core institution to advance their interests. In doing so, they adapt to the particular multilateral institutionalized form that peace operations take, which simultaneously constrains the exercise of power and allows its deployment.

The institutionalized setup of peace operations, in other words, becomes a toolbox at the disposal of a variety of actors.

Indeed, UN peace operations are home to an intense and multifaceted struggle for influence among member states. As Cunliffe observes, peacekeeping "grants the tantalizing opportunity to exercise power and influence over the direction of international affairs in excess of what would otherwise be possible if they relied purely on their own will and capacities" (2009, 334). As an institution it offers the possibility to integrate and fragment patterns of collective mobilization on the world stage. Beyond the exercise of power, peacekeeping also "serves a political function by allowing influence to be wielded without risk" (Cunliffe 2009, 323). As a site of power politics, UN peace operations are characterized by a peculiar set of struggles, which this chapter seeks to document and analyze.

We make two main claims. First, in line with the introduction to this project, we show that peacekeeping, far from attenuating power politics, rather displaces struggles for influence both in terms of sites and channels. We document how sets of informal practices within and around the UN Security Council (UNSC) lend structure to UN power politics in the realm of peace operations. Second, we demonstrate that the power politics of peacekeeping do not occur only where we might expect them (i.e., among states within sites of decision making) but permeate the implementation of peace operations on the ground. Not only are UN missions in the field driven by Council dynamics (which often have little to do with the conflict itself), they can also become instruments that local and regional actors use to further their own interests. UN peace operations, through constraints that are self-imposed or not by member states, thus create both new sites and new instruments of power politics. At the same time, power politics must adapt to the nature of peacekeeping missions, which enables but also constrains the transfer of struggles for influence across national, regional, and international spheres. Overall, then, we show that beyond the infamous dominance of the permanent five (P5) members of the Security Council, the power politics of UN peace operations are as pervasive as they are multifaceted.

Power Politics Inside and Around the Security Council

In this section, we survey the different ways in which various forms of struggle for influence structure Security Council politics, both among its members and with other states on the outside. Inside the council the main cleavage is between the P5 and the elected members (the so-called E10). Power politics between these two groups works through a wealth of informal practices, ranging from rings of consultation to a division of labor around drafting or committee chairmanships. On the outside, Security Council members often struggle for influence with the General Assembly's Fifth Committee as well as with troop-contributing countries (TCCs) and key funders.

The P5-E10 Divide

It is common wisdom that the P5 dominate the work of the Security Council, usually at the expense of elected members. This is not to say that the E10 have no leverage at all; research suggests that dominant countries are willing to spend considerable resources to rally some E10 to their cause (Vreeland and Dreher 2014). Similarly, elected members sometimes are able to play leading roles, especially on thematic issues, as their lacking "dogs in the fight" renders them less controversial players (Pouliot 2016). Overall, though, the balance of power within the council is heavily tilted in favor of the P5. As insider David Malone puts it: "In the Council the powerful impose what they can, the weak endure what they must" (2004, 617).

In this power politics, the veto is nothing more than the tip of the iceberg. The P5 owe their domination to their unparalleled institutional memory, their network of contacts in New York and beyond, their qualitatively and quantitatively superior personnel in the mission, and their in-group solidarity. For all these reasons, even without the veto, the P5 start with a tremendous advantage over elected members, especially given how fast UN waters can change. When it comes to procedure, intelligence, or precedents, elected members are essentially at the mercy of the permanent ones. As former ambassador Kishore Mahbubani (2004, 259–60) puts it, the E10 "are hobbled by the fact that much of the Council's agenda, procedures, and policies have been settled by the time each new elected member joins the Council." The previous members of the council, especially the P5, have already created

> a delicate web of understanding [around] which issues should receive real attention and which should receive pro forma attention. Within the UN community, there is also a widespread belief that a complex pattern of trade-offs has been worked out over the years. [. . .] Another impediment to the work of the E10 is the absence of any formal institutional memory in the Council, either of the proceedings in informal consultations (where most of the real decisions are hashed out) or of the record of implementation or non-implementation of the Council's decisions.

P5-E10 power politics works primarily through informal practices. Recent years have witnessed an upsurge of studies about "informal governance" (Stone 2011) in world politics, thanks to which powerful actors get around formal rules of sovereign equality. The Security Council is a particularly compelling case in that there has been a significant trend toward more informality over the past few decades. Early movements toward informalization were already perceptible during the Cold War, as the number of "informal meetings of whole" started to grow at the expense of council public sessions. As Loie Feurle explains: "Although no guidelines for the conduct of informal consultations exist in the Provisional Rules, over the years a set of unwritten rules has developed" (1985, 287). The trend has grown steadily ever since, to the point that after the Cold War, argues Malone, "'informals,' closed to all non-Council members and most Secretariat staff and leaving no formal record, became the norm. Nonmembers were in the dark and had to scramble for information, feeding off scraps in antechambers, a thoroughly humiliating experience" (2004, 630).

The power politics of informality take two main forms within the Security Council. First, the body works along rings of consultation, so to speak, by which some members are much more central in the negotiations than others. The core consists of the P3 (France, the UK, and the US), which initiate the vast majority of draft resolutions and negotiations within the council. Second come the other two permanent countries, China and Russia, whose views are sought especially on texts that are likely to be met with some resistance. The next ring consists of those few E10 that are closely aligned with the P3, usually North Atlantic Treaty Organization (NATO) and EU members. On some occasions these E10 countries are brought into the fold earlier than Beijing and Moscow, especially if the issue requires Western solidarity. The last circle of consultation comprises other E10, including larger ones at times. Here is how one French official described the practice of concentric negotiation in a 2011 interview:

> Should France want a text through, there is a step-by-step process: (1) measure the level of support with P3; if US not supportive, at least ensure no opposition—France and the UK have a huge level of intimacy, with the same reflexes; (2) go to close friends, at the time Germany and Portugal; (3) go to regional leader (e.g., Lebanon); (4) check with Russia and China; if against, go to the full format at 15; if receptive, then work within P5 to avoid E10 coalitions.

This peculiar way of negotiating matters greatly because each further ring tends to lock down the space for change. Once the P5 have agreed on a text, for instance, it becomes difficult for the E10, whether individually or as a group, to push amendments through. The more horse trading has already occurred, in other words, the less room there is for influence downstream.

This power politics has not been attenuated by the advent of social media, despite its unsettling effects for diplomacy in general. Indeed, "it is not unheard of for draft resolutions to be shared with the E10 for the first time just hours before they are put to a vote. With increasing frequency, draft resolutions also seem to be 'strategically leaked' beforehand by those in the know, usually to gain the upper hand in the fierce media battles waged around controversial Council files in the age of the Internet, blogs, and Twitter" (Von Einsiedel, Malone, and Stagno Ugarte 2016, 833). Private meetings of the P5 are not rare, either in a "cigar room" adjacent to the council or inside one of the permanent missions.

Increasingly, the P5 also initiate negotiations at the "experts" (i.e., junior) level in order to facilitate influence: "This involves the P5 'experts' having a first cut at the drafting before the text is circulated to others. It is quite common for decisions to be negotiated at the junior level in 'round robin' emails without any meetings at all. This tends to increase the marginalisation of the elected members" (Keating 2016, 147). When it comes to peacekeeping operations (PKOs), for instance, in the years 2009–11, France proposed or supported, alone or with others, an average of two-thirds of resolutions adopted by the Security Council (Tardy 2013).

The second form of informal power politics within the council has to do with the division of labor between the P5 and the E10. The core practice here is that of recognizing a "pen holder" for each item on the agenda. As David Ambrosetti explains, pen holding "presupposes practices such as a special monitoring of the situation, the drafting of resolutions or presidential statements (at the very least), the constant negotiation with UNSC delegations (particularly the main financial contributors to the UN peace operations budget), discussions with the secretariat services (when discussing operational options and available means or the appointment of UN representatives and senior staff in the field), and working with troop contributing states" (2012, 69). Pen holders, which came to replace so-called groups of friends over the past decade or so, find themselves at the center of the concentric circles described previously (see also Goddard and Nexon, this volume, on networks and power politics). For instance, in the run-up to the UN Mission in South Sudan (UNMISS), "the US became the so-called 'penholder' given its close relationship with South Sudan. This meant that it drafted the resolution and negotiated it with the other members—first with France and the UK (P3), later with China and Russia (P5) and finally with the elected members (E10)" (Dijkstra 2015, 33).

In this division of labor, France currently takes the lead over several conflicts in Western Africa (Central African Republic, DRC, Ivory Coast, Mali) while the UK similarly covers its former colonies (Darfur, Sierra Leone, but also Somalia, Libya, Syria, and Yemen). The US often controls items that are more directly related to its global interests (e.g., Iran, Iraq, North Korea, or terrorism more broadly). Exceptionally, some E10s have been lead nations, including in recent years Australia and Germany on Afghanistan or Japan on Timor. Elected members often take charge of thematic issues, such as women and conflict, small arms, and the like. Ultimately, the pen holder system amounts to a massive concentration of power, in that it marginalizes the council presidency and those interested member states (E10 and beyond) that used to organize into groups of friends to monitor particular peace operations.

The other informal practice that sustains a division of labor within the council has to do with committee chairmanships. Article 29 of the UN Charter states, "The Security Council may establish such subsidiary organs as it deems necessary for the performance of its functions." The number of such committees has consistently grown over the years, and today most peace operations mandated by the council contain sanctions that are monitored by such a body. What is interesting from a power politics perspective is that most committees are chaired by an E10, according to an informal distribution traditionally decided by the P5. Chairing is, of course, a double-edged sword, in that it confers influence but also constrains its actual exercise. Until recently, each year during the fall, as the term of half of the elected members came to an end, P5 ambassadors met informally to allocate the positions for the following year. On the face of it, allowing E10 member states to chair committees may sound like an overture from the P5, but in practice it is a form of directed delegation, often close to co-optation, which also puts the E10 in a tough spot because of the very steep learning curve involved.

Troop Contributors, Funders, and the General Assembly

At the intergovernmental level, power politics are not limited to the P5-E10 relationship. The rest of UN membership is also involved in three main ways: as TCCs, as funders, and as members of the General Assembly (or GA, which controls the UN budget). To begin with the latter, it is important to note that even though the Security Council formally decides on peace operations mandates, it is not institutionally empowered to vote their budget. This is the prerogative of the assembly, and more specifically of the Advisory Committee on Administrative and Budgetary Questions (ACABQ) as well as the Fifth Committee. While it would be greatly exaggerated to say that the GA exerts influence over the council, the fact remains that oftentimes "Fifth Committee decision-making effectively becomes a partial re-negotiation of mandates."[1] The GA also has the Special Committee on Peacekeeping Operations (C34), which has increasingly become controlled by the developing world: "Non-Western troop contributors have used the General Assembly's Special Committee on Peacekeeping Operations (the C34) as one platform for these arguments, virtually paralyzing it" (Gowan 2016, 759).

The main power politics between the Security Council and the rest of UN membership concerns those countries that contribute troops to, as well as those that pay for, peace operations. The composition of UN missions has dramatically changed since the end of the Cold War heralded the golden age of peacekeeping in the 1990s. In early 1995 nine Western countries—France, the UK, Canada, Poland, Netherlands, Norway, Denmark, Spain, and Sweden—provided about a third of the 63,500 peacekeepers deployed by the UN in the field. In late 2017 these countries had dropped from the top twenty TCCs and were providing just about 2,900 out of over 90,000 peacekeepers. As of September 2017, the top ten contributors of uniformed personnel to UN missions included four African states (Ethiopia, Rwanda, Ghana, and Senegal), five South Asian states (Bangladesh, Pakistan, India, Indonesia, and Nepal), and one North African state (Egypt).[2]

Meanwhile, funding for UN peacekeeping missions is still disproportionately provided by Western and advanced industrialized states, with the US, Japan, France, Germany, and the UK providing over 50 percent of peacekeeping funding in 2017.[3] In other words, this is another instance of "a de facto division of labor. Powerful nations finance PKOs while weaker nations staff them" (Kathman and Melin 2016, 11).

This power politics matters in several ways. For one thing TCCs have had a tough time wielding any influence over the mandating of peace operations, which is jealously guarded by council members. The poor quality of the consultations between the Security Council and TCCs has long been a sore point. TCCs have complained that consultations occur only a day or two before a mandate is supposed to be (re)negotiated, which makes it impossible for them to have meaningful input. They also argue that they are provided too little information about ongoing operations (Security Council Report 2016, 13). Security Council members regularly refuse to share drafts of ongoing negotiations with TCCs, thus presenting them with a fait accompli. Reciprocally, "P3 diplomats grouse that many troop contributors' representatives seem unwilling to engage on substance" (Gowan 2016, 759).

For another thing, the funding of UN peace operations gives way to a power politics of staffing that is particularly fierce. It is well-known that rich Western countries have controlled senior positions within the UN hierarchy for a while: France has claimed the post of undersecretary general (USG) in the Department of Peacekeeping Operations (DPKO), and the USGs for peacekeeping have all been French nationals since Kofi Annan's tenure. The Department of Political Affairs (DPA) is similarly understood to be a US fiefdom, while the Office for the Coordination of Humanitarian Affairs (OCHA) remains a British prerogative. These appointments matter a great deal because the UN civil service is heavily involved in the making of peace operations, whether through reporting and gathering facts, addressing the council in informal sessions, or drafting mandate proposals. As three experts confirm: "It is partly because of this central role of the Secretariat that the P3 place great pressure on the Secretary-General to ensure that the three main 'peace and security departments' are headed by nationals of their respective countries" (Von Einsiedel, Malone, and Stagno Ugarte 2016, 835). The nomination of special representatives of the secretary general (SRSGs) has similarly been heavily politicized in the past.

Beyond senior positions, funders also wield influence over lower-rank staffing. It is worth emphasizing that "out of the 921 total staff working in DFS [Department of Field Support] and DPKO only 247 (26.82%) hold permanent/continuing appointments whereas 674 (73.18%) hold fixed-term or temporary appointments" (Trettin and Junk 2014, 15). Similarly, in 2014 more than 30 percent of the DPA's total resources at headquarters came from voluntary funding (United Nations 2015, 33). The abundance of positions dependent on voluntary funding paves the way to an informal politics that favors rich countries. Cunliffe confirms this dynamic with numbers: "It does not seem that heavy Southern contribution to peacekeeping today has introduced any significant shift to appointing Southern personnel in the Department. Indeed, quite the opposite: in 2005, just under two-thirds of the long-term personnel in the Department came from Northern states; in 2006, 38.5 per cent of the Department was composed of Northern personnel and in 2007 the figure stood at 44.3 per cent" (2009, 328).

In sum the power politics of peace operations take the form of a complex division of labor between UN member states in which influence is unequally distributed and struggles abound. Institutionally, this dynamic works along formal procedures but also informal practices that have developed over time, from pen holding to senior staffing.

The Power Politics of Peacekeeping in the Field

The previous section has shown how power is exercised in the institutional setting of UN headquarters. This section moves away from New York, the decision-making hub, to investigate the power politics of UN peace operations in the field by focusing on two of its manifestations. First, we argue that, far from being contained in sites of decision making, power politics permeates the implementation of UN peace operations on the ground by creating a disjuncture between the official mandate and what the operation can really accomplish. Second, we show that, in a context where UN peace operations are increasingly taking sides and becoming parties to the conflicts in which they intervene, peace operations can be used by local actors to further their own agenda. Rather than victims of great power politics, states that host peace operations are players in their own right.

Power Politics versus the Mandate

As the previous section showed, UN peace operations in the field cannot be understood without reference to power politics between states at UN headquarters. Once the Security Council has issued a mandate, its implementation continues to be dramatically affected by "the state of political relations among the members of the Security Council, especially its five permanent members (P5), and the impact of those relations at any one point on the dynamics of Council decision-making" (Berdal 2018, 4). In other words, "the global politics of peacekeeping are not and cannot be separated from the local dimensions of peacekeeping" (Rhoads 2016, 8). Peace operations are not driven only (or even mostly) by dynamics on the ground but also by political dynamics within the Security Council, which can sometimes contradict these missions' official mandate. Rather than responding to needs on the ground, they often respond to political imperatives that have little to do with resolving conflict and building peace.

It is clear, for instance, that since its deployment in 1999, the UN mission in the DRC (MONUC, followed by the UN Organization Stabilization Mission in the Democratic Republic of Congo [MONUSCO]) has taken political and military positions that reflect not only developments in the field but also developments within the Council. The mission was deployed in the context of a war that involved no fewer than ten African states, fighting in changing regional alliances and with the implicit backing of different individual Security Council members. Though the war formally ended in 2003, the DRC's neighbors continued to intervene in the country by sponsoring non-state groups. MONUC was deployed in this difficult context, with the mandate to use "all necessary means" to protect civilians. However, divisions and competing alliances within the Security Council meant that the mission's use of force was erratic and inconsistent. Historically, France has supported the DRC government while the UK and the US have aligned behind its neighbor Rwanda, which has waged a proxy war in the country (Cook 2010).

These diverging political alliances meant that, although the mission was mandated to robustly protect civilians, it often failed to go after Rwanda-backed armed groups. The strength with which the mission decided to confront (or not) armed groups had little to do with how much they threatened civilians. Rather, it reflected shifting regional alliances as well as periods of alignment or misalignment among the P3 (Rhoads 2016). During periods of alignment, the mission had the full backing to undertake robust actions and did go after armed groups. During periods of misalignment, however, the mission was wary of undertaking robust actions, despite its mandate to do so, as it was not sure that these would be backed up by the Security Council (Breakey and Dekker 2014).

Given the influence of New York power politics on the implementation of peacekeeping mandates in the field, peace operations cannot be understood simply as problem-solving instruments of conflict resolution (Bellamy 2004). They also constitute both instruments of power and one of the many battlefields on which power politics are fought.

The Power Politics of Taking Sides

If political dynamics from New York have such an important influence on peace operations in the field, does this mean that host governments are powerless? Critical analyses of UN peace operations have rightly emphasized their neoimperial and neocolonial nature (Cunliffe 2012), with one prominent scholar going as far as arguing that "the contemporary practice of peacebuilding"—with its emphasis on building liberal institutions meant to prevent the reoccurrence of conflict—"may be viewed as a modern rendering of the *mission civilisatrice*" (Paris 2002, 368). It is easy to think of UN peace operations as an imposition from the "international community" onto a weak target state. This is especially true in a context where peace operations' mandates are negotiated behind closed doors within the Security Council, with little consultation with the state that is to host a mission. It is therefore not surprising that "most member states actively resist efforts to be on the Council's agenda" and use their allies in the council to prevent it from happening (Security Council Report 2016, 5).

While the power imbalance between the Security Council and host states cannot be understated, it is also true that these states are not powerless in the face of international peacekeeping intervention. Rather than victims of power politics, host states are also players. Because UN peace operations are supposed to be deployed only with the consent of the host state, these states can threaten to withdraw consent to pressure the UN to align more closely with their own interests. Consent is one of the three core principles of UN peacekeeping and is key to legitimizing UN peace operations; without consent, the UN would be engaging in peace enforcement rather than peacekeeping (United Nations 2008). Because of this concern for legitimacy, host states that are unhappy with UN peace operations can argue that these missions do not respect their consent and therefore that "they are not being true to [their] professed values" (Hurd 2005, 503) rather than challenging them head-on. Host states have also been known to take more coercive action by refusing visas to UN staff, limiting the areas that the UN mission has access to, shutting down UN communications, or simply requesting the mission to leave.[4]

More important, UN peace operations can constitute important resources for governments that face opposition. While UN peace operations are supposed to abide by the principles of consent, impartiality, and nonuse of force (except in self-defense or defense of the mandate), they have taken increasingly assertive positions that challenge all three concepts. The UN continues to claim that peace operations are impartial, but in many cases they are clearly taking sides (Rhoads 2016) and in increasingly militarized ways. In four cases (Haiti, the DRC, the Central African Republic, and Mali), the Security Council has deployed missions with the mandate to "stabilize" the host country. While stabilization is an ill-defined concept (Gorur 2016), the four stabilization missions share one key characteristic: they are mandated to support the state against non-state armed actors. Many observers have pointed out that this directly puts in jeopardy the traditional peacekeeping principle of impartiality (Bellamy and Hunt 2015; Hunt 2017; Mac Ginty 2012).

In this context UN peace operations are not only an instrument of power politics for Security Council members; they can also be used by host states to maintain and consolidate their power. While states are internationally recognized legal entities, they may possess little local legitimacy. Challenged governments may be keen to paint their opponents as "threats to international peace and security" (Fisher and Anderson 2015) and to welcome a UN peace operation willing to take sides and bring them military support. In the DRC, for instance, the UN stabilization mission, MONUSCO, has participated in joint operations with the Congolese army against opposing armed groups, despite credible allegations that the Congolese army itself was involved in numerous human rights abuses (Berdal 2018). These actions prompted former USG for UN peace operations Alain Le Roy to remark that MONUSCO had become a "kind of gun for hire . . . President Kabila's own private military company" (Rhoads 2016, 150). His successor, Jean-Marie Guéhenno, similarly notes that the UN "[became] almost an auxiliary of the government" (2015, 159).

UN peace operations can therefore become an invaluable instrument for host states, giving them both the legitimacy and the resources to carry out actions that they would not have been able to undertake otherwise.

Regional Power Politics—Neighboring States Making the Most of Peacekeeping Missions

UN peace operations are mandated to tackle conflicts that extend beyond the borders of the host country. Peacekeeping missions are thus set amid regional dynamics that are key in understanding the struggle for influence of state and non-state actors. UN peace missions must be conceived as both opportunities and challenges for states to strengthen their influence relative to their neighbors, to their own constituencies, and to international interlocutors. This section investigates power dynamics related to domestic, regional, and international struggles for influence by countries bordering peacekeeping missions: (1) neighboring states pulled in a common objective to compensate for the shortcomings of a peacekeeping mission's mandate and capability; (2) neighboring states resisting being pushed out of a host country through the implementation of a peacekeeping mandate; (3) neighboring states engaging in a peace operation to facilitate the implementation of its mandate.

The following recent cases illustrate each of these power dynamics: the Force Conjointe du G5 Sahel (FC-G5 Sahel) in relation to the United Nations Multidimensional Integrated Stabilization Mission in Mali (MINUSMA); the organization of neighboring states, such as Rwanda, Uganda, and Burundi, relative to the implementation of MONUSCO; and the provision of troops by Rwanda, Uganda, and Ethiopia to reinforce UNMISS and the African Union–United Nations Mission in Darfur (UNAMID).[5]

Peacekeeping Mission as an Opportunity to Open a New Area of Influence: The Case of FC-G5 Sahel

Peacekeeping operations provide opportunities for bordering states to enhance their influence vis-à-vis their own constituencies, neighboring states (including the country hosting the UN mission), and international interlocutors. In 2017 the G5 Sahel, comprising Burkina Faso, Mali, Mauritania, Chad, and Niger, launched the Force Conjointe du G5 Sahel with the following four objectives: to combat terrorism and drug trafficking; to contribute to the restoration of state authority and the return of displaced persons and refugees; to facilitate humanitarian operations and the delivery of aid to affected populations; and to contribute to the implementation of development strategies in the G5 Sahel region (ICG 2017a, 2). The force represented both a new structure and a new mechanism to address key regional security issues excluded by the mandate of MINUSMA, notably the lack of a UN counterterrorist strategy (Boutellis and Fink 2016; Karlsrud 2019; Attree, Street, and Venchiarutti 2018; Charbonneau 2017).[6] The organization of this common force, conceived as part of an additional burden-sharing mechanism of security challenges facing the UN, creates a new locus for domestic, regional, and international influence (Karlsrud 2019). In this context the identification of gaps in peace operations' mandates is instrumentalized in the power play of domestic and regional actors and represents opportunities in creating new sites of power politics.

The FC-G5 Sahel is meant to facilitate monitoring and coordination among member states. It serves as an incentive structure for states in the region to engage in, join, or continue existing mobilization against common threats to their sovereignty (Desgrais 2018), notably terrorist activities and the traffic of illegal arms and goods. Heads of each member state in the FC-G5 explicitly endeavored to make the most of this new force in eradicating terrorism and suppressing irregular migration, as these are common threats to the political and economic stability of the member countries.[7]

This mobilization opens a threefold opportunity for the states involved: (1) their government leaders can reaffirm their authority over their own constituency and for their neighbors; (2) they can reinforce their appeals for further financial and military assistance from other richer UN member states (mostly the United States and France); and (3) the sacrifice of providing ground troops can reinforce their negotiating position vis-à-vis international interlocutors.

Less than a year after FC-G5 Sahel was implemented, a donor conference held in Paris resulted in over US$509 million pledged by Western allies for the Force Conjointe. The financial and material investments in the creation of this parallel structure and mechanism testified to interest in the force (Karslrud 2018) and opened new areas for power struggle domestically and regionally (International Crisis Group 2017a).[8] Yet as the funding and long-term budget for the force is neither established nor secured, the punctual inflow of substantial resources and money creates incentives and opportunities for domestic and regional political elites to further their own interests (International Crisis Group 2017a, 6).[9] On the regional base, the creation of a parallel force to the UN is seen as enhancing competition for funding and sponsorship with already existing regional players, such as the Economic Community of West African States (ECOWAS), of which three members are part of the force. In the international scene, given the persistent and growing jihadi threats in the region, the force is perceived as a key partner in addressing security challenges of concern to the Western allies and as a key opportunity to reinforce cooperation mechanisms with African counterparts (Karlsrud 2019, 9).

Peacekeeping Mission as Threat to Existing Area of Influence:
The Case of MONUSCO

The struggle for influence relative to the implementation of MONUSCO's mandate contrasts with the quest pursued by members of the FC-G5 Sahel. The containment of the threat within the Malian territory and the monitoring of cross-border activities are the key objectives for the states neighboring Mali. For those neighboring the DRC, the main objective is to prevent the implementation of the peace mission's mandate, including shutting or monitoring the frontiers too closely (United Nations 2001; International Crisis Group 2017b).[10] The porosity of the Congolese borders enables traffic of goods, resources, and armed groups (International Crisis Group 2017b).[11] The successful implementation of MONUSCO's mandate implies keeping out the regional actors fueling instability in the country. Yet for neighboring states, the very porosity of the frontiers is both lucrative and key for their own political stability.[12]

The Great Lakes regional states, including Rwanda, Burundi, and Uganda, represent a complex network of political and economic interactions with significant implications for peace, security, and governance. The region has interlinked conflicts and common fundamental problems that emanate from postcolonial challenges to state building and nation building, governance issues, identity division, and structural violence. Great Lakes states are interconnected owing to cross-border dimensions, transnational identities, exploitation, and illicit trade of natural resources, small arms, resource flow, and refugees.[13] Notoriously backed by Rwanda, the M23 was composed primarily of Tutsis and opposed the Hutu Power militia, Democratic Forces for the Liberation of Rwanda (FDLR; International Crisis Group 2017b). Today, the FDLR represents the largest armed group in the area. Predominantly composed of Hutu insurgents, it is operating throughout the Kivus in eastern DRC. As this group openly opposes the Rwandan government, the Rwandese authorities have used its presence as a justification for its interventions on Congolese territory (Institute of Security Studies 2015, 8). The Allied Democratic Forces (ADF) is a Ugandan rebel group formed by a merger of various discontented sectors of Ugandan society; the Lord's Resistance Army (LRA), an insurgent armed group from northern Uganda, is now operating in northern parts of DRC; and the National Liberation Forces (FNL) is composed of Burundian rebels.[14]

The implementation of the mandate of the peacekeeping mission in DRC implies the halting of neighboring states' illegal activities within the Congolese territory. Hence MONUSCO has prompted these states to modify their activities in order to secure their access to resources and maintain their influence on the DRC. The Force Intervention Brigade (FIB) initiated by the South African Development Community (SADC) was meant to work with MONUSCO to fight regional rebel groups. It successfully defeated the M23, but when it was then requested to target the FDLR, supported by members of the SADC, main sending countries backed down their contribution to the brigade (Karslrud 2018).[15] Through their sponsorship or support of armed groups operating in DRC, regional states are thus able to secure their access to natural resources on Congolese territory (United Nations 2001).[16]

Peacekeeping as Opportunity to Reinforce Area of Influence: The Cases of UNAMID and UNMISS

States can also seek to secure or to reinforce their regional area of influence by directly engaging in peacekeeping missions in bordering countries. This is notably the case of Ethiopia in UNMISS and UNAMID and of Kenya and Uganda in UNMISS. In these cases the involvement of neighboring states is geared toward a twofold objective of containing or reducing instability while also making sure to maintain an influence on and within the host country.

In the case of Ethiopia, the shared border with South Sudan hosts communities engaged in activities in both countries. Overlapping communal tensions combined with massive population displacement threatens sovereignty and security in the two states. Ethiopia's contributing to the UN peacekeeping mission is yet another way for the country to maintain its influence over its neighbor and to show its effort to international actors to gain their diplomatic, financial, and military support of regional stabilization efforts.[17] Ethiopia's interest in the stabilization of Darfur is also suspected to be linked to the country's claim with regard to Eritrea's borders and its opposition to independence. Darfur's secession movements have been closely connected with Eritrea's claim for independence. Ethiopia thus has an interest in the type of peace accord signed and maintained in Darfur (Hassan and Ray 2009).

Kenya has a vested interest in the success of the peacekeeping mission in South Sudan. As one of the top foreign investors in the country, Kenya is concerned with securing its influence over South Sudan. It is also concerned with current and planned mega infrastructure projects to improve the exploitation and transport of goods and high-return resources, such as oil, between regional partners (notably Ethiopia).[18] Such projects are significant for the socioeconomic development of the country and are intrinsically linked to the stability of South Sudan and to the terms of the peace negotiated by the warring parties. Kenya's key contribution to UNMISS can also be understood in light of the destabilizing potential of the increasing flow of refugees fleeing ongoing violence in South Sudan. The proliferation of small arms and small weapons is also problematic.

Uganda has manifold interests in the implementation of UNMISS's mandate. Uganda's support to the peacekeeping mission aims at securing its influence in South Sudan and at regaining neighboring allies with whom to expand political and economic exchanges.[19] One key dimension of Uganda's strategy relates to its long history of competition with Khartoum for the exportation of oil.

Uganda thus aims at closer cooperation with South Sudan, notably concerning trade. This objective of building stronger ties with the country can thus be understood as both a key driver and explanatory factor for Uganda's significant contribution in the UN mission (it is among the top ten police contributors).[20]

All in all, UN peace operations are home to fierce power politics at the regional level. These take various institutional forms, often going much beyond the formal procedure established by the Security Council. Today it is not an exaggeration to say that regional power politics play a determinant role in the unfolding of UN peace operations on the ground.

Conclusion

With its exhaustive member list, the UN is an obvious locus of power politics among states. But more than a locus, peace operations, initially conceived to quell divides between and within members, have turned out to be both a unique nexus and an instrument in the struggle for influence. Struggles are reconfigured within and around peace operations, presenting challenges but also offering opportunities for asserting power that would not have existed otherwise. We have shown that this is played out at three interconnected levels: at the headquarters, in the host country, and in the regions in which these missions are established. Even though P5 countries do dominate the process, the picture we painted shows a much more complex playing field than what is usually depicted in the media and in the literature. Given the intricacies of UN peace operations, opportunities also arise for other players to struggle for influence, including nonpermanent members of the council, regional neighbors, and even local actors involved in conflicts. The power politics we described certainly do not reduce to the crude acting out of "power over resources," to use Wivel and Paul's terminology (see the introduction).

At headquarters the design of UN peace operations reflects both formal and informal power struggles between distinct circles of influence. Though the decision making around UN peace operations functions under a veneer of multilateralism that diffuses responsibility among UN member states, it remains greatly influenced by and under the control of a small number of them. UN peace operations also generate new power dynamics within the host country. We thus explain how national authorities trade consent for international presence in exchange for support vis-à-vis domestic power challengers. Finally, peacekeeping missions open windows of opportunity for host states' neighbors to renegotiate regional power balances through complementary interventions, enhanced informal presence, or formal contribution to secure networks within and outside the area of operation. UN peace operations thus frame multifaceted power politics among actors who in return use these operations to further their interest through multilevel collective mobilization, thereby making the most of evolving institutional arrangements.

Notes

1. Security Council Report, "In Hindsight: Mandating Peace Operations," *Monthly Forecast*, September 2017, http://www.securitycouncilreport.org/monthly-forecast/2017-09/in_hindsight_mandating_peace_operations.php?print=true.

2. United Nations, *Summary of Troop Contributing Countries by Ranking*, September 30, 2017, https://peacekeeping.un.org/sites/default/files/msr_30_sep_2017-2.pdf.

3. According to UN Peacekeeping, "How We Are Funded," accessed September 19, 2018, https://peacekeeping.un.org/en/how-we-are-funded.

4. Adam Day, "To Build Consent in Peace Operations, Turn Mandates Upside Down," United Nations University, Centre for Policy Research, last modified January 19, 2017, https://cpr.unu.edu/to-build-consent-in-peace-operations-turn-mandates-upside-down.html.

5. This could also be the case with Kenya and Ethiopia providing troops for the African Union Mission in Somalia (AMISOM), although AMISOM is an operation put in place by a regional organization, the African Union, to work cojointly with the UN political mission in Somalia (UNSOM). In his assessment of troop contribution to AMISOM, Williams points to additional advantages of joining peace operations: "to gain the mantle of multilateral legitimacy for continued operations" and to ease "the financial burden" (2018, 181).

6. Adopted in June 2018, UNSC Resolution 2423 "maintains the instruction for MINUSMA to help the G5 Sahel build up its security force capacities by providing operational and logistical support as well as sharing intelligence" (Attree, Street, and Venchiarutti 2018, 27).

7. Mariam Keita, "Sommet du G5 Sahel contre le terrorisme: les engagements des chefs d'Etat!" *Info Matin*, February 7, 2017, http://info-matin.ml/sommet-du-g5-sahel-contre-le-terrorisme-les-engagements-des-chefs-detat/.

8. The International Crisis Group reports, "The G5's initial budget, if it remains at €423 million for the first year, corresponds to about one year of the total budget of all the armies put together" (2017a, 6).

9. "In Niamey, . . . France and the US have developed drone facilities in a joint compound. Another USD 110 million drone base is under development . . . in the town of Agadez, known to be a main transit point for migrants and a market town for the Tuaregs. . . . With these developments, Niger is becoming . . . the second most important country for U.S. military counterterrorism operations on the continent. Italy has decided to send almost 500 troops to northern Niger to train local troops and ultimately stem migration. Germany has also established a presence in Niger, first and foremost to function as a logistic base for its 650-strong engagement in MINUSMA in neighbouring Mali, but also to support Niger with equipment and expertise" (Karlsrud 2019, 13–14).

10. "Rwanda's military appears to be benefiting directly from the conflict. . . . The Panel has noted a great integration between the military apparatus, the State (civil) bureaucracy and the business community. RPA [Rwandan Patriotic Army] finances its war in the Democratic Republic of the Congo in five ways: (a) direct commercial activities; (b) profit from shares it holds in some companies; (c) direct payments from RCD-Goma [Rassemblement congolais pour la démocratie]; (d) taxes collected by the 'Congo desk' and other payments made by individuals for the protection RPA provides for their businesses; and (e) direct uptake by the soldiers from the land" (United Nations 2001).

11. In a 2017 report, the International Crisis Group states, "Areas of competition include major projects such as the Grand Inga dam, the exploration of hydrocarbons in eastern DRC and regional logistical corridors toward South Africa, Tanzania, Angola and Kenya. And

there are also the well-documented cases of Congolese resources transiting through neighboring countries such as Uganda, Rwanda and Burundi" (2017b, 23).

12. "The illegal exploitation of resources by Burundi, Rwanda and Uganda took different forms, including confiscation, extraction, forced monopoly and price-fixing" (United Nations 2001).

13. In 2001 Rwanda had become the first exporter of these resources, even though it does not have a single one of them on its territory. Uganda had become a major exporter of diamonds, even though it has no history of diamond mining. Uganda had a fifty-fold increase in its gold export within six years, whereas Rwanda's export of coltan became twice as important followed by its producing of cassiterite (United Nations 2001).

14. MONUSCO, "The Foreign Armed Groups," https://monusco.unmissions.org/en /foreign-armed-groups. According to Ahere (2012), the FNL in the DRC has provided rationale for the Burundian army to conduct operations in the country. This echoes a UN report by a panel of experts who documented how DRC natural resources, namely, coltan, were exploited by various armed groups under the supervision of Burundi (United Nations 2002).

15. Aaron Ross, in "African Rivalries Weaken U.N. Hand against Rebels in Congo" (Reuters, October 22, https://www.reuters.com/article/us-congodemocratic-rwanda-rebels-id USKCN0IB0CY20141022?feedType=RSS&feedName=worldNews), explains how "Tanzania and South Africa—the core of the beefed-up U.N. brigade—have frosty ties with Rwanda and voiced hesitation over a military solution to the FDLR." In 2001 a panel of experts had also identified both states as benefiting from the smuggling of DRC natural resources. South Africa and Tanzania were both identified as key transit countries for resources originating in the DRC (United Nations 2002).

16. "The consequence of illegal exploitation has been twofold: (a) massive availability of financial resources for the Rwandan Patriotic Army, and the individual enrichment of top Ugandan military commanders and civilians; (b) the emergence of illegal networks headed either by top military officers or businessmen. These two elements form the basis of the link between the exploitation of natural resources and the continuation of the conflict. Other contributing factors however exist—the roles played by some entities and institutions, and the opportunistic behavior of some private companies and influential individuals. . . . Some leaders in the region bear a direct responsibility. The Panel concludes that tough measures must be taken to bring to an end the cycle of exploitation of the natural resources and the continuation of the conflict in the Democratic Republic of the Congo" (United Nations 2001).

17. Rashid Abdi, "Ethiopia Must Continue to Help Stabilise South Sudan," Crisis Group, last modified January 30, 2017, https://www.crisisgroup.org/africa/horn-africa/ethiopia/ethiopia -must-continue-help-stabilise-south-sudan.

18. Paul Odhiambo and Augustus Muluvi, "Impact of Prolonged South Sudan Crisis on Kenya's Economic and Security Interest," *Africa in Focus* (blog), March 12, 2014, https://www .brookings.edu/blog/africa-in-focus/2014/03/12/impact-of-prolonged-south-sudan-crisis-on -kenyas-economic-and-security-interests/.

19. IRIN News, "Regional Interests at Stake in the South Sudan Crisis," March 19, 2014, http://www.irinnews.org/report/99802/regional-interests-stake-south-sudan-crisis.

20. United Nations, *Summary of Troop Contributing Countries.*

CHAPTER 11

Variable Geometry: Power and Institutions in the European Union

John A. Hall and Frédéric Mérand

Any inquiry seeking to explore the interactions between power and institution-alization must place the European case at the forefront of attention. For this is the continent where institutionalization has grown fastest in the modern world, leading Europhiles at times to declare that the powers of nation-states have been contained, even removed, by the creation of a thick surrounding web of agreements of all sorts. We cannot follow such optimistic voices, much as we might like to, given the obvious presence of countervailing arguments. Instead we will offer a picture of variability in the relations between power and institutions. This should be understood in two senses. First, brute power most certainly stands behind institutional development, both enabling it at times and curtailing it in different circumstances. Second, the precise relation between power and institutions varies between different fields—and of course over the historical record.

Our chapter has three parts. First, an account of the basic physiognomy of what has become the European Union is required to get a proper sense of the nature of this remarkable arrangement. Second, attention turns to six crises that have rocked the European Union in the most recent years. Third, we explain how the crises were handled, noting differences in effectiveness and paying particular attention to the dialectic of power and institutionalization. Like other scholars, we identify a process of "politicization" that affects both European institutions and member states' relation to them. Politicization puts power struggles at the heart of Brussels: not only among states but also among other organized groups. The conclusion begins by noting the problem of writing about a moving target, for history is, as Arnold Toynbee once put it, "on the move again." This makes some of our analyses at best reasoned guesses, and it pushes us to speculate on the possibilities of leadership.

The Burdens of History

European history in the late nineteenth and mid-twentieth century is a record of endless horror and disaster; war, famine, revolution, ethnic cleansing, forced population movement, and mass murder all contributed to the loss of seventy million lives, thereby removing any claim for this part of the world to represent the core of human civilization. Given this hideous record, it is remarkable that the recovery has been so swift and so great, creating in the postwar period the most stable and prosperous decades for this region within the whole of the historical record. At least three factors lie behind this remarkable record of progress.

A crucial element was European. The extreme right had been defeated, to be replaced by Christian democracy—the most important social pillar of postwar stability. The extreme left was defeated as well, in part with American help and most certainly within the context of the Cold War. All of this is to say that there was a move to the center, to a historical class compromise based on national reconstruction and economic growth (Milward 1992). But much more was involved. The years between 1870 and 1945 had seen a marriage of empire and nation. Powers felt that security lay in the possession of territory allowing both secure sources of supply and reliable markets so that they could then be geopolitically independent (Lieven 2000). This exacerbated geopolitical tensions and caused domestic problems with nationalities when the powers sought to strengthen themselves through homogenizing policies—which, of course, often created international tensions. The fundamental difference becomes clear with this in mind. The initial and the deepest root of the European project was the move of France and Germany to cease being geopolitically independent. The agreements over coal and steel introduced interdependence between the two great continental powers. The greatest genius that was involved was French. Within a single lifetime, France had been invaded by Germany three times. When one cannot win, it makes sense to embrace instead—with the consequence in this case over time of a move from calculation to positive endorsement. The point being made deserves highlighting: power—geopolitical sense—lay behind the creation of new institutions.

Just as important was the American presence, the desire, as Lord Ismay put it, to "keep the Russians out, the Americans in and the Germans down." What is involved here is in effect the other side of the agreement between France and Germany. States face a security dilemma, at the best of times managing to achieve peace through balance of power politics. The tragedy of Europe lay in its inability to manage this in 1914. The interwar years that followed were no better, with trade suffering deeply for the failure to establish geopolitical stability. What the Europeans could not do for themselves was provided by the United States. When warring parties cannot agree, an external mediator can be essential, and so it proved in this case. The North Atlantic Treaty Organization (NATO) has been led, is led, and will most likely always be led by an American general. Europe as a whole is only a semistate, as its ultimate sovereignty depends on decisions made externally.

The third feature is, of course, the creation of the institutions of the union itself. This is a world of great complexity; the *acquis communautaire* that now faces a country wishing to join the union includes more than sixty years of accumulated legislation on anything from banking rules to hunting season. Most of these are devoted to economic affairs, making the organization as a whole very much what Marx had in mind when he spoke of states that best managed the affairs of the bourgeoisie. Thankfully more than that is involved. A concern to protect minorities matters enormously as a condition of entrance, although it is proving hard to sustain progressive pressures in that regard for states once they are admitted. It is important to highlight two points here. First, the project as a whole depended in part at crucial stages on the backing of the United States. Jean Monnet went to Washington at key moments and was able to push the project because of the help he received (Anderson 2009). Second, this very fact points to a key characteristic of the union, one that is well-known: it is an elite project, driven by the brilliance of financiers, lawyers, and politicians without much input from below (Vauchez 2014).

The European project has developed and deepened since six states founded the European Economic Community in 1957. Over the years its institutions have proved to be both resilient and flexible—in other words, "elastic" (Hofmann and Mérand 2012). Perhaps most obvious in institutional terms is the creation of a currency and a bank to support it, albeit this is an arrangement to which not all countries belong. Today, the European Union is the strongest possible version of an "*associational cluster among states with some bureaucratic structures that create and manage self-imposed and other-imposed constraints on state policies and behaviors*" (Wivel and Paul, this volume). What features form the core of the union?

The first feature has already been noted, but it is so important that it deserves to be restated and remembered in a different way. It is useful to distinguish between different levels of social interaction, from local to national to international and finally to fully transnational. It is easy indeed to place the union within this range; it is an international governmental organization, a place where heads of state and government meet and make deals (Moravcsik 1998). Bargains are struck, behind doors, with few minutes kept, and often in all-night sessions, in a way that would have been familiar to Otto von Bismarck. Many considerations stand behind this view. The European Union itself is no Leviathan: it takes only a little more than 1 percent of the union's GDP into its own pocket, meaning that class struggle and democratic politics take place within the nation-states that make up the union (Fligstein 2008). Then there is the key fact that identities within the union are national before they are transnational. There is, in fact, considerable variation here. Countries that suffered most in World War II tend to be the most Europhile, while enthusiasm for the projects rise in line with social class position (Medrano 2003). Equally there is variation in the basic claim. The Court of Justice of the European Union (CJEU) provides a measure of transnationalism while nationalist demands from below have, as we will see, gained considerable salience in the most recent years.

The second feature has been mentioned as well. In military terms Europe is a worm, collectively the second-biggest military spender but incapable of defending itself. This fact helps explains some of the most troubled postwar economic history. Money is power, and the control of guns can lead to gaining the butter. Europe in the 1970s was forced to import American inflation, caused by the hegemon's refusal to pay for Vietnam and the Great Society by taxation rather than by printing money. There is some truth to the notion that the most recent financial crisis is a spillover from American behavior. This causes great resentment, but calls for an independent European policy rarely amount to much. For one thing, there is the cost involved, especially given the inability of different countries to create a commonly funded program for procurement and action. For another, earlier suggestions that Europe did not need a defence policy as it faced no threats have faded in the light of recent Russian behavior under Putin.

But if Europe is a military worm, it is also most certainly an economic giant. The population of the union is now larger than that of the United States, while its GDP is marginally larger. Measurement of economic capability is extremely difficult; one notes, for example, the continuing lead of America in some high-tech industries, not least due to the prowess of their universities, but against this may soon have to be set the cost of internal squabbling. Still, there can be no doubt of the basic fact: the European economies are securely placed within the Organization for Economic Cooperation and Development (OECD).

The final point to be made is equally comparative. The years in which the United States was the unipolar power have not led to great success in foreign policy terms. At the time of writing, Iranian influence has expanded in the Middle East as the Kurds are yet again betrayed, with the likelihood that the Assad regime will survive in Syria. This is what realism would lead one to expect—the assembling of coalitions of weaker powers to curb hegemonic pretensions. The European story is wholly different. The six original connected countries were joined by twenty-two more, with powerful linking arrangements being made available to others. It is important to remember that the 1973 enlargement changed the character of at least one state—Ireland—whose escape from life in Britain's shadow was the background condition that allowed for the emergence of the Celtic Tiger. But the much more important point is the return to Europe of Baltic, Central European, and Balkan states. The fate of some of these states will concern us later, for some developments, as is well-known, have been deeply flawed. Nonetheless, the success of this foreign policy is perhaps the greatest of the postwar period—absolutely unimaginable in the years before it suddenly unfolded.

Six Crises That Shook Europe

Eugene O'Neill once noted, "The past is the present, isn't it? It's the future, too." That is the question that now confronts us. Will the European Union retain its character as an international arrangement, lacking military power but blessed with prosperity? The question is a poignant one for obvious reasons. Not so long ago American writers were concerned with the emergence of a European super-power. In more recent years, the opposite mood has dominated assessments of the European Union—sclerotic, crisis ridden, and all too prone to complete collapse. Let us begin by listing—and by analyzing—the crises, noting in advance a general law of life and of politics. One crisis feels like one crisis, and two like two. But there is limited time to deal with problems, and three crises can have the intensity of four. This sort of iteration can degrade fast, with six crises gaining such huge intensity as to no longer be manageable.

Mentioning six crises in the last paragraph was not innocent. At all times there are niggles and problems in any organization, but six genuine crises have affected the European Union in recent years. We outline each of these crises, paying attention to the interactions between power and institutionalization involved in each. This is followed by analysis of the manner in which the different crises were handled. The union is managing these crises, less through solutions than through endless muddle; dangers remain, but the chances of complete collapse have been minimized.

The referendum of 2016 deciding in favor of Britain leaving the European Union has a claim, at first sight, to be the most serious crisis that the union has faced (Matthijs 2017). Most important in this regard is the general background condition, namely, that of a change in the character of nationalism. Traditionally, nationalism was often an elite affair, a means by which society could be organized to allow it to compete more effectively in the world arena. In Denmark the elite was wholly in favor of joining the euro in September 2000, but the referendum went the other way. Male voters outside Copenhagen, at times unemployed and characteristically lacking high education standards, voted against ever closer union. This was an early sign of nativist nationalism, of the revolt of those unable to swim easily in a larger world, in part owing to lack of linguistic competence, and prone to resentment at being left behind. This is the world most graphically theorized by Karl Polanyi ([1944] 2001) in one of the great books to emerge from Austro-Hungary. Capitalism demands endless change, but the pain that this involves can lead to a call for society to protect itself. This syndrome was most certainly present in the British case, allied to resentment at the presence of outsiders, both from outside and from within the union. But the huge risk of Brexit would not have been envisaged but for a British peculiarity, that of an upper class, key elements of which had never reconciled themselves to the loss of empire. This upper class was thereby stuck in the illusion of Britain's "punching above its weight," of its still being a great enough power to survive alone (Rhodes 2016).

This latter point deserves consideration, for it suggests that Brexit is perhaps not the greatest crisis faced by the union. Elements within Britain never wanted to join in the first place, something which is not true of any other large country. And a rather important point follows from this. It is often forgotten that Immanuel Kant's much cited proposal for perpetual peace left a role within it for the continuation of war. Memory is important in life, Kant argued, and the members of the liberal league were likely to remain peaceful when they could see the deleterious effects of war outside their own pacific union (Doyle 1983). One can sense the European Union bracing itself for continued existence as the costs of Brexit become ever more apparent.

A greater threat to the union is the "future of the euro" (Matthijs and Blyth 2015). After almost a decade of nominal convergence and currency stability, the eurozone turned into a freak show when Greece announced it had largely underreported its government debt and Ireland and Spain ran to the rescue of their bankrupt banking sectors with oversized bailouts. This led markets to fear that other eurozone members, notably Portugal, Italy, and Cyprus, may have to default. The Great Recession that had begun in 2007–8 turned into a sovereign debt crisis, which the EU was ill equipped to address. Why? To prevent moral hazard, the Stability and Growth Pact adopted with the creation of the single currency imposed strict budgetary rules that were meant to bring all members in line. But what could the EU do when these rules were either broken or wholly inadequate for countercyclical measures? While considerable financial help was ultimately extended to Greece, Ireland, and Portugal, it came with a dire reputational cost for Brussels, soon portrayed as the heartless champion of neoliberal austerity. And while the Irish economy rebounded, Southern countries remained stuck in a downward spiral of economic stagnation, unsustainable budgets, and uncompetitive industries.

Of course, the incomplete architecture of the eurozone is largely to blame for this mess. In typical neofunctionalist fashion, the designers of the euro believed that monetary union would spill over and lead to macroeconomic coordination, a common EU treasury, and perhaps even joint economic stabilizers (Marsh 2013). The comfortable illusion of nominal interest convergence between 1999 and 2007 explains in part why political reforms didn't happen the way they should have. In the end, the crisis led to important "economic" initiatives to complement the "monetary" union, such as the banking union, the European Stability Mechanism (ESM), and stronger economic guidance through the European Commission, but they still fall short of a federal model with substantial transfers to address asymmetric shocks and economic divergences.

Yet underneath this is something much more serious. The growing conflict between northern nations that want risk reduction and southern nations that want risk sharing is founded on a toxic mix of divergent economic interests, opposing economic philosophies, and enduring nationalisms. It results in a lack of solidarity that is incompatible with European unification. This is a complex matter. Of course, there have been problems with the economies of much of southern Europe, but we need to understand the larger context—and can do so by remembering the plan that John Maynard Keynes put forward at Bretton Woods. The world economy suffers both when countries have surpluses and when they have deficits, in Keynes's view, and he accordingly sought to deal with both problems (Skidelsky 2001). The power of the great surplus country of the time, the United States, meant that Keynes's plan was not adopted. But the problem of fiscal imbalances is a real one. It is known quite generally, as Ben Bernanke (2005) claimed, that a fiscal imbalance was the cause of the 2008 financial crisis. The huge Chinese surplus was lent to the United States, allowing for the growth of subprime mortgages. A similar situation evolved within Europe. Germany's enormous surpluses allowed countries such as Ireland and Greece to borrow— and to do so at interest rates made artificially low by the presence of Germany's powerful economy within the currency union of the euro. Balancing the European economy requires Germany to absorb more of its own surplus, something that has been made difficult by Chancellor Gerhard Schroeder's neoliberal changes since these changes diminished working-class purchasing power. In that sense the eurozone is a microcosm of global economic imbalances, but one that has political meaning.

The refugee crisis is the third challenge faced by the EU, and politically the most explosive one. In a way, the specter of immigration has haunted Europe at least since the 1970s, when Western European labor markets closed their doors to guest workers without precluding family reunion. Immigrants stayed, which was not to everybody's liking. Meanwhile, in the East, immigration was not even on the agenda. As Hanspeter Kriesi (2016) and others have shown, an "integration-demarcation" cleavage crystallized in the 1980s and 1990s, allowing radical right parties, such as the National Front in France, to reshape the political landscape away from the traditional left-right opposition. This was mostly a domestic problem until such parties decided to also take on the EU (Hobolt and de Vries 2016). Then, in the summer of 2015, between one and two million Syrian, Eritrean, and Afghan refugees reached Hungarian, Austrian, German, and Danish borders—and the migrant crisis became a European one, fueling the populist challenge to the EU (see the sixth crisis).

Why did migration become a European problem? In fact, "2015 was not a turning point" (Guiraudon 2018). Since the 1990s the European Union had actually developed a set of collective rules to deal with the external dimension of the free movement of peoples, a formative treaty right that became more tangible when border controls were abolished in the Schengen area. Formal immigration remained a member state competence, but to prevent asylum shopping, the Dublin Convention established the principle that asylum requests must be processed in the first European country of arrival. Given the geography of migration, this meant Greece and Italy. Unable to cope with the rising tide, the Greek and Italian governments let refugee-status seekers go through their territory undocumented. While some destination or transit countries erected barriers, Angela Merkel opened Germany's arms, effectively putting an end to ill-conceived rules that apportioned the burden unfairly and inefficiently. To alleviate the stress on well-intentioned or badly situated countries, the European Commission came with the audacious plan to Europeanize the allocation of refugee seekers. But it faced a wall of negligence and foot-dragging, if not outright opposition. To stem the tide, Brussels and Berlin then turned to Turkey, striking an unpalatable deal whereby Ankara stopped migrants before they reach Greek shores in exchange for European discretion vis-à-vis Recep Tayyip Erdoğan's authoritarian drift.

The refugee crisis was instrumentalized in domestic political contexts, especially in Hungary and during the Brexit referendum, exacerbating a fourth European crisis: the rise of internal protectionism. Images of refugees roaming chaotically through the Continent, threatening local identities, jobs, and security, were collapsed with a distinct phenomenon: the free movement of peoples, goods, services, and capital. Since 1957 these four factors of production make up the core of the EU treaties, which treat them as fundamental freedoms. For a long time, they seemed to pose little problem. In reality the movement of services and capital remained highly constrained by domestic rules, and much to the chagrin of economists, European workers moved very little, especially in comparison with workers in the US.

This changed drastically in the first decade of the twenty-first century. First, propelled by financial globalization, the internet, EU market rules, and the adoption of the euro, capital started to move much more quickly across the Continent, creating a fertile ground for tax evasion, fiscal optimization, *délocalisation*, and financial instability. Second, the EU pushed the Bolkestein directive, an attempt to liberalize the market for services, embodied by the infamous Polish plumber, which turned into a public relations disaster during the 2005 French referendum on the constitutional treaty. And third, the accession of eastern countries expanded the supply of European citizens willing to move west to fill job opportunities. In some countries, like the UK, the easterners' presence became synonymous with the government's inability to manage migration. In others, like France, where easterners were much fewer, the theme of the neoliberal race to the bottom mobilized the public against the "detached workers" directive, which allows firms to import temporary workers from the rest of Europe. Whether of capital, services, or peoples, "free movement" has become the main target of populist parties, right and left, that seek a return to national sovereignty (Mounk 2018).

A fifth crisis is caused by the incomplete settlement reached with Russia after the end of the Cold War. While relations with Russia were always more important in the corridors of Brussels' other international institution, NATO, the EU was also founded as a capitalist and democratic club of US allies. The accession of neutral states (Ireland in 1973 and then Sweden, Austria, and Finland in 1995) changed little about the union's "western" alignment and security protection. Far from settling accounts in a renewed European security architecture (François Mitterrand's preference in 1990), eastern enlargement exacerbated tensions between the EU and Moscow. The union's desire to extend an eastern partnership to former Soviet satellites, letting open the prospect of accession, encouraged pro-democratic, pro-Western movements, notably in Ukraine, which caused grief and stimulated aggressiveness in Moscow. When the EU tempered its enthusiasm, many observers—and especially some of its most militant eastern members, Poland and the Baltic states—blamed it for making false promises and not coming to Ukraine's support.

The war in Ukraine showed the immense advantages obtained by former Soviet bloc countries that joined the EU and NATO on time, but also the strategic gamble the EU took in extending its hand to them (Haukkala 2015). While the risk of a formal Russian attack on any EU member state is minimal, enlargement has been put on hold for quite a while by Russia's intransigence—with the exception, perhaps, of the western Balkans. The question is what to do with neighbors that will remain neighbors. On the surface all EU governments support increasing defense spending to deal with an unnamed resurgent threat on the eastern front. But on the specifics of foreign policy, the EU is as divided as ever between southern and western members (France, Italy, Germany, Spain) that seek good relations with Russia, and thus strongly oppose further enlargement, and a northern-eastern group (Baltics, Poland) that wants the EU to take on a firmer stance vis-à-vis Russia. The latter are weakened by the exit of their only western ally, the UK, but populist leaders in Hungary or Austria play a dangerous game of cozying up to Putin while seeking to undermine the EU.

These five crises come together in a last, ongoing one: the rise of populism. Anti-European, feeding off ill-managed migration patterns and growing inequality, implicitly or explicitly supported by Russia, populists experienced their greatest victory during the Brexit referendum. But populism is by no means limited to the UK. During the crisis, fringe and established antisystem parties managed to turn themselves into credible political alternatives all over the continent (Mudde 2016). Although France's National Front had been considered a threatening force since Jean-Marie Le Pen's electoral upset in 2002, it is their Italian and Austrian cousins that stormed into office. Since 2018 the Freiheitliche Partei Österreichs (FPÖ) and the Lega have controlled important ministries (notably Home Affairs) and a large part of the government agenda in Vienna and Italy. In Eastern Europe Viktor Orban's authoritarian populist strategy is emulated by former communists and nationalists alike, from Warsaw to

Bratislava. Meanwhile, even marginal parties such as the Alternative für Deutschland can blackmail mainstream government parties thanks to their growing electoral force.

Although most of these parties come from the radical right tradition, not all do. Before it was tamed by international creditors, Greece's Syriza came to power on a populist agenda. In coalition with the Lega, the Movimiento 5 Stelle sees itself as progressive, and in France Jean-Luc Mélenchon's France Insoumise has become as powerful as Le Pen's National Front. There is probably little the EU, as an international institution, can do to address populism, but there is no denying that European integration is supported by the very same forces that aggrieve populist voters: social liberalism and the free circulation of people (Norris and Inglehart 2018). In turn, domestic populism infuses the power politics of member state governments with aggressive nationalism, which turns the EU into a less comfortably institionalized place.

The Return of Politics

A variable geometry of power politics and collective institutions explains how the first five crises we discussed were handled. While European institutions gained considerable strength through the Brexit and eurozone crises, they remained ineffective to deal with the refugee crisis and Russia. As for the sixth crisis, the rise of populism, it remains in full swing with, if the reader forgives us the expression, a positive outlook.

It would be wrong in our view to underestimate the union's institutional consolidation since 2010 (Dehousse and Boussaguet 2014). Although it remains lacking, eurozone governance has been strengthened by a fiscal compact "with teeth" since it gives considerable macroeconomic and budgetary surveillance powers to the European Commission. The European Central Bank has also expanded its authority with the banking union, which includes a single supervisory and resolution mechanism. The reaction to Brexit and Russia has generated a new consensus on the need to increase the commission's role in defense affairs, notably through a beefed-up security budget. Politically, the commission gained prominence by leading the EU in Brexit negotiations, but more important, the European executive has successfully protected the four freedoms underpinning the single market that were threatened by the UK's request for decoupling, convincing the remaining twenty-seven member states that this constituted the core principle of the European project. While the EU's resettlement and relocation plan for refugees is considered a failure in practice, the commission has managed to get the idea approved in theory—no small feat—and it has transformed Frontex into a credible European Border and Coast Guard Agency.

At the same time, large states have also expanded their role and influence in European politics. The "polycrisis" led to an intensification of European summits, the "European Council" of heads of state and government that has become the main instrument of crisis management and policy leadership. In the economic sphere, the Eurogroup of eurozone finance ministers has become the key decision-making forum (Bickerton, Hodson, and Puetter 2015). Now, these two institutions embody intergovernmentalism and the domination of large and rich states, especially Germany, which projects incommensurable economic and symbolic power. Between 2010 and 2017, this has meant that Chancellor Angela Merkel and Finance Minister Wolfgang Schäuble were Europe's most powerful politicians, without whom no important decision could be made. They were flanked by a reliable group of smaller leaders, for example, the Dutch, the Finnish, or the Slovaks, who rarely expressed dissent. Italy, Portugal, Spain, and France were often isolated.

Germany does not win all the time. On the refugee crisis, for example, Merkel was able to set the agenda but she faced mounting opposition among eastern leaders that eventually defeated her plans. In addition, intergovernmental structures mean that even small member states are capable of halting what they see as going against their national interest. By reducing the domestic "win-set" of pro-European forces, the rise of nationalism and populism empowers national leaders who threaten Armageddon if they are outvoted in the council or even criticized in parliament. Viktor Orban is the most prominent example of this tendency (Lendvai 2017).[1] This is not to mention areas, such as fiscal policy, in which the rule of unanimity protects delinquents such as Malta and Cyprus. On agenda setting, however, it is hard to find policy areas in which France, Italy, and the UK managed to get their ideas through, at least on substance. One exception may be the Greek crisis, during which Schäuble eventually conceded to saving the country from bankruptcy, albeit with strong conditionality. Despite his ambition for France to play a historic role in European integration, it is far from evident that Emmanuel Macron will shift his country to the winning side.

While the parallel growing authority of European institutions and member states may appear to be a win-win evolution, strengthening European governance through more infrastructural power, it has heightened the degree of conflict on different levels. In Brussels "politicization" is the new name of the game. It refers to "an increase in polarization of opinions, interests or values and the extent to which they are publicly advanced towards policy formulation within the EU" (de Wilde 2011). When Jean-Claude Juncker became president of the European Commission in 2014, after he had won the first transnational presidential campaign between *Spitzenkandidaten* during parliamentary elections, he said he would lead a "political Commission." This means several things: the enhanced legitimacy of an elected president with a program, his reliance on a political coalition of Christian Democrats, Social Democrats, and Liberals to govern, the explicit willingness to engage with domestic politics and address member state interests—all of which run counter to the idea of an impartial, neutral, and technocratic international secretariat that many member states would prefer to see.

For those who want to make the EU more visible, more powerful, more responsive to cleavages, and thus perhaps more democratic, a bit like a federal state, politicization is a compelling strategy. But it is also a potentially dangerous one if opposition to specific EU actions turns into opposition to the EU itself (Hix and Bartolini 2006; Papadopoulos and Magnette 2010). In Brussels the return of politics has been accompanied by haggling over posts, decisions that can be explained less by rule following than by the desire to please a government from the same political family, and conversely a tendency to step on toes that no commission had since Jacques Delors. Within member states politicization is associated with the increased salience of European issues on domestic politics; each election (in the Netherlands, Austria, France, the Czech Republic, etc.) seems to be interpreted as a referendum on the EU. Not surprisingly, as people become more aware of what the EU does, they like it less. After forty years of "permissive consensus," we have entered the era of the "constraining dissensus" (Hooghe and Marks 2009).

In the heydays of supranationalism, a "political Europe" meant "more Europe," or more federalism. Today, it can also mean that interstate and cross-national conflicts are exposed in public, bringing open antagonism in the corridors of Brussels (van Middelaar 2013). The long-standing cleavage between pro-European and Euroskeptic forces is well documented. It is largely embedded in the domestic politics of member states and also in the European Parliament (Hurrelmann, Gora, and Wagner 2015; Helbling, Hoeglinger, and Wüest 2010). But three additional cleavages have emerged in the past decade (Hutter, Grande, and Kriesi 2016). The first cleavage is economic. It pits (Nordic) creditor against (southern) debtor nations and has so far prevented a major deepening of the economic and monetary union. The second cleavage is cultural. Focused on migration and the rule of law, it opposes liberals, concentrated in the West, and conservatives, who tend to be overrepresented in the East. This cleavage has made it difficult to make progress on a common asylum policy. The last cleavage, which has been paid less attention in the public opinion literature, is geopolitical; it distinguishes governments and parties that seek to accommodate Russia from governments and parties that want to challenge it. Although France and Germany have recently moved toward a less accommodationist position, the impact of that cleavage on the EU's external policy is considerable.

These four political cleavages increasingly structure European institutions but could also undermine them, forcing governments to become more or less prone to cooperate with each other inside European institutions. They could also bring about differentiated integration, encouraging core groups to move along, while leaving the discontent or the laggard by the wayside (Schimmelfennig and Winzen 2014). Whether they strengthen, weaken, or truncate international institutions, these cleavages point to a degree of politicization that is quite unique among international institutions, suggesting that power politics goes beyond traditional interstate bargaining. They reflect the fact that the EU has accrued more authority than any other organization (de Wilde and Zürn 2012). For that reason, politicization is unlikely to be reversed.

In sum, although it is self-evident that states seek to use the EU as an instrument to pursue their goals, what distinguishes Europe from other regions is that power politics has come to mean more than "*the efforts by states to influence the formulation, application, and enforcement of the rules and regulations of a given institution as well as the control of bureaucratic positions and allocation of resources within it*" (Wivel and Paul, this volume). Increasingly, European power politics involves "politics based on the use of power to influence the actions and decisions of actors that claim, or exercise, authority over a political community" (Goddard and Nexon 2016, 3). That is, it includes not only interstate struggles but also distributional and cultural politics among organized groups and people. Combined with the increased salience of European symbols, this makes the "politics of everyday Europe" (McNamara 2015).

Conclusion: The Question of Leadership

In the preceding section, we have alluded to the Franco-German couple and its substitution by German leadership during the polycrisis. If "Merkozy" was not taken very seriously, "Merkhollande" never caught on. According to the late Ulrich Beck (2013), the question of a European Germany had once again been replaced by a German Europe.

Who really exerts leadership in Europe? In comparison with other regional contexts, Europe is remarkable for its balance of bloody power politics and strong international institutions. As we have argued throughout this chapter, this balance is of variable geometry. The European Central Bank and the Court of Justice are the only European institutions that are truly able to impose their authority. Their independence and reach were designed by member states precisely for that purpose. On regulatory issues and anything for which there is a legal basis to protect the free movement of goods, services, capital, and peoples, the room for compromise is wider because majority is the rule, which means that the European Commission enjoys some autonomy in setting the agenda and forging deals.

But as anyone who has spent time in Brussels knows, the influence of member states—and especially large ones—always looms large. Among the twenty-seven member states, two have always stood out. Between 1957 and 2000, the Franco-German axis, couple, or engine played the key role. France had the nuclear weapon, a seat on the Security Council, and global ambitions. Germany had money and political stability. On occasions France and Germany were guided or supported by a foreign power, the US, or the EU institutions they had created. Washington and Brussels sometimes helped the two countries with often diametrically opposed views to strike deals. But neither the US nor the EU was ever able to really counter an agreement a French president and a German chancellor would reach.

After 2000 the dominant view became that of a stark choice between German leadership or no leadership. Although the rise of German power after reunification matters, the reason is also institutional. On the economy it is quite clear that Germany has and continues to exert leadership as the widely perceived paymaster. Because it signs the check, Berlin has been careful to keep the Eurogroup and the ESM strictly intergovernmental. On migration, despite real communitarian inroads since the 1990s, most member states have been reluctant to follow Germany's (and the commission's) lead. The ability of Berlin to push others around is more limited when there is no money involved.

The UK gone, we see three possible scenarios for the foreseeable future. Each scenario hinges on a specific configuration of institutional dynamics and domestic politics in key member states. Note that we exclude the EU's unravelling, which remains unlikely even after Brexit and the very real possibility of more populist victories.

The first scenario is a further consolidation of institutional power in Brussels after the haphazard, emergency-driven advances of the past decade (White 2015). This could take the shape of a new treaty in which the president of the commission is merged with the president of the European Council; a European finance minister is appointed to head a real treasury for the eurozone, able to issue eurobonds; the EU is given a substantive role in defense cooperation; and unanimity is lifted for issues such as fiscal policy. Possible if a coalition of Social Democrats and Greens ever take over the German government while France remains in the hands of a pro-European president, this scenario is not likely at this stage.

The second scenario will depend on whether Emmanuel Macron's gamble pays off. He is the first French president to have been elected on a salient pro-EU platform. Rather than promising a reform of European institutions that would shield the "French model," he has committed to implementing French reforms that would help convince Germany to move toward political union around the eurozone. Beyond the specifics, which may evolve according to political expediency, his strategy is to put France back in a leadership position, along with Germany and with the UK out of the way. At the European level, he wants to lead a progressive, pro-European coalition against conservative, nationalist forces. If he succeeds (and more than a five-year mandate may be required to pass judgment), small, recalcitrant, ineffective, or supranational EU partners may be in for a ride. The power of great powers will be firmly established, but in the thickest institutional context ever seen. Although the Free Democratic Party's presence in the German government would have delivered a stronger blow to his ideal, the difficult formation of a Christian Democratic Union (CDU)–Social Democratic Party (SPD) coalition has lowered Macron's ambitions, especially with regard to eurozone reforms. Here again, the German partner seems to be missing.

The last scenario is muddling through, and as students of European history, we know it is the most likely. The EU has survived the worst crisis of its history, the euro project is saved, and populist forces stagnate, which delays the need for radical reform. The institutions created after the crisis, such as the ESM and banking union, will consolidate but not significantly expand their reach. The EU's reputation and legitimacy depend more on the general economic and political climate than on the actual performance of European institutions. Political leadership will be slightly rebalanced in favor of France in the short term, but Germany remains primus inter pares. It is also probable that the eurozone and Schengen will become ever more synonymous with the EU. The UK gone, the eurozone now represents 85 percent of the EU's GDP, while Schengen covers 93 percent of the EU's population, which means that marginal member states will need to decide where they stand.

Concluding with the likelihood of muddling through is not mere intellectual laziness on our part. It is a reflection of the considerable stickiness of European institutions. Against all odds, the EU has weathered the storm of the economic and financial crisis. There was no Grexit. The eurozone did not implode. So far Brexit has been much more of a nuisance to its instigators than to Brussels. While antisystem and far right parties can be expected to continue to enjoy success in domestic politics, they have almost everywhere toned down their anti-EU rhetoric (in favor, it must be added, of not particularly savory anti-immigration platforms). What has been built still stands and the balance between power and institutions remains, but in a context where organized groups pay more attention.

Note

1. It is worth noting that as long as unanimity-1 is required to implement Article 7, the EU's institutional structure lacks practical means to discipline countries moving in an illiberal direction.

Part V

Conclusions

CHAPTER 12

The Dynamic Relations between Power Politics and Institutionalization: A Neo-Gramscian Intervention

Annette Freyberg-Inan

What Do We Know and What Don't We?

There is, in fact, a whole lot we already know. We know that power differences between states matter for the design and content of international institutions: the powerful have more influence on them, and power dynamics characterize decision-making processes within formal institutions (see, e.g., Gruber 2000; Steinberg 2002; Stone 2004; Drezner 2008; Dreher, Sturm, and Vreeland 2009; Thompson 2010; Copelovitch 2010; Lim and Vreeland 2013; Allen and Yuen 2014). Thus, power is exercised through and can be augmented by institutionalization. We also know that, while it provides them with benefits, institutionalized cooperation simultaneously constrains states in their exercise of power and may even affect their relative power positions (see, e.g., Lake 1999; Ikenberry 2001; Voeten 2001; Thompson 2009; Kreps 2011; Weitsman 2014). Institutions can sometimes shift the outcomes of interaction between states away from what they would likely have been without them. Thus, institutionalization can counteract power politics.

As argued by the editors in the introduction to this volume, it makes no sense to juxtapose a world of self-help and power politics with one of institutionalization and cooperation. Not only is "institutionalized cooperation . . . often the result of the 'power politics of peace,' for example, balancing threat or power or exercising hegemony" (see also Wivel 2004), it is also evident that no matter how deeply institutionalized the politics, power struggles will never be absent from them (see the chapters by Martin-Brûlé, Pingeot, and Pouliot and by Hall and Mérand, in this volume). The previously cited and many other studies have expanded our understanding of the complex dynamics linking power politics and international institutionalization, enough so to reject as evidently silly the juxtaposition of a cliché structural realist vision of institutions as epiphenomenal to power politics with a cliché liberal-constructivist vision of power politics' death by institutions (see the chapter by Sørensen). However, as a rule, relevant international relations (IR) scholarship remains wedded to a realist-inspired view of power as material, relational, and the prerogative of states. This is also illustrated by most (though not all) contributions to this volume. I will instead advocate a neo-Gramscian perspective and argue that we need to leave state centrism and strictly material and relational conceptions of power behind to shed more light on the central question posed by this volume: *What is the relationship between power politics and institutionalization? Can the latter constrain or even overcome the former?*

How would we know if it can? Institutionalization constraining power politics would emphatically *not* have to mean that states would no longer be key actors in world politics nor that it would no longer matter how powerful states are vis-à-vis their peers. However, it *would* have to mean that relative power would at least occasionally fail to predict the policy outcomes of international interaction. Explicitly or implicitly, all contributions to this volume admit that this may well happen or in fact does happen. Yet all fail to embed this recognition in a fully developed analytical framework, and most fail to take seriously the opening this constitutes for potential fundamental change to world affairs. The reason for the second lacuna is their commitment to various versions of IR realism. Realist-inspired contributions to the debate adopt a state-centric ontology and predominantly material and relational conceptions of power.[1] These theoretical commitments, while delivering a range of valuable payoffs, also result in several blind spots when one explores the relationship between institutionalization and power. The remainder of this section will show how. The next section will then develop my own neo-Gramscian take and explain its added value. It will show how we can recognize that power politics remains a core feature of international relations even as international institutions are becoming ever more numerous and comprehensive, and yet simultaneously take a more open stance with respect to the possibility of political transformation.

Realist Contributions

Opening the conversation in this book, the chapters by Barkin and Weitsman and by Ripsman divert the discussion from the relationship between power politics and institutionalization to the Abbott and Snidal (1998) question: Why do states (including great powers) spend so much time, resources, and influence on international institutions? Obviously, this is puzzling from a structural realist point of view suspecting such institutions of irrelevance. As pointed out by Ripsman, neoclassical realism moves us significantly beyond structural realist accounts by pointing out that while "states construct foreign policy to respond to international imperatives," "domestic political arrangements . . . have an intervening influence between systemic pressures and national foreign policy responses." This also helps explain why states, and even great powers, find benefits in setting up, joining, maintaining, and supporting international institutions. In his contribution Ripsman also shows that the perceived legitimacy associated with operating through international institutions and thereby bestowed on the policies of institutionally cooperating states matters both domestically and internationally with direct consequences for governmental power. This is an important observation to which I will return later. However, remaining wedded to realism, Ripsman does not see this as potentially enhancing the power of institutions in ways that could transform world politics away from a predominance of relative state power. It is not clear why not. From a range of alternative theoretical perspectives, one may legitimately ask whether (and when) the power payoffs of the legitimacy (and other benefits) granted by institutionalized cooperation may not lead to an "embedded realism"—or even an "embedded liberalism" (see the chapter by Rosamond)—in which state decision making is in fact so heavily constrained by institutional commitments that power has in good part gone elsewhere.

Barkin and Weitsman's "realist institutionalism" addresses the same question and comes closer to the position I will defend later. It is evidently true that institutions both bestow power and pose constraints on its operation (see also Barnett and Duvall 2005), and it is useful to know how they do so, as the authors begin to show. It is furthermore important to relax the focus on formal institutions, which characterizes most of this book, to understand that power also operates through and is constrained by *informal* institutions, unwritten rules, and norms. However, also in this contribution, a realist commitment to state centrism prevents us from fully grasping the dynamics of interaction between power politics and institutionalization as processes that transcend interstate relations. On the positive side, Barkin and Weitsman come closest to actually theorizing the relevance of the legitimacy benefits for state policy provided by institutions for both domestic and international audiences. This is made possible by taking on board constructivist thought on power as both material and ideational (e.g., Barnett and Duvall 2005; Mattern 2001; Krebs and Jackson 2007; Barkin 2010). This is not a bad idea, but I argue that there is a better one: a neo-Gramscian take on the power politics–institutionalization dynamic is more appropriate because it allows us to analyze the workings of material and ideational power *together* and to see how such complex power can become embedded in institutions in ways that can both enhance and undermine the operation of power politics.

Lobell and Nicholson's contribution in part 4 of this volume takes up one side of the power politics–institutionalization dynamic and addresses the question of how institutions *limit* the pursuit of power. Their answer is that they operate as structural modifiers (see Snyder 1996), affecting states' interaction capacity, competition, socialization, and, hence, behavior. They make the important observations that structural modifiers may be ideational and that a hegemon might not be necessary to create and enforce the rules, both of which are crucial to understand the transformative potential of institutionalization. However, they remain wedded to both structuralism and a predominantly material conception of power when they argue that "successful practices [i.e., socialization] are determined by the structure of the system itself and not by individual leaders, their regime type, or leaders' beliefs and ideas." I will argue later that we should instead include ideas as immaterial sources of power *within* our conceptualization of structure, which simultaneously grants a greater role to agency and thus to potential for change than found in materialist structuralist accounts. This allows us to see more comprehensively why and how institutionalization both enables and constrains the operation of power and also how, as implied by Lobell and Nicholson, international socialization does not *necessarily* have to lead state behavior to diverge from realpolitik, as often uncritically assumed by liberal-constructivist approaches.

Wivel and Paul's contribution in part 3 takes up the opposite side of the power politics–institutionalization dynamic and addresses the question how institutions *enable* the pursuit of power. It specifically focuses on the ways in which they can support states' soft-balancing strategies. Once again, institutions are characterized as important sources of legitimacy for state policy, in addition to other benefits. This contribution also sheds important light on how institutionalization can actually counteract the logic of power politics, by arguing that "states use institutional soft balancing to counter violations of the rules of the game in international relations, in particular when these violations are committed by great powers." Also, that "states use institutional soft balancing in cases of threats and violations of the territorial integrity of friendly states and coalition partners" cannot but strengthen the consensus on which the relevant institutions are based, thus contributing to stabilizing institutionalization trends. In this manner, we can see how the use of institutions for soft balancing may not only reduce the amount of international aggression (thus having a pacifying effect) but also strengthen the trend of institutionalization itself. In response to the question of how institutionalization may enhance power politics, this contribution thus ends up arguing (at least in part) that power politics may enhance institutionalization. It grasps the dynamic relationship between the two without explicitly theorizing it and stops just short of recognizing the transformative potential entailed.

Carson and Thompson put the two sides of the power politics–institutionalization dynamic together by studying how institutions both constrain and enable the pursuit of power. They focus specifically on how this happens through international organizations' regulation of access to and usability of information.

Information as a source of power within organizations can serve to further entrench the advantages of already powerful states, "but it can also make it possible for relatively weak states to leverage information-power dynamics to 'punch above their weight-class.'" This not only (1) shows how institutionalization may counteract power politics but also (2) clearly recognizes the relevance of ideational sources of power, as in fact "the power effects of information appear to be decoupled from more traditional [i.e., material] sources of power." The authors also (3) relax the bias in favor of power as relational, by looking at how it can be diffused and embedded in institutional environments. All three observations are important for the argument I will make later. However, while Carson and Thompson rightly claim to occupy a theoretical middle ground by taking both state power and institutions seriously, I hold that we must more radically break with the realist departure point, leave state centrism more fully behind, and operate systematically with a broader definition of power as foreshadowed but not explicitly advocated in the contributions discussed so far. This will equip us to explore whether and how we can perceive institutionalization as affecting in significant ways, perhaps even transforming or altogether outgrowing, power politics.

Alternative Contributions

This volume also includes several contributions by nonrealist scholars. How do they take up the challenge of theorizing the relationship between power and institutions away from the realist ontology, and how does my contribution relate to theirs? The chapters by Martin-Brûlé, Pingeot, and Pouliot and by Hall and Mérand both illustrate how power politics operate within and around institutional contexts. While Martin-Brûlé, Pingeot, and Pouliot show this for UN peacekeeping operations, Hall and Mérand do so for European Union member-state relations and (crisis) governance. In both contexts institutional embedment "enables but also constrains the transfer of struggles for influence across national, regional, and international spheres" (Martin-Brûlé, Pingeot, and Pouliot). The presence, shape, and functioning of institutions affect such struggles, as they are, in turn, affected by them.

Stacie Goddard, in her analysis of revisionism in and through institutions, confirms that "institutions both enable and constrain power politics." She usefully breaks with much received wisdom by insisting that revisionism can be exercised from within institutions; that institutions do not necessarily "tame" the revisionists within them; that, on the contrary, institutional dynamics may also undermine participating status quo powers; and that, precisely by employing institutions, revision or power transition do not necessarily have to take violent forms. An important take-home message here is that revisionism, or in fact much more broadly, the seeds of intentional structural change, tends not to lie outside a system with its institutions, but *within* it. This seems to be remaining true no matter how (or how deeply) politics are institutionalized. This means, on the one hand, that we have no reason to expect institutionalization to move us *beyond* power politics. On the other hand, it is no reason to jump to the conclusion that institutions are epiphenomenal. After all, important changes—also changes in power relations—are facilitated and steered by them. In this sense, institution-al(ized) politics *are* power politics. From this insight arises an important dilemma, which I will discuss in the second part of this chapter.

Georg Sørensen reiterates the starting point of the volume that "strong liberalism's" transformative optimism is just as unrealistic as claims that institutions are irrelevant for international governance. He takes the position of a "skeptic and hopeful liberalism," observing, on the one hand, that in many areas governance is barely "good enough," piecemeal, or gridlocked but, on the other, that much governance is taking place because of and through institutions, which seem by and large resilient. Sørensen further agrees with Cox and Sinclair (1996) "that a stable and legitimate order is founded on a fit between a power base, . . . a common collective image of order expressed in values and norms, and an appropriate set of institutions." Yet he fails to go further with this important insight: in the obvious absence of such an order, we need to be concerned with the processes taking place on and between all three levels identified by Cox (the material, the ideational, and the institutional), as together they determine the nature of international order along with its perceived legitimacy and stability.

My later argument lays the foundations for such an investigation. In so doing it connects most closely with the chapter by Ben Rosamond, who also observes that most definitions of power politics, including the one suggested by the editors of this volume, carry strong realist connotations. Being concerned with "who gets what, when, and how" from a state-centric and materialist point of view leads them to treat states as "the powers," power as a resource, and power dynamics as relational. Basing himself on Susan Strange (1994a, 1998), Rosamond argues that, instead, we need to be able to see power as structural and structural power as drawing on "collective understandings and intersubjectivities." Placing what I see as excessive emphasis on the nonmaterial dimension of (power) structures, he argues: "The structures of world politics, rather than being material in essence or exogenous to action, are best seen as intersubjective, that is, rooted in collective understandings that in turn define the parameters of actor behavior in both technical and normative senses." Further, he rightfully observes that "actor behavior, premised [inter alia, I would add] on these broad intersubjectivities, both produces concrete material effects and (through practice) reproduces and reifies the intersubjective structure," making it "robust." Last, "intersubjective structures can be made 'real' [again, I add inter alia] through the design and maintenance of institutions that internalize their logic." Rosamond here makes important points, which I will link later in a broader, systematic argument.

The Challenge Ahead

Most contributions to this volume have worked with a realist-inspired view of power and a focus on formal and intergovernmental institutions at the expense of other forms. Both of these biases need to be left behind if we want to achieve the goals laid out by the editors: we want to understand better why and how institutions evolve, decay, or regenerate. We want to know more about how institutions can be tools of revisionism (see the chapter by Goddard) or power transition and in this way support peaceful change. It is no accident that this scholarly interest arises now: global systemic power transition is on the horizon, and as scholars belonging to the declining hegemony, we would rather the transition, if it must come, be peaceful. How could this work? The editors are on the right track when they suggest that this means that we need to "go beyond an intentional goal-oriented understanding of power" and also when they observe that "it makes little sense to decouple materialist measures of power from how policymakers understand power and [its] legitimate use" (see also Guzzini 1993). But we need to go further than that. In this volume we have found examples of midlevel theorizing leading to a "more eclectic, but also more open, understanding of international relations" than that characterizing the interparadigm debates on institutions and power politics. But what overall lessons can we draw? Here I take up the editors' challenge to reconnect the foregoing "to more general discussions and concerns on the nature of international relations and state behavior."

Reconceptualizing Power Politics and Institutionalization from a Neo-Gramscian Perspective

All the above contributions have made sensible claims regarding the coexistence of power politics and institutionalization in contemporary world politics. But they all suffer from blind spots following from their shared realist ontological commitments or do not go far enough in drawing theoretical conclusions from diverging ontologies or empirical observations. It is clear that realists' answer to the question of whether institutionalization may lead us away from power politics by reducing the impact of relative state power on collective policy outcomes *has to* be no. The remainder of this contribution will show that it is possible to accept the basic realist assumption that power politics remains a core feature of international relations while at the same time international institutions are becoming ever more numerous and comprehensive, and yet adopt a more open stance with respect to the possibility of political transformation and to theorize this stance. To this end I adopt a neo-Gramscian perspective that, aside from its openly normative stance in favor of overcoming the status quo, differs from the realist-inspired takes in this volume in five key analytical respects, which will be unpacked later:[2] (1) it adopts a broader definition of power that explicitly includes nonmaterial power resources and can see power as diffuse and structurally embedded; (2) it enables us to understand the key role of legitimacy for embedding power in institutions, rendering it structural, and so stabilizing world orders; (3) it thereby also becomes less wedded to a state-centric ontology, allowing room for politics to operate through other types of actors and channels; (4) it uses the language of hegemony to comprehend the ways in which power structures, thus defined, become stabilized, including through international institutionalization; (5) it reveals the paradox of institutions becoming *empowering* by providing legitimacy precisely to the extent that they are perceived as *counteracting* power politics. I briefly explain each of these points and conclude on how this perspective helps us understand both continuity and change in contemporary world affairs.

The first key intervention made by a neo-Gramscian reconceptualization of the power politics–institutionalization dynamic is an abandonment of the stress on material at the expense of ideational power and a move to theorize the two together. Gramsci (1971) conceptualized power as combining material and ideational components and thereby as exercised as a mixture of force and consent. While rule by force alone is unsustainable, rule by consent alone is no rule. It is wherever force and consent are mixed that power can be enacted in ways that have lasting political effects. This means that alongside material capabilities, resources affecting the ability to let others see the world as one would like them to and to persuade them to share one's point of view are absolutely crucial components of power (see, e.g., Cox and Schechter 2003). This is not something previous contributions to this volume disagree with, as we will also see, but it is not something most foreground sufficiently.

Gramsci used the term "hegemony" to capture a dynamic political structure in which power is exercised as a mixture of force and consent. The concept merges the material and ideational components of power, makes them inseparable, and reveals their interdependence. In the words of Cox and Sinclair, it is

> a structure of values and understandings about the nature of order that permeates a whole system of states and non-state entities. . . . Such a structure of meanings is underpinned by a structure of power, in which most probably one state is dominant but that state's dominance is not sufficient to create hegemony. Hegemony derives from the dominant social strata of the dominant states in so far as these ways of doing and thinking have acquired the acquiescence of the dominant social strata of other states. (1996, 151)

Reconceptualizing power in this manner has five important implications. First, while the material bases of hegemony remain absolutely crucial (Strange 1988a; see also Grieco and Ikenberry 2003), the structures that represent the set of opportunities and constraints faced by political actors now include ideational alongside material components (Strange 1996). Knowledge, ideas, concepts, theories, language, traditions, conventions, norms, rules, and other immaterial components of social life become *part of* power structures. They are not merely structural modifiers, as suggested by Lobell and Nicholson in this volume.

Second, the moment we theorize ideational and material components of power together, we can no longer so easily tie power to particular actors. Following Gramsci (1971), hegemony is a form of power that connects states to civil societies and is embodied in manifold political, cultural, and social practices. Power is not owned by states but is socially embedded and diffused in society and its institutions (see Herman and Chomsky 1988). Power becomes less relationally defined, and more diffuse, not the property of specific actors as much as an attribute of social structures. This insight makes clinging to state centrism impossible (see also Scholl and Freyberg-Inan 2013), as we can see how power is enacted by a variety of types of actors, across levels of governance, in varying coalitions. This does not mean that it is impossible to locate, but it does mean that seeking the effects of power politics exclusively in relations between states overlooks a great deal of how power operates both to support and to undermine the translation of power differences between interacting political entities into political outcomes. This is far from trivial, as today state centrism does not equip us to see how power is increasingly concentrated in transnational networks and a transnational ruling class (Sklair 1997) and contested between transnationalized social groups defined on class, ideological, and other bases.[3] A neo-Gramscian conception of power as operating through hegemony is, in short, more useful for understanding the transnationalizing and multilevel governance world we live in.

Third, we can now see how institutions, both formal and informal, become key components in stabilizing power relations and constructing and maintaining hegemony. In the Marxist tradition, Gramsci (1971) theorized how in advanced capitalist societies the bourgeoisie used all manner of institutions to persuade subordinated classes to internalize its values and goals and to conceive of them as general interest. Dominant groups in this way present their rule as legitimate and are enabled to rule largely through consent. This is precisely how international institutions operate today to support the rule of internationally dominant actors. From good governance norms via the Washington Consensus through World Trade Organization rulings, from military alliance commitments via Security Council resolutions to responsibility to protect (R2P), international institutions serve to present and enforce the interests of powerful actors as an international common sense, which becomes increasingly difficult to contest as such institutionalization progresses. As Barkin and Weitsman write, the responsibilities and rules of international organizations "support and reinforce particular worldviews, thereby supporting those countries that share those worldviews. . . . It is generally the case that the most efficient way to get others to do what one wants them to do is to convince them that it is what they want to do, or that it is the right thing to do. And institutions can be an effective way of creating the legitimacy and knowledge that can do this convincingly" (see also Goddard

2009b). This is rule by consent supported by institutionalization and the way institutionalization *supports* power politics.

Fourth, we have by now been repeatedly confronted with the key role of legitimacy. Perceived legitimacy is an absolutely crucial ideational power resource (see, e.g., Finnemore and Toope 2001). This has also become clear in previous contributions to this volume. For example, Wivel and Paul have shown how perceived legitimacy is crucial for the success of institutional soft-balancing strategies. Carson and Thompson have shown how it matters for harvesting the benefits of informational asymmetries: "To the extent that information advantages render arguments more credible and legitimate, they could lend states increased authority to set negotiating agendas and could be used for more effective strategizing and persuasion in the conduct of bargaining." A neo-Gramscian perspective, however, brings added value by helping us understand *why and how* legitimacy is so important for linking the processes of power politics and institutionalization: perceived legitimacy is a prerequisite for consent, and institutions provide cheap compliance with the power relations they embody to the extent that they are perceived as legitimate.

This, fifth, reveals an important paradox. As Abbott and Snidal (1998) also argue, a major source of legitimacy for international institutions is precisely that they are seen to counteract power politics. On the one hand, international institutions do allow states (and other actors) to act out interests and reflect power relations. On the other hand, their usefulness depends on their being perceived as not reflecting power relations to the full extent (and thus as not merely reproducing the interests of the powerful). To the extent that they are seen as mere transmission belts for the parochial interests of most powerful actors, they will lose legitimacy in the eyes of all observers that do not align with those interests, and they will be substantially weakened, if not abandoned, as a result.[4] Thus, from the perspective of states (and other actors), to be able to harness the benefits of institutionalization, it is important to ensure that institutions are perceived as transcending power politics. And only to the extent that they are *seen* to transcend power politics may they actually end up doing so. This, then, is the paradoxical way institutionalization can *counteract* power politics. It also creates a challenge for reflexive scholarship: showing how institutionalization fits the logic of power politics undermines the potential for institutionalization to move us out of a realist world.

Conclusion

By adopting a neo-Gramscian perspective, I have been able to pull together a series of important observations made in the previous contributions, which stopped short of theorizing them systematically, owing to their commitment to realist ontological premises or the lack of a systematic alternative framework. Power is both material and ideational. It is relational but also diffuse. It cannot be straightforwardly tied to states but is shared by other types of actors and embedded in social structures, which in this day and age are to a significant extent transnationalized. Institutions are the means by which power is structurally embedded. For this process to be successful, their perceived legitimacy is crucial. This, finally, means that institutions are empowered to the extent that they are seen as transcending power politics. This institutional power can be used either to entrench or to outgrow the power structures that supported the institution in the first place. But to the extent that it is seen to do the former, the institution is weakened, and its power political benefits evaporate.

Such an approach can, last, help us comprehend both continuity and change in the interplay between power politics and institutionalization. By becoming structurally embedded through institutionalization, power relations become stabilized and continue to have effects also after relative state power has shifted. As Barkin and Weitsman write, "Institutional histories are path dependent." Moving beyond state centrism and expanding our concept of power allows us to see that hegemony can continue after the hegemon is gone. This is what we are witnessing today, in an age in which the US-led global northwest has lost its post–Cold War unipolar status, but its rule over global governance still continues to be hegemonic. But importantly, the neo-Gramscian vision of power structures is not deterministic but dynamic. Institutionalization can stabilize such structures, but it can also undermine them. It can do so gradually by creating an "embedded realism," in which states transfer power to institutions for reasons of rational self-interest, but thereby lock themselves into a trajectory of change away from a realist world. It may do so also in more radical ways through contestation over the forms institutionalization should take. Herein may lie hope for peaceful systemic change. This can be studied through the neo-Gramscian concept of counterhegemony, which helps us think through how current orders can be challenged from within, drawing on the same sorts of resources that support the status quo in order to challenge its common sense (Rajagopal 2003, 2006; Sanbonmatsu 2004; Juris 2008; Opel and Pompper 2003; Starr 2000). In short, a neo-Gramscian approach can show why the juxtaposition of power politics with institutionalization is a false one, as the two processes are in fact tightly intertwined. By understanding that and how this is the case, we understand how they go hand in hand but also become better able to see how each process might become destabilized and thus detect possible sources of fundamental change in world affairs.

Notes

1. The contribution by Lobell and Nicholson in addition entails a commitment to structuralism. The other versions of realism we encounter in this book allow more room for agency. My critique extends to them all.

2. Explicitly neo-Gramscian accounts appear much more frequently in international political economy (IPE; e.g., Cox 1986; Cox and Sinclair 1996; Cox and Schechter 2003; Gill

1993, 2000; Rupert 1995; Eschle and Maiguashca 2005; Stephen 2009, 2011) than in the literature on international security. But in the debate surrounding institutionalization and power politics, a neo-Gramscian intervention seems called for, as critical IPE has done considerably more work on understanding the structural workings of power than security studies. See also the chapter by Rosamond.

3. The importance of the transnational dimension of institutionalization is also recognized in the chapters by Sørensen and Rosamond. Goddard as well recognizes the relevance of institutionalized networks, even as she unfortunately focuses her chapter narrowly on networks among states.

4. This dynamic is all too familiar, for example, to observers of European Union politics: efforts to develop common EU policy are routinely hindered by weaker member states' perceptions of disproportionate influence of some of the more powerful. When such perceptions are less prominent, all, including the strong, members stand a greater chance of actually being able to act on their interests.

CHAPTER 13

International Order and Power Politics

Daniel H. Nexon

In their introductory chapter to this volume, Wivel and Paul define power politics as "*the contestation among individual states using their particular resources and bargaining strength to influence the structure of relations and the conduct of other actors*" and argue that "in the context of institutions," this involves "*the efforts by states to influence the formulation, application, and enforcement of the rules and regulations of a given institution as well as the control of bureaucratic positions and allocations of resources within it.*"

At first glance this formulation reflects a relatively straightforward extension of realist principles. For realists international politics is, at heart, a struggle for power and position among states. Contemporary realists, as Barkin and Weitsman (chapter 2, this volume) discuss, tend to explain this timeless feature of world politics with reference to international anarchy. Because world politics lacks a common authority to make and enforce rules, states ultimately must rely on their own capabilities to secure their political autonomy. In some accounts this inclines states to maximize power—to seek to dominate their neighbors (Mearsheimer 2001). In others it leads them to privilege their security and, if they behave prudently, eschew threatening efforts at achieving regional or global hegemony (Waltz 1979). In neoclassical realism how states respond to the distribution of power depends on domestic political factors (Rathbun 2008; Rose 1998). Thus, in most contemporary flavors of realism the anarchical character of international order means that international politics lacks the kind of highly articulated divisions of labor found in domestic societies. Structural variation reduces to the distribution of capabilities and perhaps a few other factors, such as the relative efficacy of offensive and defensive operations (Goddard and Nexon 2005; LaRoche and Pratt 2017).

But if we look closer, we see tensions between a realist-inflected approach to power politics that takes institutions seriously and the states-under-anarchy framework. If anarchy is the ordering principle of international politics—and the only relevant form of structural variation concerns the distribution of military and economic capabilities across states—then institutions should matter only at the margins. This holds if we focus, as most chapters in this volume do, on formal international institutions. The same is true if we expand our purview—as Rosamond (chapter 5, this volume) emphasizes in his discussion of "collective understandings and intersubjectivities"—to informal institutions: social conventions around which expectations of behavior converge (Buzan 1993; Finnemore 1996).[1]

But Wivel and Paul rightly argue that power politics involves efforts to *structure relations and the conduct of actors*. This takes us into the domain of the old agent-structure debate that formed the basis of constructivist criticisms of realism: the claim that, first, states, as well as other actors, and, second, international orders mutually shape one another (Finnemore and Sikkink 1998; Wendt 1999; Wight 1999). Wivel and Paul's formulation requires a broader understanding of international structure than the distribution of capabilities and, at a minimum, requires qualifying the degree that anarchy exhausts international order. It suggests, rightly, that formal and informal institutions are part of the texture of world politics. Indeed, power politics, properly understood, involves active efforts to shape that texture. Power politics maintains and alters the relations, norms, and institutions that order world politics. And those norms, those relations, and those institutions structure how states, and other actors, conduct power politics (Goddard and Nexon 2016; Nexon 2009b, chap. 2).

A robust approach to the nexus between power politics and international institutions means that international order varies across time and space. It is no accident that Wivel and Paul emphasize, on the one hand, the institutionalization of world politics in recent decades and, on the other hand, changes in the institutional landscape driven by the rise of new powers, such as China's role in creating the Shanghai Cooperation Organization (SCO) and the Asian Infrastructure Investment Bank (AIIB). As Goddard (chapter 8, this volume) quotes Ikenberry (2011, 12), international orders are, *at a minimum*, "manifest in the settled rules and arrangements between states that define and guide their interaction." Contributors to this volume, in turn, often emphasize the tight connection between this broader understanding of international order and power politics. To incorporate even formal institutions into a realist-inflected understanding of power politics means treating *international order as means, medium, and object of power political competition*. This has always been, or should always have been, the case for realism. But the positioning of realism in opposition to, most recently, liberalism and constructivism distracted realists from embracing this research agenda (Goddard and Nexon 2016).[2]

In sum, the states-under-anarchy framework cannot supply us with the necessary analytical tools to capture the dynamic relationship between power politics and international order. In the rest of this chapter, I suggest various—but, at least to my mind, related—ways that we might theoretically and analytically cash out this relationship. In doing so I draw on insights and arguments from the other chapters in the volume.[3]

I first discuss basic principles for how we should think about international power politics in terms of the dynamics of collective mobilization. I suggest that aspects of this volume point to thinking in terms of historically, geographically, and institutionally variable repertoires of power politics. I then discuss two ways of analytically parsing international order—institutional and otherwise—in terms of fields and networks. I conclude with some broader thoughts about how these apparently disparate approaches inform one another. However, I stress that whatever frameworks we use to explain international power politics, this volume implies a need for realism to expand its own analytical toolkit.

Basic Principles: Power Politics and the Dynamics of Collective Mobilization

At "the heart of power politics are processes of collective mobilization" (Goddard and Nexon 2016, 6). Power political activities involve some combination of *joint action*—pooling and directing resources to achieve an end—and *wedging*—efforts to disrupt the pooling and directing of resources by others (T. Crawford 2011; N. Crawford 2008; Nexon and Wright 2007). Consider military balancing, one of the most venerable power political strategies studied by realists. When states engage in internal balancing, they mobilize domestic resources to enhance their military power. When states form alliances, they pool their resources via joint action to respond to unfavorable shifts in the distribution of power. In both strategies leaders of states rely on a variety of *instruments*—including symbolic, cultural, economic, military, and diplomatic capital—as they persuade, coerce, cajole, and incentivize others to engage in, or eschew, such joint action.

Once we understand that "power politics" describes a particular class of activities involving collective mobilization, a number of aspects of this volume fall into place. For example, Ripsman's (chapter 3, this volume) exploration of the uses of international institutions focuses on how they provide tools for leaders to facilitate joint action or to engage in wedge strategies. They may use international institutions in ways that directly target their own citizens, such as when they use them to legitimate the use of force. They may also target other states and foreign audiences, such as when they use international institutions to delegitimize—or withhold legitimacy from—military intervention. Naming and shaming policies, in which states and non-state actors seek to compel changes in the policies of particular states, showcase similar logics (Hafner-Burton 2008; Murdie and Davis 2012).

Moreover, as a number of different chapters demonstrate, the politics *within* international organizations involve how their institutional rules and arrangements structure dynamics of joint action and wedging (see also Pape 2005; Paul 2005; Wallander and Keohane 1999). International institutions also provide collective resources in the form of, say, economic aid, legitimation, status recognition, and diplomatic capital. This gives states, and representatives of states, incentives to jockey for position within them (see Adler-Nissen 2008; Pouliot 2016). Institutions simultaneously function as sites of power politics, instruments of power politics, and objects of power political struggles.

Thinking about power politics in terms of collective mobilization also helps us to cut into the problem of states, anarchy, and international order. As I noted previously, the insights of this volume make it difficult to unproblematically adopt the states-under-anarchy framework. However, most of the contributions emphasize the centrality of states in global power politics. Freyberg-Inan (chapter 12, this volume) correctly notes that a proper understanding of the role of institutions in power politics "would emphatically *not* have to mean that states would no longer be the key actors in world politics nor that it would no longer matter how powerful states are vis-à-vis their peers."

How can we make sense of this? The answer, in my view, is that most national-states enjoy significant asymmetric advantages as sites of collective mobilization—however attenuated those advantages may be by, for instance, the process of globalization. Strong states enjoy a broad social, technological, cultural, and symbolic infrastructure for mobilizing their populations. They collect taxes, regulate exchanges across their borders, build and deploy militaries, and otherwise command extensive governance apparatuses (Nexon 2009b, chap. 2).

But states lack a monopoly on collective mobilization within, across, or among sovereign-territorial borders. Many other social sites—including transnational and domestic movements, international organizations, and corporations—both engage in, and supply contexts for, joint action. The relative importance of different *types* of social sites—states, empires, multilateral alliances, global regulatory agencies, transnational violence-wielding movements—for collective action constitutes a critical source of variation in international order (Adamson 2005, 2016; Cerny 1995; Goddard and Nexon 2016; Phillips and Sharman 2015; Spruyt 1994).

Thus, when participants in this volume discuss the growth of the number, reach, and importance of international institutions in the postwar period, they are describing changes in the dynamics of collective mobilization in world politics. We cannot make sense of contemporary power politics without taking that shifting topography into account. This does not mean, for example, that the relationship between international institutions and nation-states is necessarily zero-sum (see Avant 2016). States may use international institutions to secure their position with respect to non-state challengers (Mendelsohn 2009) or to reinforce the perquisites of nation-state status—and hence increase the symbolic, economic, and other forms of capital enjoyed by sovereign states (R. H. Jackson 1990; Buzan 2004). But it does mean that we need alternative frameworks if we want to treat international institutions in particular, and international order in general, as means, mediums, and objects of power politics.

This extends beyond accommodating transnational advocacy networks, multinational corporations, social movements, terrorist organizations, nationalist movements, and other actors and social sites. Ripsman's chapter usefully focuses our attention on *leaders* of states. International relations scholars typically find it useful to refer to states as the primary actors in international power politics; realists speak of states trying to enhance their power and security. But "leaders wish not only to maximize national interests, but also wish to stay in power" (chapter 3, this volume). This is true in both democratic and authoritarian regimes (see Weeks 2008).

Leaders frequently privilege their own political survival, their ideological goals, and even their personal accumulation of wealth over more general state interests (see Cooley 2012). As Krasner (1999) argues, leaders are often a more relevant unit of analysis than states for the study of power politics. Leaders may concede sovereignty to international patrons in order to secure their domestic political position (see Carney 1989) or accept intrusive economic assistance in order to gain advantage over their political rivals (see Vreeland 2003). Leaders may even create international institutions, and engage in alternative international order building, in order to demonstrate that their leadership is bringing status and prestige to their countries. For example, Chinese president Xi Jinping appears to be using the One Belt and One Road (OBOR) initiative, at least in part, to stake his personalist claim to leadership.[4]

Once we recognize that power politics in general, and international power politics in particular, is a subset of collective mobilization, this allows us to draw on a wide variety of theoretical insights and traditions. The basic principles outlined previously take inspiration from the literature on contentious politics (see McAdam, Tarrow, and Tilly 2001; Goddard and Nexon 2016, 5n4). The study of political contention emphasizes the dynamic, and relational, character of political contestation. The same holds for international power politics, which involves repeated interactions among participants as they seek to influence one another. Participants adjust their strategies in light of the unfolding, and sometimes unpredictable, results of their interaction.

We can see this dynamic and relational dimension of power politics in Izumikawa's (2018, 108) account of the "diplomatic tug of war" over Japan between the United States and the Soviet Union in the 1950s. His core insight is that wedging and binding tactics interact with one another. Moscow offered territorial concessions to pry Japan from its bilateral alliance with the United States, and Washington "adjusted its diplomatic strategy in order to keep Tokyo on its side." These dynamics unfolded over time, with each side altering their wedging and binding efforts to influence Japanese alignment. Izumikawa concludes that "an alliance should be regarded not as a static object, but as a . . . *dynamic equilibrium*: a situation in which a phenomenon remains stable not because its constitutive elements are static" but because "countervailing forces cancel one another out and stabilize" it (2018, 118).

While it seems likely that all power politics reduces to a limited set of basic logics, we also know that the dynamics of international power politics change markedly over time. As I noted in the preceding section, and as many of the chapters illustrate, the *specific* tools used by states—and other actors—show historical and geographical variation. This suggests that we can think of aspects of international power politics in terms of variation—national, regional, and historical—in what scholars of contentious politics call "repertoires."

As Tilly argues, "The word *repertoire* identifies a limited set of routines that are learned, shared, and acted out through a deliberate process of choice" (1993, 264). He notes that "repertoires are learned cultural creations, but . . . they emerge from struggle. People learn to break windows in protests, attack pilloried prisons, tear down dishonored houses, stage public marches," and so on. "At any particular point in history, however, they learn only a small number of alternative ways to act collectively." McAdam, Tarrow, and Tilly define repertoires as "limited ensembles of mutual claims-making routines available to particular pairs of identities" (2001, 138).

This adapts nicely to our intuitions about power politics. In world politics, states and "other 'political actors follow rough scripts to uncertain outcomes as they negotiate' diplomatic demands, trade relations, territorial disputes, and other political concerns" (Goddard, MacDonald, and Nexon 2019, 8). Contemporary scholarship tends to focus on one or two broad strategies for pursuing power politics, such as balancing and bandwagoning (Schweller 1994; Walt 1987) or deterrence and compellence (Schelling 1966). Scholars might isolate a particular claims-making routine, such as economic sanctions, to study the conditions of its success or the broad patterns associated with its use. When realists discuss different logics of power politics, they often array them along a continuum and theorize about the conditions that lead states to choose one or the other (for example, Walt 2009). But it might prove useful to treat repertoires, defined by power political logics and specific instruments, as objects of analysis in their own right. This means that innovation can emerge out of the dynamics of power political interaction; it suggests a close connection between international order and power political repertoires.

Indeed, what I find striking about Wivel and Paul's introduction is the degree that certain elements of power political repertoires, such as using international institutions to advance interests, are temporally and geographically delimited. It would have made little sense to write about the power politics of international organizations in eighteenth-century Europe. There were, with the exception of the German Empire (see Osiander 2001; Wilson 1999), no standing, bureaucratized, autonomous organizations in which representatives of leaders of states voted in advisory or binding decisions.[5] Now, the use of international organizations, as well as their creation, constitutes a standard element of power politics repertoires for states, government officials, and non-state actors (Farrell and Newman 2015, 2014). The EU, for example, strongly conditions the set of instruments that its members use to pursue power and influence, both within and beyond its borders. Yet even in the contemporary period, some regions rely more on formal institutions to manage interstate relations than others, and the character of those institutions varies (Goh 2013).

Overall, the proliferation of international institutions, and their increasing utilization, suggests a shift in power political repertoires (compare Reus-Smit 1997). Similarly, while information warfare is an ancient practice, its specific means and mediums have shifted in response to technological change in telecommunications and innovations in the use of those technologies. During the Cold War, violations of airspace and territorial waters were a routine practice, with well-developed dynamics of escalation and deescalation, among the United States and the Soviet Union. But when Russia aggressively resumed these practices, they shocked European states and led countries such as Sweden to adapt their security policies (compare Kragh and Åsberg 2017).

Theorizing International Order: Two Approaches

Contemporary realism offers two baseline approaches to international order. As we have seen, those influenced by structural realism focus on anarchy as the ordering principle of world politics. Hegemonic order theorists, in contrast, often—but not always—accept the existence of anarchy as a "deep structure" but believe that preeminent states, or sometimes coalitions of great powers, can create and uphold order in terms of rules, norms, and arrangements (see Gilpin 1981; Ikenberry 2001, 2011; Lemke 2002). The conception of order here generally tracks with English school understandings of international societies as composed of primary institutions and secondary institutions, with the former often taking the form of social institutions—such as sovereignty—and the latter often manifesting as formal institutions—such as the United Nations (Clark 2009; Goh 2013; Mendelsohn 2009; Friedner Parrat 2017). Similarly, many constructivists understand international structure in terms of intersubjective norms that operate in constitutive, prescriptive, and proscriptive terms. Others stress the distribution and nature of identification in world politics (see, e.g., Finnemore 1996; Finnemore and Sikkink 1998; Wendt 1987).

These are all fruitful ways of tackling the relationship between international institutions in particular, and order more generally, and power politics. We find variations on them in, for instance, Sørensen's (chapter 4, this volume) discussion of liberal order, Rosamond's (chapter 5, this volume) elaboration of "discursive institutionalism," and Lobell and Nicholson's (chapter 9, this volume) incorporation of nuclear taboos into generally "realist" understandings of the non-proliferation regime. Here I want to emphasize two additional frameworks: *field theory*, which is most closely associated with practice approaches to international politics (see Adler-Nissen 2008, 2012; Bigo 2012; Pouliot 2008, 2016), and *network approaches*, which are represented in this volume by Goddard's (chapter 8) contribution (see Hafner-Burton, Kahler, and Montgomery 2009; Nexon 2009b).

Field Theory

Julian Go (2008) argues for extending field theory to global politics.[6] He defines fields as "arena[s] of struggle in which actors compete for a variety of valued resources, that is, different species of 'capital' that are potentially convertible to each other" (Go 2008, 206; see also Bucholz 2016; Christin 2016; Go and Krause 2016). For Go, fields "consist of two related but analytically separable dimensions: 1) the objective configuration of actor-positions and 2) the subjective meanings guiding actors in the struggle, that is, the 'rules of the game' and particular types of cultural or symbolic capital" (2008, 206). Obviously, this requires some elaboration.

In Bourdieusian theory social fields are roughly analogous to social structure. But they carry with them a specific analytical apparatus. A key concept here is *habitus*. For Bourdieu *habitus* bridges macro- and microlevel processes. It refers to habits of the head and heart as well as the bodily comportment of individuals. The durably installed generative principle of regulated improvisation produces that individual's repertoire of practices.

Fields compromise specific spheres of social action. They involve specific "rules of the game" (or repertoires) that shape how actors relate to one another as they jockey for power, status, and influence. Bourdieu describes fields in terms of "a set of objective power relations imposed on all those who enter the field, relations which are not reducible to the intentions of individual agents or even to direct interactions between agents" (1991, 230). Position in the hierarchy of a field depends on the accumulation of field-relevant capital—that is, assets and performances valued within a field (Berling 2012, 45).

It should now be clear that my use of "capital" to describe power resources and performances in earlier parts of this chapter is deliberate. Bourdieu defines capital as "accumulated labor (in its materialized form) or its 'incorporated' embodied form which, when appropriated on a private, i.e., exclusive, basis by agents or groups of agents, enables them to appropriate social energy in the form of reified or living labor" (2011, 81). Capital comes in three basic forms, or "species": economic capital; social capital, the resources generated by network ties to individuals and institutional sites; and cultural capital, specific material tokens of higher or lower cultural standing—such as expensive works of art or, among states, highly esteemed archaeological sites. More commonly, it refers to the knowledge of prestigious cultural codes—philosophy, arts, and so forth—as well as one's habitus, which in this sense takes the form of *embodied* cultural capital.

Forms of capital also come in subtypes, or "subspecies." For example, subspecies of economic capital include currency, ownership of businesses, government bonds, and derivatives and other financial instruments. The relative value—or even existence—of subspecies of capital varies across time and space. In turn, there are, in principle, as many forms of capital as there are social fields and as many fields as there are distinct spheres of social life with their own power relations. Power relations within fields take the form of the patterns of relations among agents: the power that a particular participant in the field enjoys relative to other participants. These are putatively measurable and graphable structures of social dominance. They capture position within the field. They also manifest in terms of the rules of the game and participants' "feel" for when and how to apply them. This involves Bourdieu's emphasis on habits, dispositions, and embodiment. It relates to understandings of practices as competent performances (Adler and Pouliot 2011a).

In these terms contemporary realism adopts an extremely spare understanding of international order. In the simplest formulation, associated with structural realism, international systems are a single field in which military and economic capabilities constitute the sole forms of field-relevant capital. The distribution of military and economic capital amounts to the only important basis for relative position in international fields, that is, in terms of greater and lesser powers. Polarity—the number of great powers—provides the main way in which we graph the structure of that field.

As noted previously, a key feature of fields—and the relationship among fields—resides in the exchange rate among different forms of capital. For example, extreme skill at basketball can position an individual at the top of the field of professional basketball in the United States. Elite basketball players earn significant amounts of money: they convert their capital in basketball into economic capital and, with it, position in the economic field. More broadly, a strong position in the field of "American celebrity," in part through the bootstrapping of financial, social, and other forms of cultural capital. But extreme success—and associated capital—in the financial industry cannot "purchase" skill at basketball, which limits the ways that hedge-fund managers can exchange their financial capital for position in the field of professional basketball.

Similarly, a key wager of realist theory is that military and economic capital enjoy a high rate of exchange in world politics. States, and other social sites, can use, all things being equal, economic capital to accumulate military capital, which is why national economic strength undergirds military power. Realists also see other forms of capital—such as cultural capital produced by possession of highly esteemed archaeological sites—as relatively useless when it comes to securing great-power status.

For many realists the proposition that force is the ultima ratio of international politics translates into the idea that compliance with norms, success at the Olympics, and even enjoyment of a highly skilled diplomatic corps matter at the margins when it comes to power politics. Though the possession of broad diplomatic capital certainly enhances success at power politics, great powers can translate economic and military capital into diplomatic capital. Great powers also enjoy outsized ability to shape international norms. Thus, the overriding importance, for realists, of military and economic capital as the basis, means, and medium of international order.[7]

Realist-inflected hegemonic order theorists deploy this logic to explain the generation, maintenance, and transformation of international order. They argue, in essence, that possession of outsized military and economic capital endows states with what Bourdieu calls *metacapital*: the capacity to set the rate of exchange among kinds of capital—within and across fields—and, more broadly, to structure fields themselves. Metacapital is closely related to Bourdieu's concept of symbolic capital: certain species and subspecies of capital—whether cultural, economic, social, military, or whatever—become infused with specifically ideological meaning that renders them valuable within particular fields and thus generates a high rate of exchange for those forms of capital (Zhang 2004, 7).

When hegemons allocate status and prestige, they determine, both deliberately and inadvertently, what kinds of assets and performances matter in international pecking orders. These assets and performances resolve as forms of symbolic capital in relevant fields. Thus, American hegemony has contributed to making the "possession" of democratic regimes valuable symbolic capital for standing in world politics. It has also contributed to rendering aircraft carriers—a subspecies of military capital—important symbolic capital in the field of great-power politics (Nexon and Neumann 2018, 674–75). The exchange value of both democracy and aircraft carriers may change in the future, with the rise of Chinese authoritarian capitalism or the development of new military capabilities that become closely associated with great-power status.

The importance of membership in international organizations as a form of symbolic capital for, on the one hand, international standing and, on the other hand, domestic legitimation might help explain their proliferation. Beijing obviously sees the AIIB as a mechanism to influence the field of international development as well as enhance its relative position within it. But like OBOR, it may also serve as symbolic capital to demonstrate China's status as a great power, and even future hegemon, to both international and domestic audiences. These kinds of initiatives supply the Chinese leadership with symbolic capital within fields of Chinese political competition. Whether oriented toward domestic or international audiences, it matters that Beijing seeks to perform, or embody, great-power status using scripts laid down by Western powers in general, and the United States in particular. At the same time, doing so has the potential to alter international order in consequential ways.

International organizations are more than sources of symbolic capital. They are, in their own right, fields in which states—and their officials—jockey for power and position. When states create international institutions and establish their rules of the game, they generate concrete organizational fields associated with those institutions (Vetterlein and Moschella 2014). These organizational fields, as bureaucratic organizations are prone to do, often develop relative autonomy; their rules of the game and field-relevant capital decouples, at least partially, from the power political conditions that produced them (Barnett and Finnemore 2004).

Conceptualizing international order in terms of fields allows us to incorporate both formal and informal institutions in the study of power politics. The United Nations, the International Monetary Fund (IMF), the North Atlantic Treaty Organization (NATO), the European Union, and the International Atomic Energy Agency (IAEA) are all organizational fields—which themselves may be composed of subfields. Participants in them carry both general professional habitus—as, say, diplomats, economists, military personnel, and nuclear engineers—and acclimate to specific styles of comportment and rules of the game. The combination of their dispositions, social relations, and the resources that come with their broader affiliations—most notably the states that they represent—endow them with field-relevant capital and related power positions.

As a number of scholars have already demonstrated, the analysis of international organizations and foreign-policy institutions in field-theoretic terms gives us important insight into power politics as well as international outcomes (see Adler-Nissen 2008; Pouliot 2016; Pouponneau and Mérand 2017). This kind of sensibility finds reflection in Martin-Brûlé, Pingeot, and Pouliot's discussion of the politics of peacekeeping (chapter 10, this volume).

World politics consists of complex and nested fields, some of which operate within and across formal institutions and others which capture informal institutions. The IAEA nests within a broader non-proliferation field, in which it is one social site among many. This kind of nesting makes, as many of the contributors to this volume stress, the stakes of power politics in such social sites potentially quite high—even though daily operations in international institutions may reflect mundane organizational practices, bureaucratic political struggles, and other parochial dynamics unrelated to the interstate struggles that form the primary interest of realist scholars (Adler-Nissen 2008; Pouliot 2016; Adler-Nissen and Pouliot 2014).

Along these lines recall my earlier discussion of Ripsman's insights on collective mobilization and countermobilization strategies. In these terms Ripsman's insights suggest that support from international organizations often functions as a form of symbolic capital for leaders seeking to legitimate their policies domestically or secure compliance from other states. Denying that symbolic capital can make both more difficult. Blocking UN authorization for the American-led intervention in Iraq probably contributed to the inability to secure Turkey as a base of operations and otherwise raised the costs of the Iraq War (Nexon 2009a, 343–44). At the same time, the struggle within the UN over authorization was itself a case of power politics, in which specific field-relevant capital in the Security Council played a role.

It follows, I think, that we can parse international order in terms of the topography of these fields—crucially, first, the nature of field-relevant capital and, second, the exchange rate of different types of capital across fields. This provides a way of understanding "how processes of social construction create" a wide variety of "*strategic contexts* through which actors pursue power politics" (Musgrave and Nexon 2018, 6). The crucial move is to recognize states—including hegemons and great powers—may produce, shape, and shove international, institutional, and regional fields. They do so across a variety of issue domains, from non-proliferation to banking regulation to international development.

But such fields, contra realism, do not quickly reduce to great-power military and economic capabilities. Military and economic capital are not necessarily highly fungible across all the fields that make up international politics. Even great powers and hegemons emerge, operate within, and find their power political endeavors shaped by international, institutional, and regional fields of various kinds. They are not just "field makers" but also "field takers" (Musgrave and Nexon 2018, 20). Moreover, non-state actors, such as transnational advocacy networks, news media, and corporations, can both influence such fields and compete within them.

The relative autonomy of fields—the fact that they channel power-political competition even for dominant states—finds reflection, as Paul Musgrave and I (2018) have argued, in the American effort to send a manned mission to the lunar surface—collectively referred to as Project Apollo. This mission can be understood as an effort to achieve a high-profile "first" in space exploration. The United States invested truly staggering resources into the project because of deep concern that Soviet "firsts"—Sputnik and Yuri Gagarin's 1961 earth orbit—had damaged American standing in the international science-and-technology field.

Position in the science-and-technology field had previously been important to the US-Soviet rivalry, which, in the early Cold War, extended beyond traditional power politics to the question of which system best reflected the modern future of humankind. But space emerged, almost overnight, as a critical symbolic resource in the Cold War. Kennedy and his advisers worried that, absent Project Apollo, the United States would prove unable to compete for allies among the "new nations" emerging from decolonization and perhaps have a more difficult time maintaining the allegiance of core allies in Europe and Asia.

Consider also Pouponneau and Mérand's (2017, 123–24) account of how France shifted from a facilitator to an opponent of nuclear proliferation. The key, they argue, involves the interaction between changes in the "international division of labor" and domestic fields in France. The "non-proliferation norm became, beginning in the 1970s, an increasingly valuable resource for a group of French diplomats involved in nuclear affairs." These diplomats "entrenched non-proliferation norms in French policy by promoting a new role for France in global politics." The change, therefore, involved the "evolution of domestic bureaucratic and political fields, which refracted changes in the international system," including shifts in the balance of power—the great-power field—brought about by the end of the Cold War and the collapse of the Soviet Union. Here we have the intersection of international power politics, domestic power political struggles for position and influence, and the non-proliferation regime.

There are other field-theoretic approaches through which we can study international organizations (see, e.g., Fligstein and McAdam 2012). For example, Vetterlein and Moschella (2014) draw from notions of organizational fields to explain policy change in the IMF. They develop a taxonomy of change based on the degree of openness of the organization involved and the position that the organization occupies within the relevant field.

To take another example, Kornprobst and Senn offer a theory centered on "rhetorical fields": they "understand a social field as a semi-autonomous social space in which actors contest, decontest and reproduce background ideas (doxa) through their foreground communication (debate)" (2016, 301, 309). The two examine how a variety of actors successfully "contested ordering principles" that formed taken-for-granted assumptions in the international nuclear weapon field. As a number of chapters in this volume note, the study of the power politics of international order and institutions remains radically incomplete without attention to rhetoric and symbolic claims (see N. Crawford 2002; Krebs and Jackson 2007; Ward 2017).

Regardless of what particular variant of theory we choose, field analytics should help to enable a richer understanding of power politics. Elements of international order become a means, medium, and object of power politics, not only in relations *among* states and *within* them but also in terms of a broader variety of actors that participate in specific fields, including international organizations.

Networks

In his important review of the concept of social capital, Portes (1998, 3–4) quotes Bourdieu's account of social capital as the "aggregate of the actual or potential resources which are linked to possession of a durable network of more or less institutionalized relationships of mutual acquaintance and recognition." The structure of social ties in which individuals operate allows them to access "market resources" and to "increase their cultural capital through contact with experts or individuals or refinement" or through affiliation "with institutions that confer valued credentials."

Membership in international institutions generates social capital for those officials who circulate through them and, in consequence, for the governments who send those officials. This social capital has important implications for international power politics, especially understood in terms of collective mobilization. As Henke argues, "US-led coalition-building efforts are influenced by the *entirety* of bilateral and multilateral ties that connect the United States to a third party" (2017, 410). This "breadth of institutions matters because it allows officials to gather information on the potential coalition partner's deployment preferences beyond straightforward security considerations—such as what kind of economic and political considerations affect its willingness to join coalitions." In the terminology of the prior section, states can bootstrap military capital from social capital and its specialized international form: diplomatic capital.

This kind of analysis points in a different, but nonexclusive, direction from field-theoretic accounts of international order. Field analysis focuses on "the typology of social difference" within a field, while network analysis stresses "intersubjective connections" between social sites (Fourcade 2007, 1022). Goddard's contribution to this volume (chapter 8) lays out the crucial assumptions of a network approach to international order. She focuses on how institutional affiliation, understood in terms of social ties and networks, *positions* states in ways that influence the nature of, and toolkits available to, revisionist states.

But as Goddard also notes, thinking about international order in terms of social networks—patterns of alliances, trade, diplomacy, and the like—gives us important leverage over its topography. Positions within those networks create power asymmetries. These can involve, say, differential social capital, which Henke stresses in terms of access to information.[8] But international order can also involve relations of dependency and control generated by occupying, say, a central position in a specific network. For example, the United States reaps important benefits, including leverage, from its centrality in global finance (Oatley et al. 2013).

As I have argued elsewhere, American hegemony has produced a network of basing and access agreements as well as interorganizational and interpersonal ties across national militaries. The structure of these ties provides not only infrastructure power for the United States but opportunities for weaker states to influence American policy (Cooley and Nexon 2013; Kreiger, Souma, and Nexon 2015). For example, in the period surrounding the 2008 war between Russia and Georgia, Tbilisi leveraged interpersonal ties with US officials to construct itself as an important strategic asset. Moreover, these affective connections led officials in Washington and Tbilisi to overestimate their counterpart's credibility when it came to, on the one hand, the restraint of the Georgian regime in the face of Russian provocation and, on the other hand, the willingness of the United States to intervene to protect Georgia (Cooley and Nexon 2016).[9] A few points merit special attention here:

First, many of these kinds of ties—embodied in basing arrangements, joint military exercises, and routine consultations—are themselves "international institutions," regardless of whether they center around NATO or other international security organizations.

Second, they structure not only power relations between the United States and its partners but also the opportunities and strategies of other states. China, for example, is seeking to build its own network of bases and strategic partnerships, but it finds itself entering a relatively rich ecology of US-centered security relations. Thus, its growing network of allies and partners often involve "weak links" in this ecology: countries where the US is relatively absent, is indifferent, or faces strained relationships.

Third, a focus on the structure of ties and networks captures the dynamic relationship among actors, power politics, and international order—even when relatively institutionalized networks reflect dynamic transactions among social sites. This insight provides another way of grasping international order as means, medium, and object of power politics—and of understanding how power political maneuvers can transform order.

Indeed, I find it helpful to think of networks as the infrastructure of global order. In conjunction with field-theoretic frameworks, this provides us with a sense of international order as a dynamic ecology in which states—and other actors—pursue power and position. Especially in the postwar period, formal international organizations have become a critical part of that ecology. They channel the pursuit of influence, become sites of contestation in their own right, and even emerge as participants in power politics in their own right. Their increasing complexity affects power political repertoires, such as the apparent rise in forum shopping by states (Alter and Meunier 2009). Whatever analytic tools we use, understanding the heterogeneity of international order as something like an ecology is crucial to studying power politics and international institutions (see chapter 11, this volume).

Concluding Thoughts

My reading of this volume suggests that incorporating international institutions into the study of power politics carries with it three implications for realism and realist-inflected approaches: first, the need to understand power politics in terms of the dynamics of collective mobilization, which includes integrating a broader range of instruments and strategies into our analysis of power politics than, say, balancing and bandwagoning; second, the importance of embracing a more flexible approach to the kinds of actors and social sites that matter for international power politics (but without abandoning the critical importance of states); and third, the imperative of adopting a broad range of analytical tools to understand how international order structures, and is structured by, power politics.

Such general principles allow for theoretical creativity when it comes to power politics. For those of us who remain influenced by realist sensibilities, they imply a productive conversation between realism and other theoretical approaches. Wivel and Paul (chapter 1, this volume) invoke the need for analytical eclecticism on this point (Katzenstein and Sil 2010). I agree. But we also need to think hard about matters of coherence and consistency. That is, when borrowing from different approaches, we should pay attention to similarities and differences in their scientific ontologies.[10] Where these scientific ontologies point in different directions, we need to engage in theoretical work in terms of figuring out how they "link up" to one another and, if they do not, how we can make them interoperable.

Because field theories and network approaches share a fundamentally relational ontology, it is easy to bring them into dialogue with one another (Fourcade 2007; McCourt 2016; Nexon and Pouliot 2013). Moreover, both involve sensibilities familiar to realists, such as a focus on power and position. Nonetheless, their emphasis on the social basis of power, their broader social-constructionist sensibilities, and their analytical distinctiveness from the kinds of systems theories realists usually work with (see Goddard and Nexon 2005; LaRoche and Pratt 2017) probably make them a difficult sell for many realist scholars. However, once we take the wagers of this volume seriously, then we likely need to marry realism to new analytical approaches, whether these or others.

That does not necessarily mean completely abandoning the notion that some interactions among states operate in the context of anarchy. For that matter, I think that realists get a lot right about the field of great-power competition, the historical ubiquity of certain elements of power political repertoires, and the enduring importance of military and economic capital across international fields. But as Goddard shows in her chapter with respect to network approaches, we can treat anarchy as less an overarching ordering principle than a feature of specific relations (see also McConaughey, Musgrave, and Nexon 2018; Nexon 2009b, chap. 2). As I attempted to show here, we can recode a lot of realist theory in terms of fields while incorporating the kinds of insights about power politics found in this volume.

None of this should surprise anyone, and not only because they might be familiar with my work or the work of many of this volume's contributors. If we think of power politics in terms of dynamics of collective mobilization oriented toward specific ends, then it makes sense to draw on frameworks closely associated with the study of social mobilization, contentious politics, and collective action. Relational approaches—such as those focusing on networks, fields, and repertoires—are ubiquitous in those research programs. The advantage of these, and other, approaches is that they provide ways of incorporating institutional dynamics that prove difficult if we stay within the states-under-anarchy framework.

Finally, a critical lesson of this volume concerns broadening our understanding of the toolkit of power politics. On the one hand, states routinely make claims on institutions, use institutions, and create institutions in their pursuit of power and influence. On the other hand, officials within institutions pursue power and influence using forms of field-relevant capital, and network resources that are often specific, or adapted to, those institutions. Some of the chapters of this volume also further highlight the tactics and strategies that institutions use to influence states and non-state actors (see also Barnett and Finnemore 2004; Hafner-Burton 2008). Many scholars study how non-state actors influence international organizations and the states that comprise them (Carpenter 2011; Keck and Sikkink 1998; Murdie and Davis 2012; Petrova 2016).

Such variation in repertoires should reflect differences in fields, particularly with respect to rules of the game and field-relevant capital. As a relational phenomenon, the evolution and innovation of repertoires should constitute and alter social ties and networks. Moreover, the power-political tactics and instruments— forms of capital—that constitute repertoires likely entail a limited set of logics related to, say, pooling and wedging. Thinking in these terms, I submit, might help us to develop an integrated research program on power politics.

Notes

Funding for this chapter was provided by the Norwegian Research Council under the project Evaluating Power Political Repertoires (EPOS), project no. 250419.

1. Sørensen (chapter 4, this volume) also emphasizes the importance of both kinds of institutions.

2. Ironically, in its hegemonic order variants, realism takes this research agenda much more seriously. Even there, though, the focus on hegemons as the "route" to international order limits realist insights into the politics of order (see Musgrave and Nexon 2018; Nexon and Neumann 2018).

3. One of these, a neo-Gramscian approach, is developed in Freyberg-Inan's chapter. For that reason, and the fact that I lack the expertise to do it justice, I set it aside.

4. Paul Musgrave and Daniel Nexon, "Zheng He's Voyages and the Symbolism Behind Xi Jinping's Belt and Road Initiative," *The Diplomat*, December 22, 2017, https://thediplomat .com/2017/12/zheng-hes-voyages-and-the-symbolism-behind-xi-jinpings-belt-and-road -initiative/.

5. Another exception, if one squints hard enough, might be the Catholic Church.

6. This section, including its text, relies heavily on Nexon and Neumann (2018).

7. Of course, as Barkin and Weitsman (chapter 2, this volume) note, classical realists saw national power resources in broader terms; classical realists admitted a wider range of capital into their understanding of international fields, including diplomatic and cultural capital.

8. See also Carson and Thompson's chapter, which stress how variation in access to information creates power asymmetries.

9. For an analysis of how social networks shaped bargaining over Turkish support for the Iraq War, see Henke (2018).

10. Patrick Thaddeus Jackson and I argue that the scientific ontologies of theories concern "the actors that populate world politics, such as states, international organizations, individuals, and multinational corporations"; "the contexts and environments within which those actors find themselves"; "their relative significance to understanding and explaining international outcomes"; "how they fit together, such as parts of systems, autonomous entities, occupying locations in one or more social fields, nodes in a network, and so forth"; "what processes constitute the primary locus of scholarly analysis, for example, decisions, actions, behaviors, relations, and practices"; and "the inter-relationship among elements of those processes, such as preferences, interests, identities, social ties, and so on" (2013, 531–32).

References

Abbott, Kenneth W., and Duncan Snidal. 1998. "Why States Act through Formal International Organizations." *Journal of Conflict Resolution* 42 (1): 3–32.

Abdelal, Rawi, and Sophie Meunier. 2010. "Managed Globalization: Doctrine, Practice and Promise." *Journal of European Public Policy* 17 (3): 350–67.

Abdelal, Rawi, and John G. Ruggie. 2009. "The Principles of Embedded Liberalism: Social Legitimacy and Global Capitalism." In *New Perspectives on Regulation*, edited by David Moss and John Cisternino, 151–62. Cambridge, MA: Tobin Project.

Acharya, Amitav. 2016. *Why Govern? Rethinking Demand and Progress in Global Governance.* Cambridge: Cambridge University Press.

Ackerman, Bruce A. 1991. *We the People: Foundations.* Vol. 1. Cambridge, MA: Belknap Press of Harvard University Press.

Adamson, Fiona B. 2005. "Globalization, Transnational Political Mobilization, and Networks of Violence." *Cambridge Review of International Affairs* 18 (1): 21–49.

———. 2016. "Spaces of Global Security: Beyond Methodological Nationalism." *Journal of Global Security Studies* 1 (1): 19–35.

Adler, Emanuel. 1997. "Seizing the Middle Ground: Constructivism in World Politics." *European Journal of International Relations* 3 (3): 319–63.

———. 2013. "Constructivism in International Relations: Sources, Contributions, and Debates." In *Handbook of International Relations*, edited by Walter Carlsnaes, Thomas Risse and Beth A. Simmons, 112–44. London: Sage.

Adler, Emanuel, and Michael N. Barnett, eds. 1998. *Security Communities.* Cambridge: Cambridge University Press.

Adler, Emanuel, and Vincent Pouliot. 2011a. "International Practices." *International Theory* 3 (1): 1–36.

———, eds. 2011b. *International Practices.* Cambridge: Cambridge University Press.

Adler-Nissen, Rebecca. 2008. "The Diplomacy of Opting Out: A Bourdieudian Approach to National Integration Strategies." *Journal of Common Market Studies* 46 (3): 663–84.

———, ed. 2012. *Bourdieu in International Relations: Rethinking Key Concepts in IR.* New York: Routledge.

Adler-Nissen, Rebecca, and Vincent Pouliot. 2014. "Power in Practice: Negotiating the International Intervention in Libya." *European Journal of International Relations* 20 (4): 889–911.

Ahere, John. 2012. "The Peace Process in the DRC: A Transformation Quagmire." *ACCORD Policy and Practice Brief* 20 (December): 1–7.

Allan, Bentley B. 2017. "Producing the Climate: States, Scientists, and the Constitution of Global Governance Objects." *International Organization* 71 (1): 131–62.

Allen, Susan Hannah, and Amy T. Yuen. 2014. "The Politics of Peacekeeping: UN Security Council Oversight across Peacekeeping Missions." *International Studies Quarterly* 58 (3): 621–32.

Allison, Graham T. 1969. "Conceptual Models and the Cuban Missile Crisis." *American Political Science Review* 63 (3): 689–718.

Alter, Karen J., and Sophie Meunier. 2009. "The Politics of International Regime Complexity." *Perspectives on Politics* 7 (1): 13–24.

Ambrosetti, David. 2012. "The Diplomatic Lead in the United Nations Security Council and Local Actors' Violence: The Changing Terms of a Social Position." *African Security* 5 (2): 63–87.

Anderson, Perry. 2009. *The New Old World*. London: Verso.

Antoniades, Andreas. 2007. "Examining Facets of the Hegemonic: The Globalization Discourse in Greece and Ireland." *Review of International Political Economy* 14 (2): 306–32.

Archer, Clive. 2015. *International Organizations*. 4th ed. London: Routledge.

Art, Robert J. 1980. "To What Ends Military Power?" *International Security* 4 (4): 3–35.

Art, Robert J., and Kenneth N. Waltz. 1983. "Technology, Strategy, and the Uses of Force." In *The Use of Force*, edited by Robert J. Art and Kenneth N. Waltz, 1–33. Lanham, MD: University Press of America.

Asada, Sadao. 2007. "Between the Old Diplomacy and the New: The Washington System and the Origins of Japanese-American Rapprochement." In *Culture Shock and Japanese-American Relations: Historical Essays*, edited by Sadao Asada, 84–105. Columbia: University of Missouri Press.

Attree, Larry, Jordan Street, and Luca Venchiarutti. 2018. *United Nations Peace Operations in Complex Environments: Charting the Right Course*. London: Saferworld.

Avant, Deborah D. 2016. "Pragmatic Networks and Transnational Governance of Private Military and Security Services." *International Studies Quarterly* 60 (2): 330–42.

Avant, Deborah D., and Oliver Westerwinter, eds. 2016. *The New Power Politics: Networks and Transnational Security Governance*. New York: Oxford University Press.

Bacharach, Samuel B., and Edward J. Lawler. 1980. *Power and Politics in Organizations*. San Francisco: Jossey-Bass.

Bachrach, Peter, and Morton S. Baratz. 1962. "Two Faces of Power." *American Political Science Review* 56 (4): 947–52.

————. 1970. *Power and Poverty: Theory and Practice*. New York: Oxford University Press.

Baldwin, David A. 1979. "Power Analysis and World Politics: New Trends Versus Old Tendencies." *World Politics* 31 (2): 161–94.

————. 1985. *Economic Statecraft*. Princeton, NJ: Princeton University Press.

————, ed. 1993. *Neorealism and Neoliberalism: The Contemporary Debate*. New York: Columbia University Press.

————. 2002. "Power and International Relations." In *Handbook of International Relations*, edited by Walter Carlsnaes, Thomas Risse, and Beth Simmons, 177–91. London: Sage.

Bariff, Martin L., and Jay R. Galbraith. 1978. "Intraorganizational Power Considerations for Designing Information Systems." *Accounting, Organizations and Society* 3 (1): 15–27.

Barkin, J. Samuel. 2010. *Realist Constructivism: Rethinking International Relations Theory*. Cambridge: Cambridge University Press.

Barnett, Michael N. 1992. *Confronting the Costs of War: Military Power, State, and Society in Egypt and Israel*. Princeton, NJ: Princeton University Press.

————. 1997. "The UN Security Council, Indifference, and Genocide in Rwanda." *Cultural Anthropology* 12 (4): 551–78.

Barnett, Michael, and Raymond Duvall. 2005. "Power in International Politics." *International Organization* 59 (1): 39–75.

Barnett, Michael N., and Martha Finnemore. 1999. "The Politics, Power, and Pathologies of International Organizations." *International Organization* 53 (4): 699–732.

————. 2004. *Rules for the World: International Organizations in Global Politics*. Ithaca, NY: Cornell University Press.

Beasley, W. G. 1987. *Japanese Imperialism, 1894–1945*. Oxford: Clarendon Press.

Beck, Ulrich. 2013. *German Europe*. Cambridge: Polity Press.

Beckfield, Jason. 2003. "Inequality in the World Polity: The Structure of International Organization." *American Sociological Review* 68 (3): 401–24.

Beker, Avi. 1988. *The United Nations and Israel: From Recognition to Reprehension*. Lexington, MA: Lexington Books.

Bellamy, Alex J. 2004. "The 'Next Stage' in Peace Operations Theory?" *International Peacekeeping* 11 (1): 17–38.

Bellamy, Alex J., and Charles T. Hunt. 2015. "Twenty-First Century UN Peace Operations: Protection, Force and the Changing Security Environment." *International Affairs* 91 (6): 1277–98.

Bello, Walden F. 2013. *Capitalism's Last Stand? Deglobalization in the Age of Austerity*. New York: Zed Books.

Bennett, Andrew, and Colin Elman. 2006. "Complex Causal Relations and Case Study Methods: The Example of Path Dependence." *Political Analysis* 14 (3): 250–67.

Berdal, Mats. 2018. "The State of UN Peacekeeping: Lessons from Congo." *Journal of Strategic Studies* 41 (5): 721–50.

Berenskoetter, Felix, and Michael J. Williams, eds. 2007. *Power in World Politics*. London: Routledge.

Berling, Trine Villumsen. 2012. "Bourdieu, International Relations, and International Security." *Theory and Society* 41: 451–78.

Bernanke, Ben S. 2005. "The Global Saving Glut and the U.S. Current Account Deficit." Homer Jones Lecture, Saint Louis, MO, April 14.

Betzold, Carola. 2010. "'Borrowing' Power to Influence International Negotiations: AOSIS in the Climate Change Regime, 1990–1997." *Politics* 30 (3): 131–48.

Bickerton, Christopher J., Dermot Hodson, and Uwe Puetter. 2015. "The New Intergovernmentalism: European Integration in the Post-Maastricht Era." *Journal of Common Market Studies* 53 (4): 703–22.

Biermann, Frank, Philipp Pattberg, Harro van Asselt, and Fariborz Zelli. 2009. "The Fragmentation of Global Governance Architectures: A Framework for Analysis." *Global Environmental Politics* 9 (4): 14–40.

Bigo, Didier. 2012. "Pierre Bourdieu and International Relations: Power of Practices, Practices of Power." *International Political Sociology* 5 (3): 225–58.

Bjola, Corneliu, and Markus Kornprobst, eds. 2011. *Arguing Global Governance: Agency, Lifeworld and Shared Reasons*. London: Routledge.

Blainey, Geoffrey. 1988. *The Causes of War*. 3rd ed. Basingstoke: Macmillan.

Blanchard, Jean-Marc F., and Norrin M. Ripsman. 2013. *Economic Statecraft and Foreign Policy: Sanctions, Incentives and Target State Calculations*. London: Routledge.

Bosco, David L. 2009. *Five to Rule Them All: The UN Security Council and the Making of the Modern World*. Oxford: Oxford University Press.

———. 2014. *Rough Justice: The International Criminal Court in a World of Power Politics*. Oxford: Oxford University Press.

Bourdieu, Pierre. 1991. *Language and Symbolic Power*. Cambridge, MA: Harvard University Press.

———. 2011. "The Forms of Capital (1986)." In *Cultural Theory: An Anthology*, edited by Imre Szeman and Timothy Kaposy, 81–93. Malden, MA: Wiley-Blackwell.

Boutellis, Arthur. 2015. "Can the UN Stabilize Mali? Towards a UN Stabilization Doctrine?" *Stability* 4 (1). https://stabilityjournal.org/articles/10.5334/sta.fz/print/.

Boutellis, Arthur, and Naureen Chowdhury Fink. 2016. *Waging Peace: UN Peace Operations Confronting Terrorism and Violent Extremism*. New York: International Peace Institute.

Brands, H. W. 2004. "George Bush and the Gulf War of 1991." *Presidential Studies Quarterly* 34 (1): 113–31.

Breakey, Hugh, and Sidney Dekker. 2014. "Weak Links in the Chain of Authority: The Challenges of Intervention Decisions to Protect Civilians." *International Peacekeeping* 21 (3): 307–23.

Brooks, Stephen G. 1997. "Dueling Realisms." *International Organization* 51 (3): 445–77.

Brooks, Stephen G., G. John Ikenberry, and William C. Wohlforth. 2013. "Don't Come Home, America: The Case against Retrenchment." *International Security* 37 (3): 7–51.

Brooks, Stephen G., and William C. Wohlforth. 2008. *World Out of Balance: International Relations and the Challenge of American Primacy.* Princeton, NJ: Princeton University Press.

———. 2016. "The Rise and Fall of the Great Powers in the Twenty-First Century: China's Rise and the Fate of America's Global Position." *International Security* 40 (3): 7–53.

Broome, André. 2014. *Issues and Actors in the Global Political Economy.* Basingstoke: Palgrave Macmillan.

Brown, Bill. 2003. *A Sense of Things: The Object Matter of American Literature.* Chicago: University of Chicago Press.

Brown, Michael E., Owen R. Coté Jr., Sean M. Lynn-Jones, and Steven E. Miller, eds. 2010. *Going Nuclear: Nuclear Proliferation and International Security in the 21st Century.* Cambridge, MA: MIT Press.

Brown, Stuart. 2013. *The Future of U.S. Global Power: Delusions of Decline.* Basingstoke: Palgrave Macmillan.

Bucholz, Larissa. 2016. "What Is a Global Field? Theorizing Fields beyond the Nation-State." In *Fielding Transnationalism,* edited by Julian Go and Monika Krause, 31–60. Malden, MA: John Wiley & Sons.

Bueno de Mesquita, Bruce, and Randolph M. Siverson. 1995. "War and the Survival of Political Leaders: A Comparative Study of Regime Types and Political Accountability." *American Political Science Review* 89 (4): 841–55.

Bueno de Mesquita, Bruce, Alastair Smith, Randolph M. Siverson, and James D. Morrow. 2003. *The Logic of Political Survival.* Cambridge, MA: MIT Press.

Bukovansky, Mlada. 2002. *Legitimacy and Power Politics: The American and French Revolutions in International Political Culture.* Princeton, NJ: Princeton University Press.

Bunn, George. 2003. "The Nuclear Nonproliferation Treaty: History and Current Problems." *Arms Control Today* 33 (10): 4–10. https://www.armscontrol.org/act/2003_12/Bunn.

Burns, Richard Dean, and Joseph M. Siracusa. 2013. *A Global History of the Nuclear Arms Race: Weapons, Strategy, and Politics.* Santa Barbara, CA: Praeger Security International.

Busch, Marc L., Eric Reinhardt, and Gregory Shaffer. 2009. "Does Legal Capacity Matter? A Survey of WTO Members." *World Trade Review* 8 (4): 559–77.

Büthe, Tim, and Walter Mattli. 2011. *The New Global Rulers: The Privatization of Regulation in the World Economy.* Princeton, NJ: Princeton University Press.

Buzan, Barry. 1993. "From International System to International Society: Structural Realism and Regime Theory Meet the English School." *International Organization* 47 (3): 327–52.

———. 2004. *From International to World Society? English School Theory and the Social Structure of Globalisation.* Cambridge: Cambridge University Press.

Buzan, Barry, Charles A. Jones, and Richard Little. 1993. *The Logic of Anarchy: Neorealism to Structural Realism*. New York: Columbia University Press.

Buzan, Barry, and Richard Little. 1996. "Reconceptualizing Anarchy: Structural Realism Meets World History." *European Journal of International Relations* 2 (4): 403–38.

Búzás, Zoltán I. 2013. "The Color of Threat: Race, Threat Perception, and the Demise of the Anglo-Japanese Alliance (1902–1923)." *Security Studies* 22 (4): 573–606.

Cameron, Angus, and Ronen Palan. 2004. *The Imagined Economies of Globalization*. London: Sage.

Campbell, John L., and John A. Hall. 2015. *The World of States*. London: Bloomsbury.

Cappella Zielinski, Rosella. 2016. *How States Pay for Wars*. Ithaca, NY: Cornell University Press.

Carnegie, Allison, and Austin M. Carson. 2018. "The Disclosure Dilemma: Nuclear Intelligence and International Organization." Unpublished paper. Columbia University and University of Chicago.

Carney, Christopher P. 1989. "International Patron-Client Relationships: A Conceptual Framework." *Studies in Comparative International Development* 24 (2): 42–55.

Carpenter, R. Charli. 2011. "Vetting the Advocacy Agenda: Network Centrality and the Paradox of Weapons Norms." *International Organization* 65 (1): 69–102.

Carr, Edward Hallett. 1946. *The Twenty Years' Crisis, 1919–1939: An Introduction to the Study of International Relations*. London: Macmillan.

Cerny, Philip G. 1995. "Globalization and the Changing Logic of Collective Action." *International Organization* 49 (4): 595–625.

———. 2000. "The New Security Dilemma: Divisibility, Defection and Disorder in the Global Era." *Review of International Studies* 26 (4): 623–46.

———. 2010. *Rethinking World Politics: A Theory of Transnational Neopluralism*. New York: Oxford University Press.

Chapman, Terrence L., and Dan Reiter. 2004. "The United Nations Security Council and the Rally 'round the Flag Effect." *Journal of Conflict Resolution* 48 (6): 886–909.

Charbonneau, Bruno. 2017. "Intervention in Mali: Building Peace between Peacekeeping and Counterterrorism." *Journal of Contemporary African Studies* 35 (4): 415–31.

Chasek, Pamela, and Lavanya Rajamani. 2003. "Steps toward Enhanced Parity: Negotiating Capacity and Strategies of Developing Countries." In *Providing Global Public Goods*, edited by Inge Kaul, 245–62. Oxford: Oxford University Press.

Checkel, Jeffrey T. 2005. "International Institutions and Socialization in Europe: Introduction and Framework." *International Organization* 59 (4): 801–26.

Chiozza, Giacomo, and Hein E. Goemans. 2003. "Peace through Insecurity: Tenure and International Conflict." *Journal of Conflict Resolution* 47 (4): 443–67.

Christin, Angèle. 2016. "Is Journalism a Transnational Field? Asymmetrical Relations and Symbolic Domination in Online News." In *Fielding Transnationalism*, edited by Julian Go and Monika Krause, 212–34. Malden, MA: John Wiley & Sons.

Clark, Ian. 2005. *Legitimacy in International Society*. Oxford: Oxford University Press.

———. 2009. "Towards an English School Theory of Hegemony." *European Journal of International Relations* 15 (2): 203–28.

Claude, Inis L. 1962. *Power and International Relations*. New York: Random House.

Clegg, Liam. 2013. *Controlling the World Bank and IMF: Shareholders, Stakeholders and the Politics of Concessional Lending*. Basingstoke: Palgrave Macmillan.

Clift, Ben. 2014. *Comparative Political Economy: States, Markets and Global Capitalism*. London: Palgrave Macmillan.

Clift, Ben, and Ben Rosamond. 2009. "Lineages of British International Political Economy." In *Handbook of International Political Economy*, edited by Mark Blyth, 95–111. London: Routledge.

Clift, Ben, and Cornelia Woll, eds. 2013. *Economic Patriotism in Open Economies*. London: Routledge.

Cogan, Jacob Katz. 2009. "Representation and Power in International Organization: The Operational Constitution and Its Critics." *American Journal of International Law* 103 (2): 209–63.

Cohen, Benjamin J. 2008. *International Political Economy: An Intellectual History*. Princeton, NJ: Princeton University Press.

Cohen, Wesley M., and Daniel A. Levinthal. 1990. "Absorptive Capacity: A New Perspective on Learning and Innovation." *Administrative Science Quarterly* 35 (1): 128–52.

Colgan, Jeff D., and Robert O. Keohane. 2017. "The Liberal Order Is Rigged: Fix It Now or Watch It Wither." *Foreign Affairs* 96 (3): 36–45.

Collard-Wexler, Simon. 2006. "Integration under Anarchy: Neorealism and the European Union." *European Journal of International Relations* 12 (3): 397–432.

Cook, Christopher R. 2010. "American Policymaking in the Democratic Republic of the Congo 1996–1999: The Anti-Kabila Bias and the Crushing Neutrality of the Lusaka Accords." *African and Asian Studies* 9 (4): 393–417.

Cooley, Alexander. 2012. *Great Games, Local Rules: The New Great Power Contest in Central Asia*. New York: Oxford University Press.

Cooley, Alexander, and Daniel Nexon. 2013. "'The Empire Will Compensate You': The Structural Dynamics of the U.S. Overseas Basing Network." *Perspectives on Politics* 11 (4): 1034–50.

———. 2016. "Interpersonal Networks and International Security." In Avant and Westerwinter 2016, 74–102.

Cooper, Andrew F. 2010. "The G20 as an Improvised Crisis Committee and/or a Contested 'Steering Committee' for the World." *International Affairs* 86 (3): 741–57.

Copelovitch, Mark S. 2010. "Master or Servant? Common Agency and the Political Economy of IMF Lending." *International Studies Quarterly* 54 (1): 49–77.

Costalli, Stefano. 2011. "The Impact of International Politics on Commercial Flows in the Age of Globalization." *World Political Science* 7 (1).

Cox, Robert W. 1986. "Social Forces, States and World Orders: Beyond International Relations Theory." In *Neorealism and Its Critics*, edited by Robert O. Keohane, 204–54. New York: Columbia University Press.

Cox, Robert W., and Michael G. Schechter. 2003. *The Political Economy of a Plural World: Critical Reflections on Power, Morals and Civilization*. London: Routledge.

Cox, Robert W., and Timothy J. Sinclair. 1996. *Approaches to World Order*. Cambridge: Cambridge University Press.

Crawford, Neta. 2002. *Argument and Change in World Politics*. Cambridge: Cambridge University Press.

———. 2008. "Wedge Strategy, Balancing, and the Deviant Case of Spain, 1940–1941." *Security Studies* 17 (1): 1–38.

Crawford, Timothy W. 2011. "Wedge Strategies in Power Politics." *International Security* 35 (4): 155–189.

Cronin, Bruce, and Ian Hurd, eds. 2008. *The UN Security Council and the Politics of International Authority*. London: Routledge.

Crouch, Colin. 2011. *The Strange Non-Death of Neoliberalism*. Cambridge: Polity Press.

Cunliffe, Philip. 2009. "The Politics of Global Governance in UN Peacekeeping." *International Peacekeeping* 16 (3): 323–36.

———. 2012. "Still the Spectre at the Feast: Comparisons between Peacekeeping and Imperialism in Peacekeeping Studies Today." *International Peacekeeping* 19 (4): 426–42.

Dahl, Robert A. 1957. "The Concept of Power." *Behavioral Science* 2 (3): 201–15.

———. 1961. *Who Governs? Democracy and Power in an American City*. New Haven, CT: Yale University Press.

———. 1999. "Can International Organizations Be Democratic? A Skeptic's View." In *Democracy's Edges*, edited by Ian Shapiro and Casiano Hacker-Cordón, 19–36. Cambridge: Cambridge University Press.

Daku, Mark, and Krzysztof J. Pelc. 2017. "Who Holds Influence over WTO Jurisprudence?" *Journal of International Economic Law* 20 (2): 233–55.

Dallek, Robert. 2005. *Lyndon B. Johnson: Portrait of a President*. Oxford: Oxford University Press.

Damro, Chad. 2012. "Market Power Europe." *Journal of European Public Policy* 19 (5): 682–99.

Davis, Christina L., and Sarah Blodgett Bermeo. 2009. "Who Files? Developing Country Participation in GATT/WTO Adjudication." *Journal of Politics* 71 (3): 1033–49.

Dehousse, Renaud, and Laurie Boussaguet. 2014. "L'impact de la crise sur la gouvernance européenne." *Pouvoirs* (2): 7–18.

Desgrais, Nicolas. 2018. "La Force conjointe du G5 Sahel ou l'émergence d'une architecture de défense collective propre au Sahel." *Les Champs de Mars* 30 (1): 211–20.

DeSombre, Elizabeth R., and Joanne Kauffman. 1996. "The Montreal Protocol Multilateral Fund: Partial Success Story." In *Institutions for Environmental Aid: Pitfalls and Promise*, edited by Robert O. Keohane and Marc A. Levy, 89–126. Cambridge, MA: MIT Press.

Deudney, Daniel. 1996. "Binding Sovereigns: Authorities, Structures, and Geopolitics in Philadelphian Systems." In *State Sovereignty as Social Construct*, edited by Thomas J. Biersteker and Cynthia Weber, 190–239. Cambridge: Cambridge University Press.

De Wilde, Pieter. 2011. "No Polity for Old Politics? A Framework for Analyzing the Politicization of European Integration." *Journal of European Integration* 33 (5): 559–75.

De Wilde, Pieter, and Michael Zürn. 2012. "Can the Politicization of European Integration Be Reversed?" *Journal of Common Market Studies* 50 (1): 137–53.

Diamond, Patrick, Peter Nedergaard, and Ben Rosamond. 2018. *Routledge Handbook of the Politics of Brexit*. London: Routledge.

Dickinson, Frederick R. 1999. *War and National Reinvention: Japan in the Great War, 1914–1919*. Cambridge, MA: Harvard University Press.

Dijkstra, Hylke. 2015. "Shadow Bureaucracies and the Unilateral Control of International Secretariats: Insights from UN Peacekeeping." *Review of International Organizations* 10 (1): 23–41.

Dinan, Desmond, Neill Nugent, and William E. Paterson. 2017. "Conclusions: Crisis without End." In *The European Union in Crisis*, edited by Desmond Dinan, Neill Nugent, and William E. Paterson, 360–75. London: Palgrave Macmillan.

Donnelly, Jack. 2000. *Realism and International Relations*. Cambridge: Cambridge University Press.

Donno, Daniela. 2010. "Who Is Punished? Regional Intergovernmental Organizations and the Enforcement of Democratic Norms." *International Organization* 64 (4): 593–625.

Downs, George W., David M. Rocke, and Peter N. Barsoom. 1996. "Is the Good News about Compliance Good News about Cooperation?" *International Organization* 50 (3): 379–406.

Doyle, Michael W. 1983. "Kant, Liberal Legacies, and Foreign Affairs." *Philosophy and Public Affairs* 12 (3): 205–35.

Dreher, Axel, Jan-Egbert Sturm, and James Raymond Vreeland. 2009. "Development Aid and International Politics: Does Membership on the UN Security Council Influence World Bank Decisions?" *Journal of Development Economics* 88 (1): 1–18.

Drezner, Daniel W. 2008. *All Politics Is Global: Explaining International Regulatory Regimes*. Princeton, NJ: Princeton University Press.

———. 2009. "The Power and Peril of International Regime Complexity." *Perspectives on Politics* 7 (1): 65–70.

———. 2012. *The Irony of Global Economic Governance: The System Worked*. New York: Council on Foreign Relations, October 2. https://www.cfr.org/report/irony-global-economic-governance.

Dumouchel, Joelle. 2018. "The Invention of Financial Stability: How Problematization Impacts Regulatory Reform." Unpublished paper. University of Copenhagen.

Eaton, Sarah, and Richard Stubbs. 2006. "Is ASEAN Powerful? Neo-realist versus Constructivist Approaches to Power in Southeast Asia." *Pacific Review* 19 (2): 135–55.

Edelstein, David M. 2002. "Managing Uncertainty: Beliefs about Intentions and the Rise of Great Powers." *Security Studies* 12 (1): 1–40.

Ella, Doron. 2016. "China and the United Nations Framework Convention on Climate Change: The Politics of Institutional Categorization." *International Relations of the Asia-Pacific* 17 (2): 233–64.

Eschle, Catherine, and Bice Maiguashca, eds. 2005. *Critical Theories, World Politics and the "Anti-Globalization Movement."* London: Routledge.

European Commission. 2017. *Resilience, Deterrence and Defence: Building Strong Cybersecurity for the EU.* Brussels. https://publications.europa.eu/en/publication-detail/-/publication/794f8627-985b-11e7-b92d-01aa75ed71a1.

European Council. 2003. *European Security Strategy: A Secure Europe in a Better World.* Brussels.

Evan, William M., and Bret B. Hays. 2006. "Dual-Use Technology in the Context of the Non-proliferation Regime." *History and Technology* 22 (1): 105–13.

Farrell, Henry, and Abraham L. Newman. 2014. "Domestic Institutions beyond the Nation-State: Charting the New Interdependence Approach." *World Politics* 66 (2): 331–63.

———. 2015. "The New Politics of Interdependence: Cross-National Layering in Trans-Atlantic Regulatory Disputes." *Comparative Political Studies* 48 (4): 497–526.

Ferguson, Chaka. 2012. "The Strategic Use of Soft Balancing: The Normative Dimensions of the Chinese-Russian 'Strategic Partnership.'" *Journal of Strategic Studies* 35 (2): 197–222.

Feurle, Loie. 1985. "Informal Consultation: A Mechanism in Security Council Decision-Making." *NYU Journal of International Law and Politics* 18: 267–308.

Finnemore, Martha. 1996. *National Interests in International Society.* Ithaca, NY: Cornell University Press.

———. 2009. "Legitimacy, Hypocrisy, and the Social Structure of Unipolarity: Why Being a Unipole Isn't All It's Cracked Up to Be." *World Politics* 61 (1): 58–85.

Finnemore, Martha, and Judith Goldstein. 2013. "Puzzles about Power." In *Back to Basics: State Power in a Contemporary World*, edited by Martha Finnemore and Judith Goldstein, 3–17. New York: Oxford University Press.

Finnemore, Martha, and Kathryn Sikkink. 1998. "International Norm Dynamics and Political Change." *International Organization* 52 (4): 887–917.

Finnemore, Martha, and Stephen J. Toope. 2001. "Alternatives to 'Legalization': Richer Views of Law and Politics." *International Organization* 55 (3): 743–58.

Fisher, Jonathan, and David M. Anderson. 2015. "Authoritarianism and the Securitization of Development in Africa." *International Affairs* 91 (1): 131–51.

Fleming, J. Marcus. 1962. "Domestic Financial Policies under Fixed and under Floating Exchange Rates." *IMF Staff Papers* 9 (3): 369–80.

Fligstein, Neil. 2008. *Euroclash: The EU, European Identity, and the Future of Europe.* Oxford: Oxford University Press.

Fligstein, Neil, and Doug McAdam. 2012. *A Theory of Fields.* New York: Oxford University Press.

Fortna, Virginia Page. 2003. "Scraps of Paper? Agreements and the Durability of Peace." *International Organization* 57 (2): 337–72.

Fourcade, Marion. 2007. "Theories of Markets and Theories of Society." *American Behavioral Scientist* 50 (8): 1015–34.

Frankel, Benjamin. 1993. "The Brooding Shadow." In *The Proliferation Puzzle: Why Nuclear Weapons Spread and What Results*, edited by Zachary S. Davis and Benjamin Frankel, 7–78. London: Frank Cass.

———. 1996. "Restating the Realist Case: An Introduction." In *Realism: Restatements and Renewal*, edited by Benjamin Frankel, ix–xx. London: Frank Cass.

Freedman, Lawrence. 1989. *The Evolution of Nuclear Strategy.* 2nd ed. London: Macmillan.

Friedner Parrat, Charlotta. 2017. "On the Evolution of Primary Institutions of International Society." *International Studies Quarterly* 61 (3): 623–30.

Fuhrmann, Matthew. 2012. *Atomic Assistance: How "Atoms for Peace" Programs Cause Nuclear Insecurity.* Ithaca, NY: Cornell University Press.

Fukuyama, Francis. 1989. "The End of History?" *National Interest* 16: 3–18.

Gaddis, John Lewis. 1986. "The Long Peace: Elements of Stability in the Postwar International System." *International Security* 10 (4): 99–142.

Gardam, Judith Gail. 2004. *Necessity, Proportionality, and the Use of Force by States.* Cambridge: Cambridge University Press.

Gavin, Francis J. 2010. "Same as It Ever Was: Nuclear Alarmism, Proliferation, and the Cold War." *International Security* 34 (3): 7–37.

Germain, Randall D. 2016. "Susan Strange and the Future of IPE." In *Susan Strange and the Future of Global Political Economy*, edited by Randall D. Germain, 1–18. London: Routledge.

Germann, Julian. 2014. "German 'Grand Strategy' and the Rise of Neoliberalism." *International Studies Quarterly* 58 (4): 706–16.

Gill, Stephen. 1993. *Gramsci, Historical Materialism and International Relations.* Cambridge: Cambridge University Press.

———. 2000. "Toward a Postmodern Prince? The Battle in Seattle as a Moment in the New Politics of Globalisation." *Millennium* 29 (1): 131–40.

Gilpin, Robert. 1981. *War and Change in World Politics.* Cambridge: Cambridge University Press.

———. 1987. *The Political Economy of International Relations.* Princeton, NJ: Princeton University Press.

———. 1988. "The Theory of Hegemonic War." *Journal of Interdisciplinary History* 18 (4): 591–613.

———. 2001. *Global Political Economy: Understanding the International Economic Order.* Princeton, NJ: Princeton University Press.

Glaser, Charles L. 1994. "Realists as Optimists: Cooperation as Self-Help." *International Security* 19 (3): 50–90.

———. 2010. *Rational Theory of International Politics: The Logic of Competition and Cooperation.* Princeton, NJ: Princeton University Press.

Global Environment Facility. 1999. *Expanded Opportunities for Executing Agencies: Recent Efforts and Current Proposals to Expand Opportunities for Regional Development Banks.* GEF/C.13/3. May 5–7. https://www.thegef.org/sites/default/files/council-meeting-documents/GEF.C.13.3_5.pdf.

Go, Julian. 2008. "Global Fields and Imperial Forms: Field Theory and the British and American Empires." *Sociological Theory* 26 (3): 201–27.

Go, Julian, and Monika Krause. 2016. "Fielding Transnationalism: An Introduction." *Sociological Review* 64 (2S): 6–30.

Goddard, Stacie E. 2009a. "Brokering Change: Networks and Entrepreneurs in International Politics." *International Theory* 1 (2): 249–81.

———. 2009b. "When Right Makes Might: How Prussia Overturned the European Balance of Power." *International Security* 33 (3): 110–42.

Goddard, Stacie E., Paul K. MacDonald, and Daniel H. Nexon. 2019. "Repertoires of Statecraft: Instruments and Logics of Power Politics." International Relations, forthcoming DOI: 1177/0047117819834625.

Goddard, Stacie E., and Daniel Nexon. 2005. "Paradigm Lost? Reassessing Theory of International Politics." *European Journal of International Relations* 11 (1): 9–61.

———. 2015. "The Dynamics of Global Power Politics: A Framework for Analysis." *Journal of Global Security Studies* 1 (1): 4–18.

———. 2016. "The Dynamics of Global Power Politics: A Framework for Analysis." *Journal of Global Security Studies* 1 (1): 4–18.

Goh, Evelyn. 2013. *The Struggle for Order: Hegemony, Hierarchy, and Transition in Post–Cold War East Asia.* Oxford: Oxford University Press.

Gold, Dore. 2004. *Tower of Babble: How the United Nations Has Fueled Global Chaos.* New York: Three Rivers Press.

Goldsmith, Jack. 2003. "The Self-Defeating International Criminal Court." *University of Chicago Law Review* 70 (1): 89–104.

Gorur, Aditi. 2016. *Defining the Boundaries of UN Stabilization Missions.* Washington, DC: Stimson Center.

Gowan, Richard. 2016. "The Security Council and Peacekeeping." In *The UN Security Council in the 21st Century,* edited by Sebastian von Einsiedel, David M. Malone, and Bruno Stagno Ugarte, 749–70. Boulder, CO: Lynne Rienner.

Graham, Erin R. 2014. "International Organizations as Collective Agents: Fragmentation and the Limits of Principal Control at the World Health Organization." *European Journal of International Relations* 20 (2): 366–90.

Gramsci, Antonio. 1971. *Selections from the Prison Notebooks.* New York: International Publishers.

Grieco, Joseph M. 1990. *Cooperation among Nations: Europe, America, and Non-tariff Barriers to Trade.* Ithaca, NY: Cornell University Press.

———. 1995. "The Maastricht Treaty, Economic and Monetary Union and the Neorealist Research Programme." *Review of International Studies* 21 (1): 21–40.

Grieco, Joseph M., and G. John Ikenberry. 2003. *State Power and World Markets: The International Political Economy.* New York: W. W. Norton.

Grigorescu, Alexandru. 2007. "Transparency of Intergovernmental Organizations: The Roles of Member States, International Bureaucracies and Nongovernmental Organizations." *International Studies Quarterly* 51 (3): 625–48.

———. 2010. "The Accountability of Intergovernmental Organizations: New Developments or Cyclical Trends?" Paper presented at the International Studies Association Annual Convention, New Orleans, LA, February 17–20.

———. 2015. *Democratic Intergovernmental Organizations? Normative Pressures and Decision-Making Rules.* Cambridge: Cambridge University Press.

Grøn, Caroline Howard, and Anders Wivel. 2011. "Maximizing Influence in the European Union after the Lisbon Treaty: From Small State Policy to Smart State Strategy." *Journal of European Integration* 33 (5): 523–39.

Gruber, Lloyd. 2000. *Ruling the World: Power Politics and the Rise of Supranational Institutions.* Princeton, NJ: Princeton University Press.

Guéhenno, Jean-Marie. 2015. *The Fog of Peace: A Memoir of International Peacekeeping in the 21st Century.* Washington, DC: Brookings Institution Press.

Guiraudon, Virginie. 2018. "The 2015 Refugee Crisis Was Not a Turning Point: Explaining Policy Inertia in EU Border Control." *European Political Science* 17 (1): 151–60.

Gulick, Edward Vose. 1955. *Europe's Classical Balance of Power: A Case History of the Theory and Practice of One of the Great Concepts of European Statecraft.* Ithaca, NY: Cornell University Press.

Guzzini, Stefano. 1993. "Structural Power: The Limits of Neorealist Power Analysis." *International Organization* 47 (3): 443–78.

———. 2000. "The Use and Misuse of Power Analysis in International Theory." In *Global Political Economy: Contemporary Theories*, edited by Ronan Palan, 53–66. London: Routledge.

Haas, Ernst B. 1953. "The Balance of Power: Prescription, Concept, or Propaganda?" *World Politics* 5 (4): 442–77.

———. 1958. *The Uniting of Europe: Political, Social, and Economic Forces, 1950–1957.* Stanford, CA: Stanford University Press.

Hafner-Burton, Emilie M. 2008. "Sticks and Stones: Naming and Shaming the Human Rights Enforcement Problem." *International Organization* 62 (4): 689–716.

———. 2009. "The Power Politics of Regime Complexity: Human Rights Trade Conditionality in Europe." *Perspectives on Politics* 7 (1): 33–37.

Hafner-Burton, Emilie M., Miles Kahler, and Alexander H. Montgomery. 2009. "Network Analysis for International Relations." *International Organization* 63 (3): 559–92.

Hafner-Burton, Emilie M., and Alexander H. Montgomery. 2006. "Power Positions: International Organizations, Social Networks, and Conflict." *Journal of Conflict Resolution* 50 (1): 3–27.

Haftel, Yoram Z., and Stephanie C. Hofmann. 2017. "Institutional Authority and Security Cooperation within Regional Economic Organizations." *Journal of Peace Research* 54 (4): 484–98.

Haggard, Stephan, and Beth A. Simmons. 1987. "Theories of International Regimes." *International Organization* 41 (3): 491–517.

Hale, Thomas, David Held, and Kevin Young. 2013. *Gridlock: Why Global Coopera-tion Is Failing When We Need It Most.* Cambridge: Polity Press.

Hall, Peter A., and David W. Soskice, eds. 2001. *Varieties of Capitalism: The Institu-tional Foundations of Comparative Advantage.* Oxford: Oxford University Press.

Hansen, Birthe, Peter Toft, and Anders Wivel. 2009. *Security Strategies and American World Order: Lost Power.* London: Routledge.

Hart, Jeffrey. 1976. "Three Approaches to the Measurement of Power in Interna-tional Relations." *International Organization* 30 (2): 289–305.

Hassan, Salah M., and Carina E. Ray. 2009. *Darfur and the Crisis of Governance in Sudan: A Critical Reader.* Ithaca, NY: Cornell University Press.

Haukkala, Hiski. 2015. "From Cooperative to Contested Europe? The Conflict in Ukraine as a Culmination of a Long-Term Crisis in EU-Russia Relations." *Journal of Contemporary European Studies* 22 (1): 25–40.

Hawkins, Darren G., David A. Lake, Daniel L. Nielson, and Michael J. Tierney, eds. 2006a. *Delegation and Agency in International Organizations.* Cambridge: Cam-bridge University Press.

Hawkins, Darren G., David A. Lake, Daniel L. Nielson, and Michael J. Tierney. 2006b. "Delegation under Anarchy: States, International Organizations, and Principal-Agent Theory." In Hawkins et al. 2006a, 3–38.

Hay, Colin. 1996. "Narrating Crisis: The Discursive Construction of the 'Winter of Discontent.'" *Sociology* 30 (2): 253–77.

Hay, Colin, and Ben Rosamond. 2002. "Globalization, European Integration and the Discursive Construction of Economic Imperatives." *Journal of European Public Policy* 9 (2): 147–67.

He, Kai. 2008. "Institutional Balancing and International Relations Theory: Eco-nomic Interdependence and Balance of Power Strategies in Southeast Asia." *European Journal of International Relations* 14 (3): 489–518.

———. 2012. "Undermining Adversaries: Unipolarity, Threat Perception, and Neg-ative Balancing Strategies after the Cold War." *Security Studies* 21 (2): 154–91.

———. 2015. "Contested Regional Orders and Institutional Balancing in the Asia Pacific." *International Politics* 52 (2): 208–22.

———. 2018. "Role Conceptions, Order Transition and Institutional Balancing in the Asia-Pacific: A New Theoretical Framework." *Australian Journal of Inter-national Affairs* 72 (2): 92–109.

Helbling, Marc, Dominic Hoeglinger, and Bruno Wüest. 2010. "How Political Parties Frame European Integration." *European Journal of Political Research* 49 (4): 495–521.

Held, David. 2004. "Democratic Accountability and Political Effectiveness from a Cosmopolitan Perspective." *Government and Opposition* 39 (2): 364–91.

Held, David, and Mathias Koenig-Archibugi. 2005. *Global Governance and Public Accountability.* Malden, MA: Wiley-Blackwell.

Helleiner, Eric. 2010. "What Role for the New Financial Stability Board? The Poli-tics of International Standards after the Crisis." *Global Policy* 1 (3): 282–90.

Helleiner, Eric, and Andreas Pickel, eds. 2005. *Economic Nationalism in a Globalizing World.* Ithaca, NY: Cornell University Press.

Henke, Marina E. 2017. "The Politics of Diplomacy: How the United States Builds Multilateral Military Coalitions." *International Studies Quarterly* 61 (2): 410–24.

———. 2018. "The Rotten Carrot: US-Turkish Bargaining Failure over Iraq in 2003 and the Pitfalls of Social Embeddedness." *Security Studies* 27 (1): 120–47.

Herman, Edward S., and Noam Chomsky. 1988. *Manufacturing Consent: The Political Economy of the Mass Media*. New York: Pantheon Books.

Hill, Christopher. 2014. "The Particular and the General: The Challenge for Foreign Policy Studies." *International Politics Reviews* 2 (1): 31–35.

Hinsley, Francis Harry. 1982. "The Rise and Fall of the Modern International System." *Review of International Studies* 8 (1): 1–8.

Hirschman, Albert O. 1970. *Exit, Voice, and Loyalty. Responses to Decline in Firms, Organizations, and States*. Cambridge, MA: Harvard University Press.

Hix, Simon, and Stefano Bartolini. 2006. "La politisation de l'UE : remède ou poison?" *Notre Europe Policy Paper* 19.

Hobolt, Sara B., and Catherine E. de Vries. 2016. "Public Support for European Integration." *Annual Review of Political Science* 19: 413–32.

Hoffman, Aaron M. 2006. *Building Trust: Overcoming Suspicion in International Conflict*. Albany, NY: State University of New York Press.

———. 2007. "The Structural Causes of Trusting Relationships: Why Rivals Do Not Overcome Suspicion Step by Step." *Political Science Quarterly* 122 (2): 287–312.

Hoffmann, Stanley. 1973. "International Organization and the International System." In *International Organization: Politics and Process*, edited by Leland M. Goodrich and David A. Kay, 49–73. Madison: University of Wisconsin Press.

Hofmann, Stephanie C., and Frédéric Mérand. 2012. "Regional Integration: The Effects of Institutional Elasticity." In *International Relations Theory and Regional Transformation*, edited by T.V. Paul, 133–57. Cambridge: Cambridge University Press.

Hooghe, Liesbet, and Gary Marks. 2009. "A Postfunctionalist Theory of European Integration: From Permissive Consensus to Constraining Dissensus." *British Journal of Political Science* 39 (1): 1–23.

Hook, Steven W., and John W. Spanier. 2016. *American Foreign Policy since World War II*. 20th ed. Thousand Oaks, CA: Sage.

Hopkin, Jonathan, and Ben Rosamond. 2018. "Post-Truth Politics, Bullshit and Bad Ideas: 'Deficit Fetishism' in the UK." *New Political Economy* 23 (6): 641–55.

Hosoya, Chihiro. 1982. "The 1934 Anglo-Japanese Nonaggression Pact." *International Studies Quarterly* 25 (3): 491–517.

Hunt, Charles T. 2017. "All Necessary Means to What Ends? The Unintended Consequences of the 'Robust Turn' in UN Peace Operations." *International Peacekeeping* 24 (1): 108–31.

Hurd, Ian. 1999. "Legitimacy and Authority in International Politics." *International Organization* 53 (2): 379–408.

———. 2005. "The Strategic Use of Liberal Internationalism: Libya and the UN Sanctions, 1992–2003." *International Organization* 59 (3): 495–526.

———. 2008. *After Anarchy: Legitimacy and Power in the United Nations Security Council*. Princeton, NJ: Princeton University Press.

————. 2018. *International Organizations: Politics, Law, Practice.* 3rd ed. Cambridge: Cambridge University Press.

Hurrelmann, Achim, Anna Gora, and Andrea Wagner. 2015. "The Politicization of European Integration: More than an Elite Affair?" *Political Studies* 63 (1): 43–59.

Hutter, Swen, Edgar Grande, and Hanspeter Kriesi, eds. 2016. *Politicising Europe.* Cambridge: Cambridge University Press.

Hwang, Wonjae, Amanda G. Sanford, and Junhan Lee. 2015. "Does Membership on the UN Security Council Influence Voting in the UN General Assembly?" *International Interactions* 41 (2): 256–78.

Ikenberry, G. John. 2001. *After Victory: Institutions, Strategic Restraint, and the Rebuilding of Order after Major Wars.* Princeton, NJ: Princeton University Press.

————. 2011. *Liberal Leviathan: The Origins, Crisis, and Transformation of the American World Order.* Princeton, NJ: Princeton University Press.

————. 2014. "The Illusion of Geopolitics: The Enduring Power of the Liberal Order." *Foreign Affairs* 93 (3): 80–90.

————. 2017. "The Plot against American Foreign Policy: Can the Liberal Order Survive?" *Foreign Affairs* 96 (3): 2–9.

————. 2018. "The End of Liberal International Order?" *International Affairs* 94 (1): 7–23.

Ikenberry, G. John, Michael Mastanduno, and William C. Wohlforth. 2009. "Unipolarity, State Behavior, and Systemic Consequences." *World Politics* 61 (1): 1–27.

Institute for Security Studies. 2015. "Kinshasa Government Attacks FDLR Rebels without the UN." *Peace and Security Council Report*, March. https://issafrica .org/pscreport/situation-analysis/kinshasa-government-attacks-fdlr-rebels -without-the-un.

International Atomic Energy Agency. 2015. *Verification and Monitoring in the Islamic Republic of Iran in Light of United Nations Security Council Resolution 2231.* GOV /2015/53, August 14. https://www.iaea.org/sites/default/files/gov-2015-53.pdf.

International Crisis Group. 2017a. "Finding the Right Role for the G5 Sahel Joint Force." *Crisis Group Africa Report* 258 (December 12). https://www.crisisgroup .org/africa/west-africa/burkina-faso/258-force-du-g5-sahel-trouver-sa-place -dans-lembouteillage-securitaire.

————. 2017b. "Time for Concerted Action in DR Congo." *Crisis Group Africa Report* 257 (December 4). https://www.crisisgroup.org/africa/central-africa /democratic-republic-congo/257-time-concerted-action-dr-congo.

International Energy Agency. 2015. *Scenarios and Projections.* Paris. https://www.iea .org/publications/freepublications/publication/WEO2015SpecialReporton EnergyandClimateChange.pdf.

International Institute for Sustainable Development. 2009. "Summary of the Copenhagen Climate Change Conference: 7–19 December 2009." *Earth Negotiations Bulletin* 12 (459): December 22.

Iriye, Akira. 1990. "US Policy toward Japan before World War II." In *Pearl Harbor Reexamined: Prologue to the Pacific War*, edited by Hilary Conroy and Harry Wray, 17–25. Honolulu: University of Hawaii Press.

Ivanova, Maria. 2012. "Institutional Design and UNEP Reform: Historical Insights on Form, Function and Financing." *International Affairs* 88 (3): 565–84.

Izumikawa, Yasuhiro. 2018. "Binding Strategies in Alliance Politics: The Soviet-Japanese-US Diplomatic Tug of War in the Mid-1950s." *International Studies Quarterly* 62 (1): 108–20.

Jabko, Nicolas. 2006. *Playing the Market: A Political Strategy for Uniting Europe, 1985–2005.* Ithaca, NY: Cornell University Press.

Jackson, Patrick Thaddeus, and Daniel H. Nexon. 1999. "Relations before States: Substance, Process and the Study of World Politics." *European Journal of International Relations* 5 (3): 291–332.

———. 2013. "International Theory in a Post-Paradigmatic Era: From Substantive Wagers to Scientific Ontologies." *European Journal of International Relations* 19 (3): 543–65.

Jackson, Robert H. 1990. *Quasi-States: Sovereignty, International Relations, and the Third World.* Cambridge: Cambridge University Press.

Jackson, Robert H., and Georg Sørensen. 2016. *Introduction to International Relations: Theories and Approaches.* 6th ed. Oxford: Oxford University Press.

Jakobsen, Peter Viggo. 2009. "Small States, Big Influence: The Overlooked Nordic Influence on the Civilian ESDP." *Journal of Common Market Studies* 47 (1): 81–102.

James, Harold. 2002. *The End of Globalization: Lessons from the Great Depression.* Cambridge, MA: Harvard University Press.

James, Patrick. 2002. *International Relations and Scientific Progress: Structural Realism Reconsidered.* Columbus: Ohio State University Press.

Jervis, Robert. 1976. *Perception and Misperception in International Politics.* Princeton, NJ: Princeton University Press.

———. 1978. "Cooperation under the Security Dilemma." *World Politics* 30 (2): 167–214.

———. 1979. "Systems Theories and Diplomatic History." In *Diplomacy: New Approaches in History, Theory, and Policy,* edited by Paul Gordon Lauren, 216–19. New York: Free Press.

———. 1988. "War and Misperception." In *The Origin and Prevention of Major Wars,* edited by Robert I. Rotberg and Theodore K. Rabb, 101–26. Cambridge: Cambridge University Press.

———. 1989. *The Meaning of the Nuclear Revolution: Statecraft and the Prospect of Armageddon.* Ithaca, NY: Cornell University Press.

———. 1997. *System Effects: Complexity in Political and Social Life.* Princeton, NJ: Princeton University Press.

Johnson, Tana. 2014. *Organizational Progeny: Why Governments Are Losing Control over the Proliferating Structures of Global Governance.* Oxford: Oxford University Press.

Johnston, Alastair I. 2003. "Is China a Status Quo Power?" *International Security* 27 (4): 5–56.

———. 2008. *Social States: China in International Institutions, 1980–2000.* Princeton, NJ: Princeton University Press.

Johnstone, Ian. 2003. "Security Council Deliberations: The Power of the Better Argument." *European Journal of International Law* 14 (3): 437–80.

Juncker, Jean-Claude. 2016. *State of the Union Address 2016: Towards a Better Europe—A Europe That Protects, Empowers and Defends.* Strasbourg: European Commission.

Jupille, Joseph Henri, Walter Mattli, and Duncan Snidal. 2013. *Institutional Choice and Global Commerce.* Cambridge: Cambridge University Press.

Juris, Jeffrey S. 2008. *Networking Futures: The Movements against Corporate Globalization.* Durham, NC: Duke University Press.

Kaplan, Lawrence S. 1984. *The United States and NATO: The Formative Years.* Lexington: University Press of Kentucky.

Kapoor, Sony. 2010. *The Financial Crisis: Causes and Cures.* Brussels: Friedrich-Ebert-Stiftung, ETUI.

Kapstein, Ethan B., and Michael Mastanduno, eds. 1999. *Unipolar Politics: Realism and State Strategies after the Cold War.* New York: Columbia University Press.

Karlsrud, John. 2019. "From Liberal Peacebuilding to Stabilization and Counterterrorism." *International Peacekeeping* 26 (19): 1–21.

Karns, Margaret P., and Karen A. Mingst. 1990. *The United States and Multilateral Institutions: Patterns of Changing Instrumentality and Influence.* Boston: Unwin Hyman.

Kathman, Jacob D., and Molly M. Melin. 2016. "Who Keeps the Peace? Understanding State Contributions to UN Peacekeeping Operations." *International Studies Quarterly* 61 (1): 150–62.

Katsumata, Hiro. 2011. "Mimetic Adoption and Norm Diffusion: 'Western' Security Cooperation in Southeast Asia?" *Review of International Studies* 37 (2): 557–76.

Katzenstein, Peter J., and Rudra Sil. 2010. *Beyond Paradigms: Analytic Eclecticism in the Study of World Politics.* New York: Palgrave Macmillan.

Kaul, Inge, Pedro Conceição, Katell Le Goulven, and Ronald U. Mendoza. 2003. "How to Improve the Provision of Global Public Goods." In *Providing Global Public Goods*, edited by Inge Kaul, 21–58. Oxford: Oxford University Press.

Kaya, Ayse. 2015. *Power and Global Economic Institutions.* Cambridge: Cambridge University Press.

Keating, Colin. 2016. "Power Dynamics between Permanent and Elected Members." In *The UN Security Council in the 21st Century*, edited by Sebastian von Einsiedel, David M. Malone, and Bruno Stagno Ugarte, 139–56. Boulder, CO: Lynne Rienner.

Keck, Margaret E., and Kathryn Sikkink. 1998. *Activists beyond Borders: Advocacy Networks in International Politics.* Ithaca, NY: Cornell University Press.

Kelley, Judith. 2008. "Assessing the Complex Evolution of Norms: The Rise of International Election Monitoring." *International Organization* 62 (2): 221–55.

———. 2017. *Scorecard Diplomacy: Grading States to Influence Their Reputation and Behavior.* Cambridge: Cambridge University Press.

Kelstrup, Morten, and Michael C. Williams, eds. 2000. *International Relations Theory and the Politics of European Integration: Power, Security, and Community.* London: Routledge.

Kennan, George F. 1954. *Realities of American Foreign Policy.* Princeton, NJ: Princeton University Press.

Kennedy, Paul. 1987. *The Rise and Fall of the Great Powers: Economic Change and Military Conflict from 1500 to 2000.* New York: Random House.

———. 1989. *The Rise and Fall of the Great Powers: Economic Change and Military Conflict from 1500 to 2000.* New York: Vintage Books.

———. 1994. "Conclusions." In *The Fall of Great Powers: Peace, Stability, and Legitimacy,* edited by Geir Lundestad, 371–81. Oxford: Oxford University Press.

Keohane, Robert O. 1982. "The Demand for International Regimes." *International Organization* 36 (2): 325–55.

———. 1984. *After Hegemony: Cooperation and Discord in the World Political Economy.* Princeton, NJ: Princeton University Press.

———. 1986. "Reciprocity in International Relations." *International Organization* 40 (1): 1–27.

———. 1988. "International Institutions: Two Approaches." *International Studies Quarterly* 32 (4): 379–96.

———. 1993. "Institutional Theory and the Realist Challenge after the Cold War." In *Neorealism and Neoliberalism: The Contemporary Debate,* edited by David A. Baldwin, 269–301. New York: Columbia University Press.

Keohane, Robert O., and Lisa L. Martin. 1995. "The Promise of Institutionalist Theory." *International Security* 20 (1): 39–51.

———. 2010. "How International Institutions Affect Outcomes." In *History and Neorealism,* edited by E. R. May, R. Rosecrance and Z. Steiner, 49–78. Cambridge: Cambridge University Press.

Keohane, Robert O., and Joseph S. Nye, eds. 1972. *Transnational Relations and World Politics.* Cambridge, MA: Harvard University Press.

———. 1977. *Power and Interdependence: World Politics in Transition.* Boston: Little, Brown.

Keohane, Robert O., and David G. Victor. 2011. "The Regime Complex for Climate Change." *Perspectives on Politics* 9 (1): 7–23.

Kim, Moonhawk. 2008. "Costly Procedures: Divergent Effects of Legalization in the GATT/WTO Dispute Settlement Procedures." *International Studies Quarterly* 52 (3): 657–86.

Kindleberger, Charles P. 1986. *The World in Depression, 1929–1939.* 2nd ed. Berkeley: University of California Press.

Kitchen, Nicholas. 2010. "Systemic Pressures and Domestic Ideas: A Neoclassical Realist Model of Grand Strategy Formation." *Review of International Studies* 36 (1): 117–43.

Kleine, Mareike. 2013. *Informal Governance in the European Union: How Governments Make International Organizations Work.* Ithaca, NY: Cornell University Press.

Koremenos, Barbara. 2002. "Can Cooperation Survive Changes in Bargaining Power? The Case of Coffee." *Journal of Legal Studies* 31 (S1): S259–S283.

———. 2005. "Contracting around International Uncertainty." *American Political Science Review* 99 (4): 549–65.

Koremenos, Barbara, Charles Lipson, and Duncan Snidal. 2001. "The Rational Design of International Institutions." *International Organization* 55 (4): 761–99.

Kornprobst, Markus, and Martin Senn. 2016. "A Rhetorical Field Theory: Background, Communication, and Change." *British Journal of Politics and International Relations* 18 (2): 300–317.

Kragh, Martin, and Sebastian Åsberg. 2017. "Russia's Strategy for Influence through Public Diplomacy and Active Measures: The Swedish Case." *Journal of Strategic Studies* 40 (6): 773–816.

Krasner, Stephen D. 1982. "Structural Causes and Regime Consequences: Regimes as Intervening Variables." *International Organization* 36 (2): 185–205.

———. 1991. "Global Communications and National Power: Life on the Pareto Frontier." *World Politics* 43 (3): 336–66.

———. 1999. *Sovereignty: Organized Hypocrisy*. Princeton, NJ: Princeton University Press.

———. 2013. "New Terrains: Sovereignty and Alternative Conceptions of Power." In *Back to Basics*, edited by Martha Finnemore and Judith Goldstein, 339–58. New York: Oxford University Press.

Kratochwil, Friedrich, and John G. Ruggie. 1986. "International Organization: A State of the Art on an Art of the State." *International Organization* 40 (4): 753–75.

Krebs, Ronald R. 1999. "Perverse Institutionalism: NATO and the Greco-Turkish Conflict." *International Organization* 53 (2): 343–77.

Krebs, Ronald R., and Patrick Thaddeus Jackson. 2007. "Twisting Tongues and Twisting Arms: The Power of Political Rhetoric." *European Journal of International Relations* 13 (1): 35–66.

Krebs, Ronald R., and Jennifer K. Lobasz. 2007. "Fixing the Meaning of 9/11: Hegemony, Coercion, and the Road to War in Iraq." *Security Studies* 16 (3): 409–51.

Krebs, Ronald R., and Aaron Rapport. 2012. "International Relations and the Psychology of Time Horizons." *International Studies Quarterly* 56 (3): 530–43.

Kreiger, Miriam, Shannon L. C. Souma, and Daniel Nexon. 2015. "US Military Diplomacy in Practice." In *Diplomacy and the Making of World Politics*, edited by Ole Jacob Sending, Vincent Pouliot, and Iver B. Neumann, 220–55. Cambridge University Press.

Kreps, Sarah E. 2011. *Coalitions of Convenience: United States Military Interventions after the Cold War*. New York: Oxford University Press.

Kriesi, Hanspeter. 2016. "The Politicization of European Integration." *Journal of Common Market Studies* 54 (1): 32–47.

Kristensen, Peter Marcus. 2017. "After Abdication: America Debates the Future of Global Leadership." *Chinese Political Science Review* 2 (4): 550–66.

Kroenig, Matthew. 2010. *Exporting the Bomb: Technology Transfer and the Spread of Nuclear Weapons*. Ithaca, NY: Cornell University Press.

Kwon, Gi-Heon. 1995. "The Declining Role of Western Powers in International Organizations: Exploring a New Model of UN Burden Sharing." *Journal of Public Policy* 15 (1): 65–88.

Kydd, Andrew. 1997. "Game Theory and the Spiral Model." *World Politics* 49 (3): 371–400.

———. 2005. *Trust and Mistrust in International Relations*. Princeton, NJ: Princeton University Press.

Labs, Eric J. 1997. "Beyond Victory: Offensive Realism and the Expansion of War Aims." *Security Studies* 6 (4): 1–49.

Lake, David A. 1992. "Powerful Pacifists: Democratic States and War." *American Political Science Review* 86 (1): 24–37.

———. 1999. *Entangling Relations: American Foreign Policy in Its Century*. Princeton, NJ: Princeton University Press.

———. 2013. "Theory Is Dead, Long Live Theory: The End of the Great Debates and the Rise of Eclecticism in International Relations." *European Journal of International Relations* 19 (3): 567–87.

Lane, Peter J., and Michael Lubatkin. 1998. "Relative Absorptive Capacity and Interorganizational Learning." *Strategic Management Journal* 19 (5): 461–77.

Larionova, Marina, A. Sakharov, Andrey Shelepov, and Mark Rakhmangulov. 2017. "Donald Trump's Policy and International Institutions." *Monitoring of Russia's Economic Outlook* 5 (43): 11–15.

LaRoche, Christopher David, and Simon Frankel Pratt. 2017. "Kenneth Waltz Is Not a Neorealist (and Why That Matters)." *European Journal of International Relations* 24 (1): 153–76.

Lefebvre, Stéphane. 2003. "The Difficulties and Dilemmas of International Intelligence Cooperation." *International Journal of Intelligence and CounterIntelligence* 16 (4): 527–42.

Legro, Jeffrey W., and Andrew Moravcsik. 1999. "Is Anybody Still a Realist?" *International Security* 24 (2): 5–55.

Lemke, Douglas. 2002. *Regions of War and Peace*. Cambridge: Cambridge University Press.

Lendvai, Paul. 2017. *Orban: Europe's New Strongman*. London: Hurst.

Levy, Jack S. 2004. "What Do Great Powers Balance against and When?" In Paul, Wirtz, and Fortmann 2004, 29–51.

Levy, Jack S., and William R. Thompson. 2010. "Balancing on Land and at Sea: Do States Ally against the Leading Global Power?" *International Security* 35 (1): 7–43.

Lieber, Keir A., and Gerard Alexander. 2005. "Waiting for Balancing: Why the World Is Not Pushing Back." *International Security* 30 (1): 109–39.

Lieven, Dominic. 2000. *Empire: The Russian Empire and Its Rivals*. London: John Murray.

Lim, Daniel Yew Mao, and James Raymond Vreeland. 2013. "Regional Organizations and International Politics: Japanese Influence over the Asian Development Bank and the UN Security Council." *World Politics* 65 (1): 34–72.

Lipson, Charles. 1984. "International Cooperation in Economic and Security Affairs." *World Politics* 37 (1): 1–23.

———. 2003. *Reliable Partners: How Democracies Have Made a Separate Peace*. Princeton, NJ: Princeton University Press.

Little, Richard. 2007. *The Balance of Power in International Relations: Metaphors, Myths, and Models*. Cambridge: Cambridge University Press.

Lobell, Steven E. 2018. "A Granular Theory of Balancing." *International Studies Quarterly* 62 (3): 593–605.

Lobell, Steven E., Norrin M. Ripsman, and Jeffrey W. Taliaferro. 2009. *Neoclassical Realism, the State, and Foreign Policy*. Cambridge: Cambridge University Press.

Logvinenko, I. 2017. "Control and Access: Russia's Rendez-vous with Financial Globalization." Unpublished manuscript.

Mac Ginty, Roger. 2012. "Against Stabilization." *Stability* 1 (1). https://www.stabilityjournal.org/articles/10.5334/sta.ab/.

Machiavelli, Niccolo. [1532] 2003. *The Prince*. London: Penguin.

Mack, Andrew. 1975. "Why Big Nations Lose Small Wars: The Politics of Asymmetric Conflict." *World Politics* 27 (2): 175–200.

Mahbubani, Kishore. 2004. "The Permanent and Elected Council Members." In *The UN Security Council: From the Cold War to the 21st Century*, edited by David M. Malone, 253–66. Boulder, CO: Lynne Rienner.

———. 2014. *The Great Convergence: Asia, the West, and the Logic of One World*. New York: Public Affairs.

Mälksoo, Lauri. 2013. "The Tallinn Manual as an International Event." *Diplomaatia*, no. 120. https://icds.ee/the-tallinn-manual-as-an-international-event/.

Malone, David M. 2004. "Conclusion." In *The UN Security Council: From the Cold War to the 21st Century*, edited by David M. Malone, 617–52. Boulder, CO: Lynne Rienner.

Maness, Ryan C., and Brandon Valeriano. 2015. *Russia's Coercive Diplomacy: Energy, Cyber, and Maritime Policy as New Sources of Power*. Basingstoke: Palgrave Macmillan.

Manev, Ivan M., and William B. Stevenson. 2001. "Balancing Ties: Boundary Spanning and Influence in the Organization's Extended Network of Communication." *Journal of Business Communication* 38 (2): 183–205.

Manners, Ian. 2002. "Normative Power Europe: A Contradiction in Terms?" *Journal of Common Market Studies* 40 (2): 235–58.

———. 2008. "The Normative Ethics of the European Union." *International Affairs* 84 (1): 45–60.

March, James G., and Johan P. Olsen. 1998. "The Institutional Dynamics of International Political Orders." *International Organization* 52 (4): 943–69.

Marsh, David. 2013. *Europe's Deadlock: How the Euro Crisis Could Be Solved—And Why It Won't Happen*. New Haven, CT: Yale University Press.

Marsh, Kevin. 2014. "'Leading from Behind': Neoclassical Realism and Operation Odyssey Dawn." *Defense and Security Analysis* 30 (2): 120–32.

Martin, Lisa L. 1993. "Credibility, Costs, and Institutions: Cooperation on Economic Sanctions." *World Politics* 45 (3): 406–32.

———. 2017. "Institutions and the Global Political Economy." In *Oxford Research Encyclopedia of Politics*. Oxford: Oxford University Press.

Martin, Lisa L., and Beth A. Simmons. 1998. "Theories and Empirical Studies of International Institutions." *International Organization* 52 (4): 729–57.

Mason, Michael. 2008. "Transparency for Whom? Information Disclosure and Power in Global Environmental Governance." *Global Environmental Politics* 8 (2): 8–13.

Mattern, Janice Bially. 2001. "The Power Politics of Identity." *European Journal of International Relations* 7 (3): 349–97.

———. 2005. "Why Soft Power Isn't So Soft: Representational Force and the Sociolinguistic Construction of Attraction in World Politics." *Millennium* 33 (3): 583–612.

Matthijs, Matthias. 2017. "Europe after Brexit: A Less Perfect Union." *Foreign Affairs* 96 (1): 85–95.

Matthijs, Matthias, and Mark Blyth. 2015. *The Future of the Euro*. Oxford: Oxford University Press.

McAdam, Doug, Sidney Tarrow, and Charles Tilly. 2001. *Dynamics of Contention*. Cambridge: Cambridge University Press.

McConaughey, Meghan, Paul Musgrave, and Daniel H. Nexon. 2018. "Beyond Anarchy: Logics of Political Organization, Hierarchy, and International Structure." *International Theory* 10 (2): 181–218.

McCourt, David M. 2016. "Practice Theory and Relationalism as the New Constructivism." *International Studies Quarterly* 60 (3): 475–85.

McGoldrick, Fred. 2011. "The Road Ahead for Export Controls: Challenges for the Nuclear Suppliers Group." *Arms Control Today* 41 (1): 30–36.

McNamara, Kathleen. 2015. *The Politics of Everyday Europe: Constructing Authority in the European Union*. Oxford: Oxford University Press.

Mead, Walter Russell. 2014. "The Return of Geopolitics: The Revenge of the Revisionist Powers." *Foreign Affairs* 93 (3): 69–79.

Mearsheimer, John J. 1990. "Back to the Future: Instability in Europe after the Cold War." *International Security* 15 (1): 5–56.

———. 1994. "The False Promise of International Institutions." *International Security* 19 (3): 5–49.

———. 1995. "A Realist Reply." *International Security* 20 (1): 82–93.

———. 2001. *The Tragedy of Great Power Politics*. New York: W. W. Norton.

―――. 2010. "Why Is Europe Peaceful Today?" *European Political Science* 9 (3): 387–97.

―――. 2014. *The Tragedy of Great Power Politics*. Updated ed. New York: W. W. Norton.

Mechanic, David. 1962. "Sources of Power of Lower Participants in Complex Organizations." *Administrative Science Quarterly* 7 (3): 349–64.

Medrano, Juan Díez. 2003. *Framing Europe: Attitudes to European Integration in Germany, Spain, and the United Kingdom*. Princeton, NJ: Princeton University Press.

Mendelsohn, Barak. 2009. *Combating Jihadism: American Hegemony and International Cooperation in the War on Terrorism*. Chicago: University of Chicago Press.

Menon, Jayant. 2014. "From Spaghetti Bowl to Jigsaw Puzzle? Fixing the Mess in Regional and Global Trade." *Asia and the Pacific Policy Studies* 1 (3): 470–83.

Milner, Helen V. 1997. *Interests, Institutions, and Information: Domestic Politics and International Relations*. Princeton, NJ: Princeton University Press.

Milward, Alan S. 1992. *The European Rescue of the Nation-State*. Berkeley: University of California Press.

Mitchell, Ronald B. 1998. "Sources of Transparency: Information Systems in International Regimes." *International Studies Quarterly* 42 (1): 109–30.

Mitzen, Jennifer. 2014. *Power in Concert: The Nineteenth-Century Origins of Global Governance*. Chicago: University of Chicago Press.

Moe, Terry M. 2005. "Power and Political Institutions." *Perspectives on Politics* 3 (2): 215–33.

Monteiro, Nuno P. 2012. "Unrest Assured: Why Unipolarity Is Not Peaceful." *International Security* 36 (3): 9–40.

―――. 2014. *Theory of Unipolar Politics*. Cambridge: Cambridge University Press.

Monteiro, Nuno P., and Alexandre Debs. 2014. "The Strategic Logic of Nuclear Proliferation." *International Security* 39 (2): 7–51.

Monteleone, Carla. 2015. "Coalition Building in the UN Security Council." *International Relations* 29 (1): 45–68.

Moravcsik, Andrew. 1995. "Explaining International Human Rights Regimes: Liberal Theory and Western Europe." *European Journal of International Relations* 1 (2): 157–89.

―――. 1997. "Taking Preferences Seriously: A Liberal Theory of International Politics." *International Organization* 51 (4): 513–53.

―――. 1998. *The Choice for Europe: Social Purpose and State Power from Messina to Maastricht*. Ithaca, NY: Cornell University Press.

Morgenthau, Hans J. 1946. *Scientific Man vs. Power Politics*. Chicago: University of Chicago Press.

―――. 1967. *Politics among Nations: The Struggle for Power and Peace*. 4th ed. New York: Knopf.

―――. 1985. *Politics among Nations: The Struggle for Power and Peace*. 6th ed. New York: McGraw-Hill.

Mounk, Yascha. 2018. *The People vs. Democracy: Why Our Freedom Is in Danger and How to Save It*. Cambridge, MA: Harvard University Press.

Mouritzen, Hans, and Anders Wivel, eds. 2005. *The Geopolitics of Euro-Atlantic Integration.* London: Routledge.

———. 2012. *Explaining Foreign Policy: International Diplomacy and the Russo-Georgian War.* Boulder, CO: Lynne Rienner.

Mudde, Cas. 2016. "Europe's Populist Surge: A Long Time in the Making." *Foreign Affairs* 95 (6): 25–30.

Mueller, John. 1988. "The Essential Irrelevance of Nuclear Weapons: Stability in the Postwar World." *International Security* 13 (2): 55–79.

Müller, Harald. 1997. "Neither Hype nor Complacency: WMD Proliferation after the Cold War." *Nonproliferation Review* 4 (2): 62–71.

Mulligan, Shane P. 2006. "The Uses of Legitimacy in International Relations." *Millennium* 34 (2): 349–75.

Mulligan, William. 2014. *The Great War for Peace.* New Haven, CT: Yale University Press.

Mundell, Robert A. 1963. "Capital Mobility and Stabilization Policy under Fixed and Flexible Exchange Rates." *Canadian Journal of Economics and Political Science* 29 (4): 475–85.

Muñoz, Miquel, Rachel Thrasher, and Adil Najam. 2009. "Measuring the Negotiation Burden of Multilateral Environmental Agreements." *Global Environmental Politics* 9 (4): 1–13.

Murdie, Amanda M., and David R. Davis. 2012. "Shaming and Blaming: Using Events Data to Assess the Impact of Human Rights INGOs." *International Studies Quarterly* 56 (1): 1–16.

Murray, Philomena. 2010. "Comparative Regional Integration in the EU and East Asia: Moving beyond Integration Snobbery." *International Politics* 47 (3/4): 308–23.

Musgrave, Paul, and Daniel Nexon. 2018. "Defending Hierarchy from the Moon to the Indian Ocean: Symbolic Capital and Political Dominance in Early Modern China and the Cold War." *International Organization* 72 (3): 561–90.

Narang, Vipin. 2014. *Nuclear Strategy in the Modern Era: Regional Powers and International Conflict.* Princeton, NJ: Princeton University Press.

Neumann, Iver B., and Sieglinde Gstöhl. 2004. "Lilliputians in Gulliver's World? Small States in International Relations." Working Paper 2004/1. Reykjavik: Centre for Small State Studies.

———. 2006. "Introduction: Lilliputians in Gulliver's World?" In *Small States in International Relations,* edited by Christine Ingebritsen, Iver B. Neumann, and Sieglinde Gstöhl, 3–36. Seattle: University of Washington Press.

Nexon, Daniel H. 2009a. "The Balance of Power in the Balance." *World Politics* 61 (2): 330–59.

———. 2009b. *The Struggle for Power in Early Modern Europe: Religious Conflict, Dynastic Empires, and International Change.* Princeton, NJ: Princeton University Press.

Nexon, Daniel H., and Iver B. Neumann. 2018. "Hegemonic-Order Theory: A Field-Theoretic Account." *European Journal of International Relations* 24 (3): 662–86.

Nexon, Daniel H., and Vincent Pouliot. 2013. "'Things of Networks': Situating ANT in International Relations." *International Political Sociology* 7 (3): 342–45.

Nexon, Daniel H., and Thomas Wright. 2007. "What's at Stake in the American Empire Debate." *American Political Science Review* 101 (2): 253–71.

Niblett, Robin. 2017. "Liberalism in Retreat: The Demise of a Dream." *Foreign Affairs* 96 (1): 17–24.

Norris, Pippa, and Ronald Inglehart. 2018. *Cultural Backlash and the Rise of Populism: Trump, Brexit, and the Rise of Authoritarian Populism.* Cambridge: Cambridge University Press.

Nye, Joseph S. 1988. "Neorealism and Neoliberalism." *World Politics* 40 (2): 235–51.

———. 2000. "The US and Europe: Continental Drift?" *International Affairs* 76 (1): 51–60.

———. 2002. *The Paradox of American Power.* New York: Oxford University Press.

———. 2011. *The Future of Power.* New York: Public Affairs.

———. 2017. "Will the Liberal Order Survive: The History of an Idea." *Foreign Affairs* 96 (1): 10–16.

Oates, John G. 2017. "The Fourth Face of Legitimacy: Constituent Power and the Constitutional Legitimacy of International Institutions." *Review of International Studies* 43 (2): 199–220.

Oatley, Thomas, W. Kindred Winecoff, Andrew Pennock, and Sarah Bauerle Danzman. 2013. "The Political Economy of Global Finance: A Network Model." *Perspectives on Politics* 11 (1): 133–53.

O'Brien, Robert, and Marc Williams. 2016. *Global Political Economy: Evolution and Dynamics.* 5th ed. Basingstoke: Palgrave Macmillan.

O'Connor, Brendon, and Srdjan Vucetic. 2010. "Another Mars-Venus Divide? Why Australia Said 'Yes' and Canada Said 'No' to Involvement in the 2003 Iraq War." *Australian Journal of International Affairs* 64 (5): 526–48.

Opel, Andy, and Donnalyn Pompper, eds. 2003. *Representing Resistance: Media, Civil Disobedience, and the Global Justice Movement.* Westport, CT: Praeger.

Organski, A. F. K. 1968. *World Politics.* 2nd ed. New York: Knopf.

Organski, A. F. K., and Jacek Kugler. 1980. *The War Ledger.* Chicago: University of Chicago Press.

O'Rourke, Kevin H., and Jeffrey G. Williamson. 1999. *Globalization and History: The Evolution of a Nineteenth-Century Atlantic Economy.* Cambridge, MA: MIT Press.

Osiander, Andreas. 2001. "Sovereignty, International Relations, and the Westphalian Myth." *International Organization* 55 (2): 251–88.

Oye, Kenneth A. 1986. *Cooperation under Anarchy.* Princeton, NJ: Princeton University Press.

Panke, Diana. 2012. "Being Small in a Big Union: Punching above Their Weights? How Small States Prevailed in the Vodka and the Pesticides Cases." *Cambridge Review of International Affairs* 25 (3): 329–44.

Pant, Harsh V. 2011. *The US-India Nuclear Pact: Policy, Process, and Great Power Politics.* New Delhi: Oxford University Press.

Papadopoulos, Yannis, and Paul Magnette. 2010. "On the Politicisation of the European Union: Lessons from Consociational National Polities." *West European Politics* 33 (4): 711–29.

Pape, Robert A. 1996. *Bombing to Win: Air Power and Coercion in War.* Ithaca, NY: Cornell University Press.

———. 2005. "Soft Balancing against the United States." *International Security* 30 (1): 7–45.

Paris, Roland. 2002. "International Peacebuilding and the 'Mission Civilisatrice.'" *Review of International Studies* 28 (4): 637–56.

Patrick, Stewart. 2014. "The Unruled World: The Case for Good Enough Global Governance." *Foreign Affairs* 93 (1): 58–73.

———. 2016. "World Order: What, Exactly, Are the Rules?" *Washington Quarterly* 39 (1): 7–27.

———. 2017. "Trump and World Order: The Return of Self-Help." *Foreign Affairs* 96 (2): 52–57.

Paul, T.V. 2004. "Introduction: The Enduring Axioms of Balance of Power Theory and Their Contemporary Relevance." In Paul, Wirtz, and Fortmann 2004, 1–25.

———. 2005. "Soft Balancing in the Age of US Primacy." *International Security* 30 (1): 46–71.

———. 2009. *The Tradition of Non-use of Nuclear Weapons.* Stanford, CA: Stanford University Press.

———, ed. 2016. *Accommodating Rising Powers: Past, Present, and Future.* Cambridge: Cambridge University Press.

———. 2018. *Restraining Great Powers: Soft Balancing from Empires to the Global Era.* New Haven, CT: Yale University Press.

Paul, T.V., James J. Wirtz, and Michel Fortmann, eds. 2004. *Balance of Power: Theory and Practice in the 21st Century.* Stanford, CA: Stanford University Press.

Pease, Kelly-Kate S. 2003. *International Organizations: Perspectives on Governance in the Twenty-First Century.* 2nd ed. Upper Saddle River, NJ: Prentice Hall.

Pedersen, Susan. 2015. *The Guardians: The League of Nations and the Crisis of Empire.* Oxford: Oxford University Press.

Pelc, Krzysztof J. 2010. "Constraining Coercion? Legitimacy and Its Role in US Trade Policy, 1975–2000." *International Organization* 64 (1): 65–96.

Peters, Michael A. 2016. "Challenges to the 'World Order' of Liberal Internationalism: What Can We Learn?" *Educational Philosophy and Theory* 48 (9): 863–71.

Petrova, Margarita H. 2016. "Rhetorical Entrapment and Normative Enticement: How the United Kingdom Turned from Spoiler into Champion of the Cluster Munition Ban." *International Studies Quarterly* 60 (3): 387–99.

Pettigrew, Andrew M. 1972. "Information Control as a Power Resource." *Sociology* 6 (2): 187–204.

———. 1973. *The Politics of Organizational Decision-Making.* London: Tavistock.

Phillips, Andrew, and J. C. Sharman. 2015. "Explaining Durable Diversity in International Systems: State, Company, and Empire in the Indian Ocean." *International Studies Quarterly* 59 (3): 436–48.

Phillips, Nicola. 2005. "Globalization Studies in International Political Economy." In *Globalizing International Political Economy*, edited by Nicola Phillips, 20–54. Basingstoke: Palgrave Macmillan.

Pierson, Paul. 2000. "Increasing Returns, Path Dependence, and the Study of Politics." *American Political Science Review* 94 (2): 251–67.

Polanyi, Karl. (1944) 2001. *The Great Transformation: The Political and Economic Origins of Our Time*. Boston: Beacon Press.

Pollack, Mark A. 2003. *The Engines of European Integration: Delegation, Agency, and Agenda Setting in the EU*. Oxford: Oxford University Press.

Pons, Silvio. 2014. *The Global Revolution: A History of International Communism, 1917–1991*. Oxford: Oxford University Press.

———. 2015. "The Soviet Union and the International Left." In *The Cambridge History of the Second World War*, edited by John Robert Ferris, Evan Mawdsley, R. J. B. Bosworth, Joseph A. Maiolo, Michael Geyer, and J. Adam Tooze, 68–90. Cambridge: Cambridge University Press.

Portes, Alejandro. 1998. "Social Capital: Its Origins and Applications in Modern Sociology." *Annual Review of Sociology* 24 (1): 1–24.

Posen, Barry R. 2003. "Command of the Commons: The Military Foundation of US Hegemony." *International Security* 28 (1): 5–46.

———. 2014. *Restraint: A New Foundation for U.S. Grand Strategy*. Ithaca, NY: Cornell University Press.

Pouliot, Vincent. 2008. "The Logic of Practicality: A Theory of the Practice of Security Communities." *International Organization* 62 (1): 257–88.

———. 2016. *International Pecking Orders: The Politics and Practice of Multilateral Diplomacy*. Cambridge: Cambridge University Press.

Pouponneau, Florent, and Frédéric Mérand. 2017. "Diplomatic Practices, Domestic Fields, and the International System: Explaining France's Shift on Nuclear Nonproliferation." *International Studies Quarterly* 61 (1): 123–35.

Powell, Robert. 1990. *Nuclear Deterrence Theory: The Search for Credibility*. Cambridge: Cambridge University Press.

———. 2002. "Game Theory, International Relations Theory, and the Hobbesian Stylization." In *Political Science: The State of the Discipline*, edited by Ira Katznelson and Helen V. Milner, 773–78. New York: W. W. Norton.

Rajagopal, Balakrishnan. 2003. *International Law from Below: Development, Social Movements, and Third World Resistance*. Cambridge: Cambridge University Press.

———. 2006. "Counter-Hegemonic International Law: Rethinking Human Rights and Development as a Third World Strategy." *Third World Quarterly* 27 (5): 767–83.

Rapkin, David, and William R. Thompson. 2003. "Power Transition, Challenge and the Reemergence of China." *International Interactions* 29 (4): 315–42.

Rathbun, Brian. 2008. "A Rose by Any Other Name: Neoclassical Realism as the Logical and Necessary Extension of Structural Realism." *Security Studies* 17 (2): 294–321.

Ravenhill, John, ed. 2017. *Global Political Economy*. 5th ed. Oxford: Oxford University Press.

Reiss, Mitchell. 1988. *Without the Bomb: The Politics of Nuclear Non-Proliferation*. New York: Columbia University Press.

Reiter, Dan, and Allan C. Stam. 2008. *Democracies at War*. Princeton, NJ: Princeton University Press.

Renshon, Jonathan. 2016. "Status Deficits and War." *International Organization* 70 (3): 513–50.

Resende-Santos, João. 1996. "Anarchy and the Emulation of Military Systems: Military Organization and Technology in South America, 1870–1930." *Security Studies* 5 (3): 193–260.

———. 2007. *Neorealism, States, and the Modern Mass Army*. Cambridge: Cambridge University Press.

Reus-Smit, Christian. 1997. "Constructing Anarchy: The Constitutional Structure of International Society and the Nature of Fundamental Institutions." *International Organization* 51 (4): 555–89.

———. 2001. "The Strange Death of Liberal International Theory." *European Journal of International Law* 12 (3): 573–94.

Rhoads, Emily Paddon. 2016. *Taking Sides in Peacekeeping: Impartiality and the Future of the United Nations*. Oxford: Oxford University Press.

Rhodes, M. 2016. "Brexit—A Disaster for Britain and for the European Union." In *Key Controversies in European Integration*, edited by Hubert Zimmermann and Andreas Dür, 252–58. Basingstoke: Palgrave Macmillan.

Ripsman, Norrin M. 2002. *Peacemaking by Democracies: The Effect of State Autonomy on the Post–World War Settlements*. University Park: Pennsylvania State University Press.

———. 2005. "Two Stages of Transition from a Region of War to a Region of Peace: Realist Transition and Liberal Endurance." *International Studies Quarterly* 49 (4): 669–93.

———. 2009. "Conclusion: The State of Neoclassical Realism." In Lobell, Ripsman, and Taliaferro 2009, 280–99.

Ripsman, Norrin M., Jeffrey W. Taliaferro, and Steven E. Lobell. 2016. *Neoclassical Realist Theory of International Politics*. Oxford: Oxford University Press.

Rittberger, Volker, Bernhard Zangl, and Andreas Kruck. 2012. *International Organization*. 2nd ed. Basingstoke: Palgrave Macmillan.

Rosamond, Ben. 2014. "Three Ways of Speaking Europe to the World: Markets, Peace, Cosmopolitan Duty and the EU's Normative Power." *British Journal of Politics and International Relations* 16 (1): 133–48.

Rosato, Sebastian. 2011. *Europe United: Power Politics and the Making of the European Community*. Ithaca, NY: Cornell University Press.

Rose, Gideon. 1998. "Neoclassical Realism and Theories of Foreign Policy." *World Politics* 51 (1): 144–72.

Ruggie, John G. 1982. "International Regimes, Transactions, and Change: Embedded Liberalism in the Postwar Economic Order." *International Organization* 36 (2): 379–415.

Rupert, Mark. 1995. *Producing Hegemony: The Politics of Mass Production and American Global Power.* Cambridge: Cambridge University Press.

Russett, Bruce M., and John R. Oneal. 2001. *Triangulating Peace: Democracy, Interdependence, and International Organizations.* New York: W. W. Norton.

Russett, Bruce, John R. Oneal, and David R. Davis. 1998. "The Third Leg of the Kantian Tripod for Peace: International Organizations and Militarized Disputes, 1950–85." *International Organization* 52 (3): 441–67.

Rynning, Sten. 2005. *NATO Renewed: The Power and Purpose of Transatlantic Cooperation.* New York: Palgrave Macmillan.

Sagan, Scott D. 1996. "Why Do States Build Nuclear Bombs? Three Models in Search of a Bomb." *International Security* 21 (3): 54–86.

Sagan, Scott D., and Kenneth N. Waltz. 1995. *The Spread of Nuclear Weapons: A Debate.* New York: W. W. Norton.

Saltzman, Ilai Z. 2012. "Soft Balancing as Foreign Policy: Assessing American Strategy toward Japan in the Interwar Period." *Foreign Policy Analysis* 8 (2): 131–50.

Sampanis, Maria. 2012. "Comply or Defy? Following the Hegemon to Market." In *Beyond Great Powers and Hegemons: Why Secondary States Support, Follow, or Challenge*, edited by Kristen P. Williams, Steven E. Lobell, and Neal G. Jesse, 97–111. Stanford, CA: Stanford University Press.

Sanbonmatsu, John. 2004. *The Postmodern Prince: Critical Theory, Left Strategy, and the Making of a New Political Subject.* New York: Monthly Review Press.

Sandholtz, Wayne, and Alec Stone Sweet, eds. 1998. *European Integration and Supranational Governance.* Oxford: Oxford University Press.

Sandler, Todd, and John F. Forbes. 1980. "Burden Sharing, Strategy, and the Design of NATO." *Economic Inquiry* 18 (3): 425–44.

Schaefer, Brett D. 2009. "Critical Reforms Required for U.N. Peacekeeping." *Heritage Foundation Executive Summary Backgrounder* 2313 (September 8). https://www.heritage.org/report/critical-reforms-required-un-peacekeeping.

Schelling, Thomas C. 1966. *Arms and Influence.* New Haven, CT: Yale University Press.

———. 2008. *Arms and Influence.* Rev. ed. New Haven, CT: Yale University Press.

Schimmelfennig, Frank, and Thomas Winzen. 2014. "Instrumental and Constitutional Differentiation in the European Union." *Journal of Common Market Studies* 52 (2): 354–70.

Schmidt, Brian C., and Thomas Juneau. 2012. "Neoclassical Realism and Power." In *Neoclassical Realism in European Politics: Bringing Power Back In*, edited by Asle Toje and Barbara Kunz, 61–78. Manchester: Manchester University Press.

Schmidt, Vivien A. 2008. "Discursive Institutionalism: The Explanatory Power of Ideas and Discourse." *Annual Review of Political Science* 11: 303–26.

———. 2012. "Discursive Institutionalism: Scope, Dynamics, and Philosophical Underpinnings." In *The Argumentative Turn Revisited: Public Policy as Communicative Practice*, edited by Frank Fischer and Herbert Gottweiss, 85–113. Durham, NC: Duke University Press.

Scholl, Christian, and Annette Freyberg-Inan. 2013. "Hegemony's Dirty Tricks: Explaining Counter-Globalization's Weakness in Times of Neoliberal Crisis." *Globalizations* 10 (4): 619–34.

Scholte, Jan Aart. 2010. "Governing a More Global World." *Corporate Governance* 10 (4): 459–74.

Schroeder, Paul W. 1994. *The Transformation of European Politics, 1763–1848.* Oxford: Oxford University Press.

Schultz, Kenneth A. 2001. *Democracy and Coercive Diplomacy.* Cambridge: Cambridge University Press.

———. 2003. "Tying Hands and Washing Hands: The U.S. Congress and Multilateral and Domestic Institutions." In *Locating the Proper Authorities: The Interaction of International and Domestic Institutions*, edited by Daniel W. Drezner, 105–42. Ann Arbor: University of Michigan Press.

Schwartz, Stephen I. 1998. *Atomic Audit: The Costs and Consequences of U.S. Nuclear Weapons since 1940.* Washington, DC: Brookings Institution Press.

Schweller, Randall L. 1994. "Bandwagoning for Profit: Bringing the Revisionist State Back In." *International Security* 19 (1): 72–107.

———. 1997. *Deadly Imbalances: Tripolarity and Hitler's Strategy of World Conquest.* New York: Columbia University Press.

———. 1999. "Managing the Rise of Great Powers." In *Engaging China: The Management of an Emerging Power*, edited by Alastair I. Johnston and Robert S. Ross, 1–31. London: Routledge.

———. 2001. "The Problem of International Order Revisited: A Review Essay." *International Security* 26 (1): 161–86.

———. 2003. "The Progressiveness of Neoclassical Realism." In *Progress in International Relations Theory: Appraising the Field*, edited by Colin Elman and Miriam Fendius Elman, 311–48. Cambridge, MA: MIT Press.

———. 2004. "Unanswered Threats: A Neoclassical Realist Theory of Underbalancing." *International Security* 29 (2): 159–201.

Schweller, Randall L., and David Priess. 1997. "A Tale of Two Realisms: Expanding the Institutions Debate." *Mershon International Studies Review* 41 (1): 1–32.

Scribner, Richard A., Theodore J. Ralston, and William D. Metz. 1985. *The Verification Challenge: Problems and Promise of Strategic Nuclear Arms Control Verification.* Boston, MA: Birkhä.

Sechser, Todd S., and Matthew Fuhrmann. 2013. "Crisis Bargaining and Nuclear Blackmail." *International Organization* 67 (1): 173–95.

Security Council Report. 2016. *The Security Council and UN Peace Operations: Reform and Deliver.* Research Report 2. http://www.securitycouncilreport.org /atf/cf/%7B65BFCF9B-6D27-4E9C-8CD3-CF6E4FF96FF9%7D/research _report_peace_operations_may_2016.pdf.

Sell, Susan K. 2016. "Ahead of Her Time? Susan Strange and Global Governance." In *Susan Strange and the Future of Global Political Economy*, edited by Randall D. Germain, 21–32. London: Routledge.

Shinoda, Hideaki. 2000. "The Politics of Legitimacy in International Relations: A Critical Examination of NATO's Intervention in Kosovo." *Alternatives* 25 (4): 515–36.

Sil, Rudra, and Peter J. Katzenstein. 2011. "De-centering, Not Discarding, the 'Isms': Some Friendly Amendments." *International Studies Quarterly* 55 (2): 481–85.

Simpson, John. 1985. "The Non-Proliferation Treaty at Its Half-Life." In *The Nuclear Non-Proliferation Treaty*, edited by Ian Bellany, Coit D. Blacker, and Joseph Gallacher, 1–12. London: Frank Cass.

Skidelsky, Robert. 2001. *John Maynard Keynes*. Vol. 3, *Fighting for Freedom, 1937–1946*. New York: Viking.

Sklair, Leslie. 1997. "Social Movements for Global Capitalism: The Transnational Capitalist Class in Action." *Review of International Political Economy* 4 (3): 514–38.

Smith, James McCall. 2000. "The Politics of Dispute Settlement Design: Explaining Legalism in Regional Trade Pacts." *International Organization* 54 (1): 137–80.

Smith, Thomas W. 2002. "The New Law of War: Legitimizing Hi-Tech and Infrastructural Violence." *International Studies Quarterly* 46 (3): 355–74.

Snyder, Glenn H. 1984. "The Security Dilemma in Alliance Politics." *World Politics* 36 (4): 461–95.

———. 1996. "Process Variables in Neorealist Theory." *Security Studies* 5 (3): 167–92.

———. 2015. *Deterrence and Defense: Toward a Theory of National Security*. Princeton, NJ: Princeton University Press.

Solingen, Etel, ed. 2012. *Sanctions, Statecraft, and Nuclear Proliferation*. Cambridge: Cambridge University Press.

Sørensen, Georg. 2001. *Changes in Statehood: The Transformation of International Relations*. New York: Palgrave Macmillan.

———. 2004. *The Transformation of the State: Beyond the Myth of Retreat*. Basingstoke: Palgrave Macmillan.

———. 2008. "The Case for Combining Material Forces and Ideas in the Study of IR." *European Journal of International Relations* 14 (1): 5–32.

———. 2011. *A Liberal World Order in Crisis: Choosing between Imposition and Restraint*. Ithaca, NY: Cornell University Press.

———. 2016. *Rethinking the New World Order*. London: Palgrave Macmillan.

Spirtas, Michael. 1999. "French Twist: French and British NATO Policies from 1949 to 1966." *Security Studies* 8 (2–3): 302–46.

Spruyt, Hendrik. 1994. *The Sovereign State and Its Competitors: An Analysis of Systems Change*. Princeton, NJ: Princeton University Press.

Starr, Amory. 2000. *Naming the Enemy: Anti-Corporate Movements Confront Globalization*. London: Zed Books.

Stein, Arthur A. 2008. "Neoliberal Institutionalism." In *The Oxford Handbook on International Relations*, edited by Christian Reus-Smit and Duncan Snidal, 201–21. Oxford: Oxford University Press.

Steinberg, Richard H. 2002. "In the Shadow of Law or Power? Consensus-Based Bargaining and Outcomes in the GATT/WTO." *International Organization* 56 (2): 339–74.

Stephen, Matthew D. 2009. "Alter-Globalism as Counter-Hegemony: Evaluating the 'Postmodern Prince.'" *Globalizations* 6 (4): 483–98.

———. 2011. "Globalisation and Resistance: Struggles over Common Sense in the Global Political Economy." *Review of International Studies* 37 (1): 209–28.

Sterling-Folker, Jennifer, and Rosemary E. Shinko. 2005. "Discourses of Power: Traversing the Realist-Postmodern Divide." *Millennium* 33 (3): 637–64.

Stoessinger, John Georges. 2010. *Why Nations Go to War*. 11th ed. New York: St Martin's.

Stokes, Doug. 2018. "Trump, American Hegemony and the Future of the Liberal International Order." *International Affairs* 94 (1): 133–50.

Stone, Randall W. 2004. "The Political Economy of IMF Lending in Africa." *American Political Science Review* 98 (4): 577–91.

———. 2011. *Controlling Institutions: International Organizations and the Global Economy*. Cambridge: Cambridge University Press.

Stopford, John M., and Susan Strange. 1991. *Rival States, Rival Firms: Competition for World Market Shares*. With John S. Henley. Cambridge: Cambridge University Press.

Strandsbjerg, Jeppe. 2010. *Territory, Globalization and International Relations: The Cartographic Reality of Space*. Basingstoke: Palgrave Macmillan.

Strange, Susan. 1988a. "The Persistent Myth of Lost Hegemony: Reply to Milner and Snyder." *International Organization* 42 (4): 751–52.

———. 1988b. *States and Markets*. London: Pinter.

———. 1994a. *States and Markets*. 2nd ed. London: Pinter.

———. 1994b. "Wake up, Krasner! The World Has Changed." *Review of International Political Economy* 1 (2): 209–19.

———. 1996. *The Retreat of the State: The Diffusion of Power in the World Economy*. Cambridge: Cambridge University Press.

———. 1998. "What Theory? The Theory in Mad Money." Centre for the Study of Globalisation and Realisation Working Paper No. 18/98. http://wrap.warwick.ac.uk/2107/1/WRAP_Strange_wp1898.pdf.

Streich, Philip, and Jack S. Levy. 2007. "Time Horizons, Discounting, and Intertemporal Choice." *Journal of Conflict Resolution* 51 (2): 199–226.

Stulberg, Adam N., and Matthew Fuhrmann. 2013. *The Nuclear Renaissance and International Security*. Stanford, CA: Stanford University Press.

Stumpf, Waldo. 1995. "South Africa's Nuclear Weapons Programme: From Deterrence to Dismantlement." *Arms Control Today* 5 (10): 3–8.

Sullivan, Robert R. 1973. "Machiavelli's Balance of Power Theory." *Social Science Quarterly* 54 (2): 258–70.

Swank, Duane. 2003. "Withering Welfare? Globalisation, Political Economic Institutions, and Contemporary Welfare States." In *States in the Global Economy:*

Bringing Domestic Institutions Back In, edited by Linda Weiss, 58–82. Cambridge: Cambridge University Press.

Taliaferro, Jeffrey W. 2009. "Neoclassical Realism and Resource Extraction: State Building for Future War." In Lobell, Ripsman, and Taliaferro 2009, 194–226.

Taliaferro, Jeffrey W., Steven E. Lobell, and Norrin M. Ripsman. (2009). "Introduction: Neoclassical Realism, the State, and Foreign Policy." In Lobell, Ripsman, and Taliaferro 2009, 1–42.

Tallberg, Jonas. 2003. "The Agenda-Shaping Powers of the EU Council Presidency." *Journal of European Public Policy* 10 (1): 1–19.

Tannenwald, Nina. 2005. "Stigmatizing the Bomb: Origins of the Nuclear Taboo." *International Security* 29 (4): 5–49.

Tardy, Thierry. 2013. "France." In *Providing Peacekeepers: The Politics, Challenges, and Future of United Nations Peacekeeping Contributions*, edited by Alex J. Bellamy and Paul D. Williams, 115–38. Oxford: Oxford University Press.

Teitt, Sarah. 2008. "China and the Responsibility to Protect." Asia-Pacific Centre for the Responsibility to Protect. https://r2pasiapacific.org/files/451/china_and_r2P _2008_report.pdf.

Thayer, Bradley A. 1995. "The Causes of Nuclear Proliferation and the Utility of the Nuclear Non-proliferation Regime." *Security Studies* 4 (3): 463–519.

Thies, Cameron G. 2010. "State Socialization and Structural Realism." *Security Studies* 19 (4): 689–717.

Thompson, Alexander. 2006a. "Coercion through IOs: The Security Council and the Logic of Information Transmission." *International Organization* 60 (1): 1–34.

———. 2006b. "Screening Power: International Organizations as Informative Agents." In Hawkins et al. 2006a, 229–54.

———. 2009. *Channels of Power: The UN Security Council and US Statecraft in Iraq.* Ithaca, NY: Cornell University Press.

———. 2010. "Rational Design in Motion: Uncertainty and Flexibility in the Global Climate Regime." *European Journal of International Relations* 16 (2): 269–96.

Thompson, Alexander, and Daniel Verdier. 2014. "Multilateralism, Bilateralism, and Regime Design." *International Studies Quarterly* 58 (1): 15–28.

Thorhallsson, Baldur. 2006. "The Size of States in the European Union: Theoretical and Conceptual Perspectives." *European Integration* 28 (1): 7–31.

Tilly, Charles. 1993. "Contentious Repertoires in Great Britain, 1758–1834." *Social Science History* 17 (2): 253–80.

———. 1998. "Contentious Conversation." *Social Research* 65 (3): 491–510.

Tortoriello, Marco, Ray Reagans, and Bill McEvily. 2012. "Bridging the Knowledge Gap: The Influence of Strong Ties, Network Cohesion, and Network Range on the Transfer of Knowledge between Organizational Units." *Organization Science* 23 (4): 1024–39.

Trettin, Frederik, and Julian Junk. 2014. "Spoilers from Within: Bureaucratic Spoiling in United Nations Peace Operations." *Journal of International Organizations Studies* 5 (1): 13–27.

United Nations. 2001. *Report of the Panel of Experts on the Illegal Exploitation of Natural Resources and Other Forms of Wealth of the Democratic Republic of the Congo.* S/2001/357. April 12. http://www.un.org/en/ga/search/view_doc.asp?symbol=S /2001/357.

———. 2002. *Final Report of the Panel of Experts on the Illegal Exploitation of Natural Resources and Other Forms of Wealth of the Democratic Republic of the Congo.* S/2002/1146. October 16. http://www.un.org/en/ga/search/view_doc.asp?symbol =S/2002/1146.

———. 2005. *Resolution Adopted by the General Assembly on 16 September 2005: 2005 World Summit Outcome.* A/RES/60/1. October 24. http://www.un.org/en /development/desa/population/migration/generalassembly/docs/globalcompact /A_RES_60_1.pdf.

———. 2008. *United Nations Peacekeeping Operations: Principles and Guidelines.* New York: Department of Peacekeeping Operations. https://www.un.org/rule oflaw/blog/document/united-nations-peacekeeping-operations-principles -and-guidelines-the-capstone-doctrine/.

———. 2015. *Report of the High-Level Independent Panel on Peace Operations on Uniting Our Strengths for Peace: Politics, Partnership and People.* A/70/95–S/2015/446. June 17. http://www.un.org/en/ga/search/view_doc.asp?symbol=A/70/95.

Urpelainen, J. 2013. "Promoting International Environmental Cooperation through Unilateral Action: When Can Trade Sanctions Help?" *Global Environmental Politics* 13 (2): 26–45.

Vabulas, Felicity, and Duncan Snidal. 2013. "Organization without Delegation: Informal Intergovernmental Organizations (IIGOs) and the Spectrum of Intergovernmental Arrangements." *Review of International Organizations* 8 (2): 193–220.

Van Evera, Stephen. 1984. "The Cult of the Offensive and the Origins of the First World War." *International Security* 9 (1): 58–107.

———. 1990. "Primed for Peace: Europe after the Cold War." *International Security* 15 (3): 7–57.

———. 1998. "Offense, Defense, and the Causes of War." *International Security* 22 (4): 5–43.

———. 1999. *Causes of War: Power and the Roots of Conflict.* Ithaca, NY: Cornell University Press.

Van Middelaar, Luuk. 2013. *The Passage to Europe: How a Continent Became a Union.* New Haven, CT: Yale University Press.

Vauchez, Antoine. 2014. *Démocratiser l'Europe.* Paris: Seuil.

Vetterlein, Antje, and Manuela Moschella. 2014. "International Organizations and Organizational Fields: Explaining Policy Change in the IMF." *European Political Science Review* 6 (1): 143–65.

Victor, David G. 2011. *Global Warming Gridlock: Creating More Effective Strategies for Protecting the Planet.* Cambridge: Cambridge University Press.

Voeten, Erik. 2001. "Outside Options and the Logic of Security Council Action." *American Political Science Review* 95 (4): 845–58.

———. 2005. "The Political Origins of the UN Security Council's Ability to Legitimize the Use of Force." *International Organization* 59 (3): 527–57.

Von Einsiedel, Sebastian, David M. Malone, and Bruno Stagno Ugarte. 2016. "Conclusion: The Security Council and a World of Crisis." In *The UN Security Council in the 21st Century*, edited by Sebastian von Einsiedel, David M. Malone, and Bruno Stagno Ugarte, 827–77. Boulder, CO: Lynne Rienner.

Vreeland, James Raymond. 2003. *The IMF and Economic Development*. Cambridge: Cambridge University Press.

Vreeland, James Raymond, and Axel Dreher. 2014. *The Political Economy of the United Nations Security Council: Money and Influence*. Cambridge: Cambridge University Press.

Wade, Robert H. 2003. "What Strategies Are Viable for Developing Countries Today? The World Trade Organization and the Shrinking of 'Development Space.'" *Review of International Political Economy* 10 (4): 621–44.

Wæver, Ole. 1995. "Identity, Integration and Security: Solving the Sovereignty Puzzle in EU Studies." *Journal of International Affairs* 48 (2): 389–431.

———. 1996. "The Rise and Fall of the Inter-paradigm Debate." In *International Theory: Positivism and Beyond*, edited by Steve Smith, Ken Booth, and Marysia Zalewski, 149–86. Cambridge: Cambridge University Press.

———. 1998. "The Sociology of a Not So International Discipline: American and European Developments in International Relations." *International Organization* 52 (4): 687–727.

Wallander, Celeste A. 2000. "Institutional Assets and Adaptability: NATO after the Cold War." *International Organization* 54 (4): 705–35.

Wallander, Celeste A., and Robert O. Keohane. 1999. "Risk, Threat, and Security Institutions." In *Imperfect Unions: Security Institutions over Time and Space*, edited by Helga Haftendorn, Robert O. Keohane, and Celeste A. Wallander, 21–47. Oxford: Oxford University Press.

Walsh, Jim. 2005. *Learning from Past Success: The NPT and the Future of Non-Proliferation*. Stockholm: Weapons of Mass Destruction Commission.

Walt, Stephen M. 1987. *The Origins of Alliances*. Ithaca, NY: Cornell University Press.

———. 2002. "The Enduring Relevance of the Realist Tradition." In *Political Science: State of the Discipline III*, edited by Helen V. Milner and Ira Katznelson, 197–230. New York: W. W. Norton.

———. 2005. *Taming American Power: The Global Response to U.S. Primacy*. New York: W. W. Norton.

———. 2009. "Alliances in a Unipolar World." *World Politics* 61 (1): 86–120.

Waltz, Kenneth N. 1979. *Theory of International Politics*. Boston: McGraw-Hill.

———. 1981. *The Spread of Nuclear Weapons: More May Be Better*. Adelphi Papers. London: International Institute for Strategic Studies.

———. 1986. "Reflections on *Theory of International Politics*: A Response to My Critics." In *Neorealism and Its Critics*, edited by Robert O. Keohane, 322–45. New York: Columbia University Press.

———. 1988. "The Origins of War in Neorealist Theory." In *The Origin and Prevention of Major Wars*, edited by Robert I. Rotberg and Theodore K. Rabb, 39–52. Cambridge: Cambridge University Press.

———. 2000. "Structural Realism after the Cold War." *International Security* 25 (1): 5–41.

Ward, Steven. 2013. "Race, Status, and Japanese Revisionism in the Early 1930s." *Security Studies* 22 (4): 607–39.

———. 2017. *Status and the Challenge of Rising Powers*. Cambridge: Cambridge University Press.

Wargelin, Clifford F. 1997. "A High Price for Bread: The First Treaty of Brest-Litovsk and the Break-Up of Austria-Hungary, 1917–1918." *International History Review* 19 (4): 757–88.

Watson, Adam. 1992. *The Evolution of International Society: A Comparative Historical Analysis*. London: Routledge.

Watson, Matthew. 2005. *Foundations of International Political Economy*. Basingstoke: Palgrave Macmillan.

———. 2017. "Historicising Ricardo's Comparative Advantage Theory: Challenging the Normative Foundations of Liberal IPE." *New Political Economy* 22 (3): 257–72.

Weber, Katja. 1997. "Hierarchy amidst Anarchy: A Transaction Costs Approach to International Security Cooperation." *International Studies Quarterly* 41 (2): 321–40.

Weber, Steve. 1990. "Realism, Detente, and Nuclear Weapons." *International Organization* 44 (1): 55–82.

Weeks, Jessica. 2008. "Autocratic Audience Costs: Regime Type and Signaling Resolve." *International Organization* 62 (1): 65–101.

Weiss, Thomas G., and Karen E. Young. 2005. "Compromise and Credibility: Security Council Reform?" *Security Dialogue* 36 (2): 131–54.

Weitsman, Patricia A. 2004. *Dangerous Alliances: Proponents of Peace, Weapons of War*. Stanford, CA: Stanford University Press.

———. 2014. *Waging War: Alliances, Coalitions, and Institutions of Interstate Violence*. Stanford, CA: Stanford University Press.

Wendt, Alexander E. 1987. "The Agent-Structure Problem in International Relations Theory." *International Organization* 41 (3): 335–70.

———. 1992. "Anarchy Is What States Make of It: The Social Construction of Power Politics." *International Organization* 46 (2): 391–425.

———. 1999. *Social Theory of International Politics*. Cambridge: Cambridge University Press.

Wheeler-Bennett, John. 1971. *Brest-Litovsk: The Forgotten Peace, March 1918*. New York: W. W. Norton.

White, Jonathan. 2015. "Emergency Europe." *Political Studies* 63 (2): 300–318.

Widmaier, Wesley W. 2004. "The Social Construction of the 'Impossible Trinity': The Intersubjective Bases of Monetary Cooperation." *International Studies Quarterly* 48 (2): 433–53.

Widmaier, Wesley W., Mark Blyth, and Leonard Seabrooke. 2007. "Exogenous Shocks or Endogenous Constructions? The Meanings of Wars and Crises." *International Studies Quarterly* 51 (4): 747–59.

Wight, Colin. 1999. "They Shoot Dead Horses Don't They? Locating Agency in the Agent-Structure Problematique." *European Journal of International Relations* 5 (1): 109–42.

Wight, Martin. 1995. *Power Politics*. London: Continuum.

Williams, Paul D. 2018. "Joining AMISOM: Why Six African States Contributed Troops to the African Union Mission in Somalia." *Journal of Eastern African Studies* 12 (1): 172–92.

Wilson, Peter H. 1999. *The Holy Roman Empire, 1495–1806*. London: Macmillan.

Wivel, Anders. 2004. "The Power Politics of Peace: Exploring the Link between Globalization and European Integration from a Realist Perspective." *Cooperation and Conflict* 39 (1): 5–25.

———. 2008. "Balancing against Threats or Bandwagoning with Power? Europe and the Transatlantic Relationship after the Cold War." *Cambridge Review of International Affairs* 21 (3): 289–305.

———. 2017. "Realism in Foreign Policy Analysis." In *Oxford Research Encyclopedia on Politics*, 1–27. Oxford: Oxford University Press.

Wivel, Anders, and Ole Wæver. 2018. "The Power of Peaceful Change: The Crisis of the European Union and the Rebalancing of Europe's Regional Order." *International Studies Review* 20 (1): 249–64.

Wohlforth, William C. 1993. *The Elusive Balance: Power and Perceptions during the Cold War*. Ithaca, NY: Cornell University Press.

———. 1999. "The Stability of a Unipolar World." *International Security* 24 (1): 5–41.

———. 2009. "Unipolarity, Status Competition, and Great Power War." *World Politics* 61 (1): 28–57.

Wohlforth, William C., Richard Little, Stuart J. Kaufman, David Kang, Charles A. Jones, Victoria Tin-Bor Hui, Arthur Eckstein, Daniel Deudney, and William L. Brenner. 2007. "Testing Balance-of-Power Theory in World History." *European Journal of International Relations* 13 (2): 155–85.

Woods, Ngaire. 2001. "Making the IMF and the World Bank More Accountable." *International Affairs* 77 (1): 83–100.

World Trade Organization. 2015. *WTO Dispute Settlement: Resolving Trade Disputes between WTO Members*. https://www.wto.org/english/thewto_e/20y_e/dispute_brochure20y_e.pdf.

Zahra, Shaker A., and Gerard George. 2002. "Absorptive Capacity: A Review, Reconceptualization, and Extension." *Academy of Management Review* 27 (2): 185–203.

Zakaria, Fareed. 1998. *From Wealth to Power: The Unusual Origins of America's World Role*. Princeton, NJ: Princeton University Press.

Zhang, Xiaojun. 2004. "Land Reform in Yang Village: Symbolic Capital and the Determination of Class Status." *Modern China* 30 (1): 3–45.

Zürn, Michael, and Matthew Stephen. 2010. "The View of Old and New Powers on the Legitimacy of International Institutions." *Politics* 30 (1): 91–101.

Zweifel, Thomas D. 2006. *International Organizations and Democracy: Accountability, Politics, and Power.* Boulder, CO: Lynne Rienner.

Contributors

J. *Samuel Barkin*, professor of global governance, University of Massachusetts, Boston

Austin Carson, assistant professor of political science, University of Chicago

Annette Freyberg-Inan, associate professor of political science, and dean of Graduate School of Social Sciences, University of Amsterdam

Stacie Goddard, professor of political science, Wellesley College

John A. Hall, James McGill Professor of Sociology, McGill University

Steven E. Lobell, professor of political science, University of Utah

Sarah-Myriam Martin-Brûlé, associate professor of political science, Bishop's University

Frédéric Mérand, professor of political science and director of Centre d'études et de recherches internationales (CÉRIUM), Université de Montreal

Daniel H. Nexon, associate professor of government, Georgetown University

Brad Nicholson, doctoral student, Department of Political Science, University of Utah

T.V. Paul, James McGill Professor of International Relations, McGill University

Lou Pingeot, doctoral student, Department of Political Science, McGill University

Vincent Pouliot, James McGill Professor, Department of Political Science, McGill University

Norrin M. Ripsman, Monroe J. Rathbone Distinguished Professor, Department of International Relations, Lehigh University

Ben Rosamond, professor, Department of Political Science, University of Copenhagen

Georg Sørensen, professor emeritus of political science, Aarhus University

Alexander Thompson, associate professor of political science, Ohio State University

Patricia A. Weitsman, the late professor of political science and director of War and Peace Studies, Ohio University

Anders Wivel, professor with special responsibilities, Department of Political Science, University of Copenhagen

Index

Figures, notes, and tables are indicated by f, n, and t following the page number.